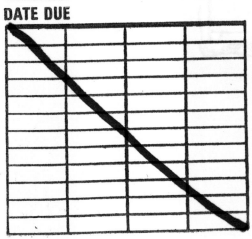

DATE DUE

Speech IN THE ELEMENTARY SCHOOL

McGraw-Hill Series in Speech

CLARENCE T. SIMON, *Consulting Editor*

Speech IN THE ELEMENTARY SCHOOL

Mardel Ogilvie

ASSISTANT PROFESSOR OF SPEECH
QUEENS COLLEGE

1954

McGRAW-HILL BOOK COMPANY, INC.

New York   Toronto   London

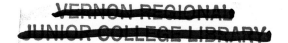

SPEECH IN THE ELEMENTARY SCHOOL

Preface

The purposes of this book are three: (1) to suggest ways to promote effective communication in the elementary school classroom, (2) to indicate the speaking activities that are part of the language-arts program, and (3) to note the part the classroom teacher plays in improving the child's speech. The author has attempted to describe types of speech activities that will engender lively and interested speaking and listening. She has tried to suggest ways of encouraging all students to participate and to explain techniques of the various speech arts that will prove effective in the classroom. Lastly, she has endeavored to show the standards of voice and diction that children should attain, to describe the speech difficulties that the child may possess, and to indicate the teacher's role in improving the voice and diction of the child.

ACKNOWLEDGMENTS

The author is indebted to Dr. Robert Thompson, Dean of State Teachers College, Fredonia, New York, who first motivated the writing of the book; to Dr. Phil Lange of Teachers College, Columbia University, who encouraged the writing along the way, read the manuscript carefully, and offered constructive criticism; to Dr. Wilbur Gilman, the head of the Speech Department at Queens College, who gave of both his time and advice freely, for his helpful counsel; and to Dr. Magdalene Kramer for her kindly criticisms and excellent suggestions for making the book more useful to the classroom teacher.

Appreciation is also due the author's colleagues in the Speech Department at Queens College. Professors Jon Eisenson and Beatrice Jacoby gave generous assistance in determining the content of the chapter on speech defects. Dr. Elizabeth Scanlan and Dr. Robert Dierlam kindly read and evaluated the chapter on dramatics. Recognition is also due Prof. Arthur Bronstein for his reading and his suggestions for the chapter on discussion and Dr. Hollis White for his guidance on the chapter on conducting meetings.

The author also acknowledges great obligation to: Mrs. Myrtle Searles, New Paltz State Teachers College, for suggestions for materials for young children; Miss Florence Morrissey, Fredonia State Teachers College, for her recommendations of children's literature and for other helpful advice; Mr. and Mrs. Philip Frankle for their assistance on the chapter on puppetry; and Miss Marie Jones, New Paltz State Teachers College, for her description and explanation of the activity of the Christmas mitten tree.

Recognition is also due Miss Vivian McCuller, Fredonia State Teachers College. On many occasions she allowed the author to borrow her third graders for speaking activities. At other times, the author learned from watching her work and play with her children. Some of the material in this book is a description of what happens in her classroom. To Dr. Ernest Hilton, former Principal of the Laboratory School at Fredonia State Teachers College, and to his staff the author is indebted for having been allowed to work with them and to learn from them.

Appreciation is expressed to Prof. Agnes Rigney, State Teachers College, Geneseo, Mrs. Joyce Cole, and Mr. Neil Croom, State Teachers College, New Paltz, and Miss Bernice Gross of East School, Long Beach, New York, for their help in obtaining meaningful photographs for the book.

Finally, the author is indebted to the proprietors of the copyrighted materials which are reprinted with their permission in this book and to whom acknowledgment is made elsewhere.

Mardel Ogilvie

Contents

1 | Guides for Teaching Speech in the Elementary School

The speech environment in a classroom should be a happy one, where many activities take place and where each child is developing his own interests and is discovering new and stimulating ideas to discuss. The activities of such a classroom in a public school suggest guides to the classroom teacher in the teaching of speech.

A Rochester teacher[1] took over a first grade where the children did not want to talk; they just sat. All the members of the class were paralyzed with inertia. She said, "The children were reluctant to take part in conversation or to participate in any form of speaking activity. They had no particular fear of speech; they just didn't feel any need for it." Obviously their school environment had been one that emphasized listening.

The most evident needs were for the children to become acquainted, to enjoy talking with each other, and to have a feeling of living together and of belonging. To these ends, the teacher planned that for the first six weeks she and the children would cook and eat lunch in the classroom. This activity stimulated free conversation and discussion. Speaking as well as listening became a necessity. In the beginning, the children offered only brief comments and rarely used complete sentences. Toward the end of the six-week period, they spoke much more fully and freely.

When the teacher read stories to them, they began to ask for their favorites and to repeat parts of the stories with her. The group frequently requested Dr. Seuss's *Horton Hatches the Egg*.[2] As might be expected, the favorite lines were:

[1] Mrs. Ruth Draggett White, Rochester, N.Y.
[2] From *Horton Hatches the Egg* by Dr. Seuss. Copyright, 1940, by Random House. Reprinted by permission of Random House.

1

> I meant what I said.
> And I said what I meant.
> An elephant's faithful
> One hundred percent.

Another story they particularly liked was *Millions of Cats* by Wanda Gág.[3] They enthusiastically spoke with the teacher:

> Cats here, cats there
> Cats and kittens everywhere
>   Hundreds of cats,
>   Thousands of cats,
> Millions and billions and trillions of cats.

The children soon became interested in enacting the stories. They frequently asked to play *The Little Red Hen,* one of their favorites. In their early dramatizations, they acted rather than spoke; they told the story largely in pantomime. However, each time they added more speaking parts. Other stories they liked to play were *The Little Family, The New House in The Forest,* and *The Little Train That Could.*

About the time they were first finding and enjoying success in adding speaking roles to their stories, they began to dramatize everyday situations. They played the roles of the family first: mother, daddy, and children. The stories were simple. Members of the family got themselves ready to go on a picnic, or, while they were eating supper, the little boy became ill, and the father went for the doctor. Then they dramatized other situations: playing store, going to the movies, telephoning friends, and being firemen.

A visit to the firehouse provided not only a subject for dramatization but also an excellent opportunity to teach speech. Planning the trip and talking about it afterward provided live and interesting topics for conversation and spontaneous short talks. The teacher taught principles of organization in a simple way by questions such as "What came first?" or "What has he left out?" The children learned other principles of speaking. When a child related how quickly the fire engine left the building, the teacher asked him how he knew. He supported his statement by reference to the authority, the fire chief.

The proposal to go to the firehouse motivated the children to gather information about different kinds of fire engines, and how they are used. They read Lois Lenski's *The Little Fire Engine;* the teacher read them other books about fire fighting. While they were trying to find out what

[3] From *Millions of Cats* by Wanda Gág. Copyright, 1928, by Coward-McCann, Inc. Reprinted by permission of Coward-McCann, Inc.

actually occurs when there is a fire, a real fire in the neighborhood greatly stimulated their interest. As the children talked about the work of the city fire department, they sounded authoritative because they knew what they were discussing.

Shortly after this trip, the children decided to go to a department store, a post office, or a zoo. The problem was an excellent one for group discussion. Jackie, the most glib child in the room, advocated a specific choice, the post office, instead of discussing the relative merits of all three choices. The teacher asked the children to consider the other two possibilities. Eventually, through the give-and-take of discussion, they decided to go to the zoo. Jackie, the advocate of the trip to the post office, learned to listen and to accept the decision made by the group.

From this trip to the zoo grew an interest in reading about animals and in writing about them. The children enjoyed reading these stories aloud. Jacob, a little shy child, was quite happy to share the poem he wrote about a squirrel:

> Once there was a frisky squirrel.
> One day he jumped into a mailbox.
> Along came the postman,
> Out jumped the squirrel.
> The postman dropped all of his letters.
> Away ran the squirrel.

He read it conversationally in a truly delightful manner: he enjoyed reading it, and the other first graders enjoyed hearing it.

Tony, a charming youngster, quiet and reserved, was a passive member of the group because he stuttered. As he became more active, he lost his reserve and entertained his classmates with his quiet but delightful sense of humor. The speech correctionist worked with Tony; the classroom teacher cooperated; both conferred with the parents. When Tony spoke a solo part in choral reading, his classmates, his parents, and his teacher were happy. The classroom atmosphere in which he lived was calm, pleasant, and relaxed. With the aid of the correctionist and his teacher and with the fine cooperation of his parents, Tony's stutter almost disappeared by the end of the year. Although the work of a speech correctionist and the cooperation of correctionist, teacher, and parents provided an ideal program for Tony, the atmosphere of this classroom alone would have done much to help Tony control his stuttering.

The children in this first grade spoke and listened in their own ways, in many different situations, in a happy, friendly environment. The teacher helped to provide interesting topics to talk about through trips and other experiences. She instilled in the children a desire to communicate in a lively fashion with their classmates. She helped them to tell their experiences in an orderly and interesting manner, to make their points clear, and to hold the attention of their classmates. As the desire to talk increased, they used speech not as an end in itself but as a tool for the communication of ideas to their classmates. Jane was not so timid about speaking. Jackie listened more carefully and did not always insist on being the solo speaker. Mary was reading in a lively, conversational way. Helen was beginning to organize what she was saying. Joe was not talking to hear himself talk but was making intelligent contributions to the discussion. Mary was taking her rightful place in the group. In a genuine way, the Helens, Marys, and Johns grew to be better speakers and happier individuals.

GUIDES FOR TEACHING SPEECH

The activities and procedures of the children and teacher in this classroom suggest the following guides to the teaching of speech in the elementary school:

THE CHILD HAS SOMETHING OF CONSEQUENCE TO SAY

In the first place, the child must have something worthwhile to say and must know what he is talking about. For his age, he is an educated person. When John told how the fire alarm was received at the station, he knew. He described accurately the fire-alarm box, its operations, and the relaying of the message to the firehouse. The tradition of public speaking from ancient times to the present has been that the speaker should be an educated person and that he should be as thoroughly informed on the topic of his speech as the circumstances permit. Furthermore, he should make every reasonable effort to obtain complete, accurate information.

THE CHILD FINDS AND ORGANIZES MATERIAL INTERESTING TO HIS CLASSMATES

The second guide is that the child selects his topic, finds and organizes materials, and makes the presentation interesting. A view frequently held is that a child who knows his subject matter and thinks soundly will be able to communicate his knowledge to his classmates. In addition, he must make his classmates listen to him, follow him readily, understand him, and feel the force of what he is saying.

The children in the classroom mentioned earlier were following this guide when they talked about fire fighting. They gathered material when they read and listened to stories about fire engines and when they visited the firehouse. The teacher questioned one child on his authority when he was telling how quickly the fire engine left the building. He explained that one of the responsibilities of the fire chief was to check how long it takes the engine to depart. The children learned to organize. The teacher asked, "What happened first?" when the child was telling about the ringing of the fire bell. Other queries, as "What did he leave out?" "What can he omit?" "What is he trying to say?" pointed up organization. The teacher asked other pertinent questions, such as "Why didn't the children listen when you were telling how a fire extinguisher works?" The simple teaching of the process of finding and organizing material interesting to listeners lays the foundation for more advanced work.

A speaker must be accurate and clear; his listeners must understand and be interested in what he is saying. Donald Bryant and Karl Wallace, in *Oral Communication*, describing a speaker, say,[4] "He must be clear and intelligible, he must be easy to follow . . . he must be able to hold the attention of his listeners to the thing in hand and to interest them, and he must persuade them to accept his proposal. These likewise were the problems of Cicero, Burke, and Webster, and the basic principles for solving the problems have not changed. . . ." These also are the problems of the speaker in the elementary and high schools.

THE CHILD COMMUNICATES HIS IDEAS TO HIS CLASSMATES

The third guide is that children learn to communicate well whether they are speaking their own words or the words of someone else. They are conveying ideas to interested hearers. They have a full understanding of what they are saying, and they feel a need to convey this understanding to their listeners. They are thinking about what they are

[4] From *Oral Communication* by D. Bryant and K. R. Wallace, p. 4. Copyright, 1948, by Appleton-Century-Crofts, Inc. Reprinted by permission of Appleton-Century-Crofts, Inc.

speaking and, at the same time, are trying to keep their classmates interested in what they are saying. As they speak the words, they are creating or re-creating thoughts and feelings to which their classmates are responding. James Winans[5] underscores two essential qualities of communication: "(1) a full realization of the content of your words as you utter them, and (2) a lively sense of communication."

The child who was reading his story about the frisky squirrel illustrates well the first quality, full realization of the content of words as

Fig. 1. Activity invites talk. (*Neil Croom, University State Teachers College, New Paltz, N.Y.*)

they are uttered. He wrote the story as the result of a series of meaningful experiences. He knew exactly what a "frisky squirrel" was. He was thinking about the full meaning as he read the story. Even though he might have been reading the words of someone else, the same principle would have held. He should know the significance of the material and should be wholly aware of it as he speaks the words.

The teacher was constantly aware of the second quality, a lively sense of communication. Frequently the children were made conscious

[5] J. A. Winans and C. K. Thomas, *Speech-making*, New York, Appleton-Century-Crofts, 1938, p. 25.

that communication is a two-way experience and that in speaking they are trying to gain a response from their listeners. The cooking of meals together prepared them for speaking and listening. The trips made interesting topics for conversation. The desire to go to one place or another motivated discussion. In this class, speaking and listening were live processes. John enjoyed telling about the new silo on his farm and was well aware of the response he was getting from his group. Mary described the new subway station at 179th Street to her classmates and held their attention. A live speaker with his mind on his topic, a responsive audience, and something worthwhile to say add up to enjoyable and purposeful communication.

THE CHILD USES SPEECH TO FOSTER SUCCESSFUL COOPERATIVE LIVING IN A SPEAKING WORLD

The fifth guide is that the child uses speech to foster successful cooperative living in a speaking world. Two requirements for this cooperative living are that (1) through speech, the child adapts himself to his social world; (2) through group discussion, he participates effectively in group decisions.

Through speaking activities, the child adapts himself to his social world. The children, in carrying out the assignments for the planning of their meals, were building satisfactory relationships. In making decisions, preparing for their trips, going on them, adjusting to the demands of the adults they met, being gracious about the hospitality accorded them, they were learning to adapt to each other and to society. Furthermore, in the play of family life, they were expanding their own horizons and observing how members of other families acted and reacted. In a childlike way they were gaining insight into their own families' behavior.

An important requirement in social adaptation is an ability to communicate successfully with others. Carrie Rasmussen[6] says, "Adequacy in self-expression obviously has much to do with the establishing of satisfying human relationships." Franklin Knower[7] states, "Good speech is a social activity. Even more important than self-expression is the function of social adaptation served by this art."

[6] C. Rasmussen, *Speech Methods in the Elementary School*, New York, Ronald, 1949, p. 4.
[7] F. Knower, "Speech Education for All American Youth," *Bulletin of the National Association of Secondary School Principals*, Vol. 32 (January, 1948), p. 13.

The second requirement for using speech in order to live effectively with others is the competent use of the techniques of group discussion. Marie Hochmuth,[8] in an article, "Speech and Society," says, "It is in group interaction that the areas of agreement are to be located and the areas of discord discovered. Group discussion provides an instrument for an examination of those opinions which everyone recognizes to

FIG. 2. Living together. (*Neil Croom, University State Teachers College, New Paltz, N.Y.*)

be a source of conflict." The children reached the decision of going to the zoo rather than to the post office through the use of group discussion. They examined the problem and defined it; they found the solutions, evaluated them, and decided on the best solution. Two aspects of the process are that (1) the group decides, and (2) the individuals must yield to the prevailing decision.

THE CHILD'S VOICE AND DICTION ARE ADEQUATE FOR COMMUNICATION

The last guide is that the child's voice and diction are free of any variations that call attention to them rather than to his speaking. The

[8] M. Hochmuth, "Speech and Society," *Bulletin of the National Association of Secondary School Principals*, Vol. 32 (January, 1948), p. 27.

teacher and the school's personnel will cooperate with the parents in helping the child with a speech difficulty to control it. Tony's stutter drew attention to how he was talking rather than to what he was saying. Because of his own efforts and those of the clinician, the teacher, and the parents, he learned to control it. The teacher made sure the child's classmates were doing all they could to help him. The voice and diction of Tony and of all the other members of his class should be clear, audible, and pleasant.

SUMMARY

There are five guides for the teaching of speech in the elementary school: (1) The child has something worthwhile to say, and he knows what he is talking about. (2) The child selects his subject matter, finds and organizes materials, supports his main idea, and makes the presentation interesting. (3) The child communicates with his audience; he keeps his mind on what he is saying and gains a response from his classmates. (4) The child uses speech to foster successful cooperative living in a speaking world. This cooperative living involves (a) the child's adapting himself through speech to his speaking world and (b) his participating effectively through group discussion in group decisions. (5) His speech is audible, clear, and pleasant.

EXERCISES

1. Visit an elementary school classroom for two hours and list the speech activities that go on during the time you are there.
2. Indicate how the various speech activities you have seen in a schoolroom follow the guides mentioned in this chapter.
3. Describe how a classroom teacher you have observed encourages his children to speak in conversation or in discussion.

BIBLIOGRAPHY

Contest Committee of the Speech Association of America, "A Program of Speech Education," *Quarterly Journal of Speech*, Vol. 37 (October, 1951), pp. 347–358. Shows the place of speech in today's society.
Eckelmann, D. H., and M. Parret, "Source Material for Speech in the Elementary Schools," *Quarterly Journal of Speech*, Vol. 36 (April, 1950), pp. 251–259. Contains excellent suggestions of bibliography for teaching speech in the elementary school. Quite comprehensive.

Gunn, M. A., "Speech in the English Program," *Elementary English*, Vol. 26 (November, 1949), pp. 399–403. Discusses two kinds of experiences in teaching speech: (1) direct teaching of the skills of speech and listening and (2) teaching through experiences which approximate the real-life situations in which pupils need both speaking and listening skills.

National Association of Teachers of Speech,[9] *Guides to Speech Training in the Elementary School*, Magnolia, Mass., Expression Co., 1943. Includes a series of articles written by authorities in the field of speech.

Peins, M., "Speech Techniques for the Classroom," *Elementary English*, Vol. 27 (November, 1950), pp. 446–449. Gives the results of a survey which indicates what techniques are used by teachers in the classroom teaching of speech.

——, "For Better Speech," *Elementary English*, Vol. 26 (November, 1949), pp. 404–406. Discusses needs and interests of children in the light of speech work.

Rasmussen, C., *Speech Methods in the Elementary School*, New York, Ronald, 1947. Contains many suggestions for teaching speech. The section on dramatics particularly good. Obviously written by a person who has worked with children.

Raubicheck, L., *How to Teach Speech in the Elementary School*, New York, Noble, 1937. Gives the history and the status of speech in the elementary school. Includes procedure on teaching sounds, oral reading, choral speaking, and creative dramatics. Corrective techniques.

Speech Association of America (Carrie Rasmussen, chairman), *The Role of Speech in the Elementary School*, Washington, National Education Association, Department of Elementary School Principals, 1946–1947. Includes articles by various authorities in the field of speech. Covers philosophy, integration of speech with other subjects, speech attitudes, basic speech skills, activities which motivate better speech, such as oral reading, choral reading, creative dramatics, and puppetry. Contains a section on the teacher's speech.

Weber, J., "Speaking and Writing in the Elementary School," *Elementary English*, Vol. 24 (April, 1947), pp. 230–236. Tells of specific children's growth in speaking and writing.

[9] Now known as the Speech Association of America.

2 Dramatics

Wherever children gather, in the playground, in the home, or in school, they pretend to be teachers, doctors, mothers, babies, cops and robbers, or Indians. They identify themselves with persons, animals, or objects. When they feel and act as they think fathers, rabbits, or little trains feel and act, they lose themselves in the playing of the roles. Teachers put this natural interest in make-believe to use in the classroom and direct it purposefully. "Creative dramatics" is children's play centered around an experience or a story and skillfully guided by a teacher into a learning experience.

Creative dramatics is distinct from children's play production and children's theater. Creative dramatics is informal, while children's play production and children's theater are more formal. Creative dramatics exists for the child, whereas play production exists for the audience. In creative dramatics, children, selected for educational reasons, make up their own dialogue and story. They produce their situation or story for themselves and their classmates with very simple scenery or none. The teacher may discuss the activity with the children and encourage freedom of interpretation and movement. From time to time, the story and the interpretation change. On the other hand, in children's play production and in children's theater, actors, selected usually because of ability, speak lines of a play written by an adult for children. They present the play before an audience with planned scenery or drapery. The teacher or director works out with his cast the meaning, movement, and interpretation of the story, which remain fairly constant from one rehearsal to the next. The difference between children's theater and play production is that in children's theater the actors are members of a theater group of a college or community, while in children's play production they are members of a club or grade in a school.

Other terms, similar to creative dramatics, are "dramatic play," "educational dramatics," "creative play," and "playmaking." As writers use the four terms, they agree that the purpose in each of the four activities is to develop individuals and not to entertain an audience. Occasionally, the children present the results of the work for an audience, but the emphasis is not on the performance but on the process. Some writers use the term dramatic play in relationship to five-, six-, and seven-year-olds and creative dramatics for the older children. They include in both definitions the concepts of acting out real situations, stories, or poems, of pantomiming, and of the game of make-believe. Others use the term dramatic play to signify play that expresses emotion. Its chief purpose is the socially acceptable release of feelings associated with unhappy experiences. Still others use the term for completely spontaneous, fragmentary make-believe. Many writers use the terms educational dramatics, playmaking, and creative play interchangeably with creative dramatics. This chapter deals with (1) creative dramatics and (2) children's play production.

VALUES OF CREATIVE DRAMATICS

Creative dramatics in the elementary school is an important part of the education of children. John Dewey,[1] in *How We Think*, writes, "Play is the chief, almost the only, mode of education for the child in the years of later infancy." Magdalene Kramer and Orville Hitchcock[2] say, "Many elementary schools use the creative play as the core of the educational program. . . . Arithmetic, reading, writing, speaking, listening, social studies are taught in relation to play developed and produced by the pupils." Winifred Ward[3] says, "Creative play is one of the strongest motivating forces for learning. . . . It promotes better understanding of people and places and, as no dialogue is written, the creative drama provides an excellent framework for expression and imagination."

LEARNING THROUGH A MEANINGFUL EXPERIENCE

The idea recurs in these writings that, in creative dramatics, children learn through a meaningful experience. Learning through a meaningful experience is the first value of creative dramatics. A group of third-grade children took a train trip to a neighboring town. After they had

---

[1] J. Dewey, *How We Think*, Boston, Heath, 1933, p. 210.

[2] M. Kramer and O. Hitchcock, "Trends in Speech Education," *School Executive*, Vol. 69 (August, 1950), p. 50.

[3] W. Ward, "Dramatics—A Creative Force," *School Executive*, Vol. 69 (August, 1950), p. 54.

paid their fares, they boarded the train, found their seats, and gave the conductor their tickets. Later, they walked to the dining car, where they ordered their lunches and paid for them. They then went back to their seats, and finally they left the train. When they returned to the classroom, they played the story of the excursion. Subsequently, they expanded it and pretended they were going to Chicago. They learned about the personnel and functions of the train crew and the route to Chicago. Travel by railroad gained significance.

ACCEPTING RESPONSIBILITIES FOR MEMBERSHIP IN A GROUP

A second value is that creative dramatics gives children a chance to be part of a working group, to accept its responsibilities, to help make its decisions, and to abide by them. Since members of the group chose Johnny to play the train conductor, he is accountable to them for his acting. He is responsible for his characterization, his dialogue, his relationships to the riders on the train, and his part in telling the story. Although he may have preferred to be the station agent, he is the train conductor. He learns to give and take and to accept criticism constructively. This experience helps him to be a resourceful and cooperative member of the group.

Through play, children take part gracefully in social living. The polite and mannerly train conductor acquires social competence. He makes sure that his riders on the train are comfortable. If they complain, he answers them quietly and courteously. In the dining car, the riders learn to order a dinner, to handle their silverware correctly, and to treat other diners kindly. They should be better equipped for living in today's society because they have had opportunities to practice the social amenities.

DEVELOPING CREATIVE ABILITY

A third value is that creative dramatics increases children's ability to produce a work of thought and imagination. Children portray the characters as they wish. They make up the lines they speak. They work out the necessary pantomime. Although the experiences take different forms, they are creative ones. A seven-year-old girl has a flair for language. Her line "Ugh, ugh, I like to waddle in the gooey, gushy, dirty mud" fits the big black hog in the story. A ten-year-old boy's portrayal of a kindly old grandfather recalling his younger days is an original and talented bit of acting. An eight-year-old's design for the plates for a witch's kitchen shows artistic ability, for the yellow and black colors and the strong, bold lines express the mood of the story. These children, through the oral expression, acting, and painting involved in creative dramatics, are expressing their ideas and exercising their imaginations.

DEVELOPING EMOTIONALLY

A fourth value is that creative dramatics helps children to develop emotionally. This emotional development occurs in three ways: (1) Children express their difficulties in dramatic play. (2) Playing out their difficulties effects a catharsis for them. (3) Timid and aggressive children mature through taking part cooperatively in the dramatic play of the group.

Children express their difficulties in dramatic play. After children have shown their feelings in play, they frequently begin to think about their problems constructively to find a way to handle the difficult situation or relationship. Sometimes they discuss the problem with the teacher, who is the sounding board for the children and an influence in a nondirective way. Although the teacher cannot and should not serve as a psychiatrist, he does gain insight into a child's problems through his play. For example, Johnny would knock out, shoot, or kill a big brother. His strong antipathy to his own brother was a result of a complicated situation in the family. This violence toward a brother was a clue that led the teacher to suspect that Johnny had a real problem. The teacher enlisted the aid of a social worker, who helped Johnny and his family. When a teacher suspects that a child has emotional difficulties, he gets help for him from the proper sources.

A catharsis occurs for children who play their difficulties. One train rider rebuked an imaginary mother who scolded and nagged. Expressing his feelings, which may have been representative of those he had for his own mother, was helpful to him. An eight-year-old girl brought powerful emotion into the open. She played the witch in *Snow White and the Seven Dwarfs* in a bloodcurdling fashion. Another time, she acted the part of a fierce, angry dragon. These experiences satisfied the emotional needs of this eight-year-old. Children possess strong feelings that they do not show because of fear of retaliation or punishment. They release these feelings through creative dramatics. Virginia Axline[4] in her book

[4] V. Axline, *Play Therapy*, Boston, Houghton Mifflin, 1943.

on play therapy explains clearly what dramatic play does for children.

Group activities in creative dramatics help the timid, shy child and the aggressive youngster to mature. The teacher encourages the shy child to play a role which brings him success and satisfaction. A group of seven-year-olds were rabbits nibbling at the farmer's lettuce. Since Mary, a timid child, wanted badly to be part of the group, she found herself nibbling lettuce. Because she enjoyed the experience, the next time she was glad to play a role. The aggressive youngster, on the other hand, also benefits, for he learns he cannot always play the lead, he must wait his turn to speak, and he must be a cooperative unit of the whole. Both types of children achieve, through their participation in creative dramatics, a degree of maturity.

SOURCES FOR CREATIVE DRAMATICS

Creative dramatics offers an active program where boys and girls broaden their horizons, think creatively, work together, and express their feelings. In creative dramatics, teachers channel children's natural interest in play into valuable experiences. A question that confronts the teacher and children is what to play.

Children dramatize their own experiences, such as the activities of the members of the family and trips and other projects of members of the class. A second source of dramatic activity is stories, poems, and rhymes. A third source includes folklore and fairy tales. Because of their lively action and clear-cut characterizations, folk and fairy stories dramatize delightfully. A fourth source, special events, holidays, or seasons, provides an impetus for dramatizations. Lastly, children improvise plays starting with a character, an object, or a situation. Probably most dramatic play originates from the children's own experiences and from stories.

EXPERIENCES

Children make everyday occurrences into a play. They pretend to be parents putting their children to bed. As they become more adept at playing, they plan more complex situations. When the little daughter becomes ill, they call a doctor; or the small son runs away. The variations of the family theme depend on the experiences and backgrounds of the children. Projects of the classroom, such as trips to the firehouse, to the toy store, to the vineyard, and to the glass blower, provide bases for dramatic play. Children play almost any childhood happening or adventure.

A third-grade group of children devised a delightful drama from a child's losing a tooth, placing it under his pillow, and receiving a shiny new dime for it. As the children planned the dramatization of the event, they had a number of ideas for the first scene, the child's going to bed. The only consistent idea was that the child always placed the tooth under his pillow. One eight-year-old boy suggested that the hero was so tired when he came home that he ran into the door and knocked his tooth loose; a seven-year-old boy, that he tied one end of a string to the tooth and the other to a door and banged the door shut; a nine-year-old girl, that the mother pulled out the hero's tooth, tucked him into bed, and read him a story. The second scene was the replacement of the tooth by a dime. The children considered four ways of accomplishing the replacement: (1) After the father had crept into the room, he removed the tooth from under the pillow, put it into his pocket, and replaced it with a dime. (2) A fairy queen, attended by fairies dancing and singing, made a ceremony of the exchange. (3) Twelve elves, marching in a military manner, contrived the substitution. (4) Squirrels performed the rite. The last scene was of the child's waking and finding the dime. Some of the children wanted to include just the discovery; some, the plans for spending the dime; others, the actual spending. Children dramatize in many ways as simple an experience as a boy's losing a tooth and receiving a dime for it.

POETRY

Children play rhymes and poetry. In the kindergarten or first grade, they play Mother Goose rhymes, such as "Little Jack Horner," "Baa-baa Black Sheep," "Humpty Dumpty," "Jack and Jill," "Georgie Porgie," and "Polly Put the Kettle On." Different children play these rhymes in various ways. One little five-year-old portrayed Jack Horner as sad and forlorn. He put his thumb slowly into the pie, and as he pulled the plum out, he examined it from every angle. He ate it deliberately and finally, in a kind of whine, said, "What a good boy am I." A seven-year-old girl, on the other hand, played Jack as a gay, mischievous imp. While she looked slyly around the room to see whether anyone was looking, she stuck in her thumb quickly, pulled out the plum, and gleefully gobbled it. She then did a little jig as she chortled, "What a good boy am I." Where the rhymes, such as "Little

Jack Horner," have an expressive character and action, they are good for dramatization.

Poetry serves as a basis for creative dramatics. Young children enjoy dramatizing Nona Duffy's "I'm an Engine," which tells of the engine's puffing past, tooting as it goes along. It rushes down the track, over the mountain, bridge, and plain. Older boys and girls like the ballad "The Raggle Taggle Gypsies," the story of a lady who very gaily leaves her lord to go off with the gypsies. Many boys and girls can participate, since there are servants who ask about their lady and gypsies who welcome her when she leaves her lord. Any number of poems inspire dramatic activity. Anthologies such as *Sung under the Silver Umbrella*,[5] prepared by a committee for the American Childhood Association, and Doane's[6] *A Small Child's Book of Verse*, organized in categories such as the out of doors and the circus, contain poems that arouse children's interest in playing roles.

STORIES

Probably teachers use stories for dramatic play more frequently than they do any other medium. Children have always played traditional stories like "The Three Bears," "The Three Billy Goats Gruff," and "The Three Little Pigs," and they still enjoy them. However, to expand their knowledge of literature, the teacher introduces them to less familiar and more modern stories. Some of these are published separately; others are published in collections such as Lucy S. Mitchell's[7] *Here and Now Story Book*, which contains stories for boys and girls in the kindergarten and first grade.

Stories for Lower Grades. Two stories that children in the lower grades enjoy dramatizing are *Benjie's Hat*,[8] with its humor of the likable small boy, and *Betsy-Lacy*[9], a story of two little girls at play. Other books, such as Lois Lenski's *The Little Airplane*[10] and *The Little Train*,[11] Robert McCloskey's[12] *Make Way for Ducklings*, C. T. Newberry's[13]

[5] American Childhood Association, *Sung under the Silver Umbrella*, New York, Macmillan, 1950.

[6] P. Doane, *A Small Child's Book of Verse*, New York, Oxford, 1948.

[7] L. S. Mitchell, *Here and Now Story Book*, New York, Dutton, 1948.

[8] M. L. Hunt, *Benjie's Hat*, Philadelphia, Lippincott, 1938.

[9] M. H. Lovelace, *Betsy-Lacy*, New York, Crowell, 1940.

[10] L. Lenski, *The Little Airplane*, New York, Oxford, 1946.

[11] L. Lenski, *The Little Train*, New York, Oxford, 1940.

[12] R. McCloskey, *Make Way for Ducklings*, New York, Viking, 1941.

[13] C. T. Newberry, *April's Kittens*, New York, Harper, 1940.

April's Kittens, Leo Politi's [14]*A Boat for Peppe*, Margaret Brown's[15] *The Little Farmer*, Virginia Burton's[16] *Mike Mulligan and His Steam Shovel*, and Alice Davis's[17] *Timothy Turtle*, are suitable for dramatic play. Teachers have used these stories successfully.

FIG. 3. "Winnie-the-Pooh." (*University State Teachers College, Geneseo N.Y.*)

Stories for Older Children. Stories for older children to dramatize are also plentiful. They include parts of books like Alice Dalgliesh's[18] *The Davenports Are at Dinner*, Richard Atward's[19] *Mr. Popper's Penguins*, Kate Seredy's[20] *The Open Gate*, Lois Lenski's[21] *The Strawberry Girl*, and Robert McCloskey's[22] *Homer Price*. Boys and girls like to stage the chapter of *Homer Price* which tells of the baking of the doughnuts and of the search for the diamond ring in one of hundreds of doughnuts.

[14] L. Politi, *A Boat for Peppe*, New York, Scribner, 1950.
[15] M. W. Brown, *The Little Farmer*, Chicago, Scott, Foresman, 1948.
[16] V. Burton, *Mike Mulligan and His Steam Shovel*, Boston, Houghton Mifflin, 1939.
[17] A. Davis, *Timothy Turtle*, New York, Harcourt Brace, 1948.
[18] A. Dalgliesh, *The Davenports Are at Dinner*, New York, Scribner, 1948.
[19] R. Atward, *Mr. Popper's Penguins*, Boston, Little, Brown, 1949.
[20] K. Seredy, *The Open Gate*, New York, Viking, 1943.
[21] L. Lenski, *The Strawberry Girl*, Philadelphia, Lippincott, 1945.
[22] R. McCloskey, *Homer Price*, New York, Viking, 1949.

The making of a doughnut machine and the doughnuts demands ingenuity from children. Ruth Sawyer Durand's[23] *Roller Skates*, a delightful story of old New York, can be converted into a play effectively and gives children a feeling for another age.

Folklore and Fairy Tales. Folklore and fairy tales lend themselves to dramatization, since the characters are clear-cut and the action is exciting. For children in the intermediate grades, stories in books like *Yankee Doodle's Cousins*[24] motivate dramatic play. The beginning story in this book might be developed in this way: the first scene tells about the decision of Sal of the Erie Canal to sponsor a fishing contest to decide which man will marry her. In the second scene, when her favorite is far behind in the contest, she hangs her red hair over the side of the boat; the fish come flying, and her favorite wins the contest. In the last scene, the wedding and the reception take place.

Botkin's[25] *Treasury of American Folklore*, now in inexpensive paper-covered form, contains folklore, songs, and stories which children of all ages like to play. A group of children in the fourth grade divided "The Tar Baby," one of the tales of this book, into the following six scenes:

SCENE I: The lion, bear, wolf, fox, giraffe, monkey, elephant, and the rabbit are planning how to get water since there is a drought. They decide to dig a well, and all are to help. The rabbit refuses. The other animals declare that, if he doesn't help, he cannot drink a drop of the water.

SCENE II: They dig the well.

SCENE III: After the animals discover the footprints of the rabbit near the completed well, they decide to catch and punish him. The bear agrees to sit by the well all night. He watches, but when he hears the song

> Cha ra ra, will you, will you, can you
> Cha ra ra, will you, will you, can you

he dances far away.

SCENE IV: The next morning, when the animals discover the footprints of the rabbit near the well, they are disgusted with the bear. That night, the monkey takes charge but the music enchants him too, and he follows it.

SCENE V: The following morning, the animals confer again, and since they decide they can trust none of the animals, they leave a tar baby near the well. The rabbit tries to seduce it with his music but fails. As he gets angry, he pokes it first with one arm, which sticks, and then his other arm, which also sticks. Finally, his legs and arms are completely stuck. When the animals find him, they are jubilant. They decide to punish him. They talk about cut-

[23] R. S. Durand, *Roller Skates*, New York, Viking, 1949.
[24] A. Malcomson, *Yankee Doodle's Cousins*, Boston, Houghton Mifflin, 1941.
[25] B. A. Botkin, *The Pocket Treasury of American Folklore*, New York, Pocket Books, 1949, p. 266.

ting off his head; the rabbit is enthusiastic about this idea. Then they suggest shooting him; again the rabbit is very happy. Finally they agree on feeding and feeding him, throwing him into the air, and letting him burst as he drops. He claims he doesn't like this suggestion at all.

SCENE VI: The animals feed and feed the rabbit. Finally, they take him to the top of the hillside, where four animals each take a paw, swing him, and drop him. As he lands on his feet, he runs off, calling

Yip, my name's Molly Cottontail
Catch me if you can.

This tale is representative of many folk tales that children find exciting.

Ghost stories appeal to boys and girls in the upper grades. Jones's[26] *Spooks of the Valley* contains stories carefully gathered from the Hudson Valley. "Old House by the River," one of the stories in this collection, dramatizes effectively since it is vivid and moves well. Children in the upper grades are interested in ghosts.

Other fairy and folk stories include Ruth Gannet's[27] *My Father's Dragon*, Pamela L. Travers's[28] *Mary Poppins and Mary Poppins Comes Back*, and stories found in collections such as *Andersen's Fairy Tales*,[29] *Greek Myths*,[30] *More Tales from Grimm*,[31] *English Fairy Tales*,[32] and Carl Sandburg's[33] *Rootabaga Stories*. *Jacoble Tells the Truth*, by Lisl Weil,[34] the story of a big green flying rabbit, is a folk tale from the Old World which attracts small children.

Seasons. Seasons offer opportunities for dramatic play. Boys and girls in the primary grades like Lois Lenski's[35] *Now It's Fall*. She has also written books depicting the activities of spring, summer, and winter. The first fall of snow, the sight of the first robin, or the first swim stimulates children to tell the story of winter, spring, or summer.

Holidays. Halloween, Christmas, and other holidays motivate creative dramatics. *Pumpkin Moonshine*, by Tasha Tudor,[36] which tells

[26] L. Jones, *Spooks of the Valley*, Boston, Houghton Mifflin, 1948.
[27] R. Gannet, *My Father's Dragon*, New York, Random House, 1948.
[28] P. L. Travers, *Mary Poppins and Mary Poppins Comes Back*, New York, Harcourt Brace, 1950.
[29] H. C. Andersen, *Andersen's Fairy Tales*, New York, Grosset & Dunlap, 1950.
[30] O. E. Coolidge, *Greek Myths*, Boston, Houghton Mifflin, 1949.
[31] W. Gág, *More Tales from Grimm*, New York, Coward-McCann, 1947.
[32] J. Jacobs, *English Fairy Tales*, New York, Grosset & Dunlap, 1932.
[33] C. Sandburg, *Rootabaga Stories*, New York, Harcourt Brace, 1922.
[34] L. Weil, *Jacoble Tells the Truth*, Boston, Houghton Mifflin, 1946.
[35] L. Lenski, *Now It's Fall*, New York, Oxford, 1948.
[36] T. Tudor, *Pumpkin Moonshine*, New York, Oxford, 1931.

of Sylvie Ann who started out to find the biggest pumpkin, provides a story that is excellent playmaking for primary students at Halloween. At Easter time, they play *The Egg Tree* by Katherine Methous,[37] in which Katy and Carl spend Easter with their cousins and grandmother. Katy, rummaging in the attic, finds an old hat box containing eggs with pictures; out of this adventure grows the egg tree with hundreds of colored eggs. Boys and girls in intermediate groups like Ruth Sawyer's[38] *The Christmas Anna Angel*, a delightful Hungarian folk tale of Christmas. At the end of this chapter, the teacher will find a list of stories and poetry of the various holidays that adapt well to dramatic work.

PROCEDURE AND DIRECTION
OF CREATIVE DRAMATICS

From the preceding discussion, it is obvious that there is a wealth of material for children to play—poetry, stories, experiences suggested by activities at home and at school, holidays, and seasons. But the teacher sometimes must encourage boys and girls to participate in creative dramatics. Furthermore, through the use of certain procedures and techniques, he guides them so that the experience is a profitable one. The children must adapt the story or experience and must portray consistent characters who tell the story effectively. One requirement is that the playing of the story or experience appeals to the children.

MOTIVATION

The teacher frequently motivates children to act a story or situation. How he stimulates them depends on the interests of the boys and girls in his class. He knows that Ginny's interest is horses since she rides every spare moment she has. She reads about horses, paints horses, and writes about horses. He realizes Jack is an enthusiastic and intelligent baseball fan. He may use Ginny's interest in horses and Jack's in baseball as an incentive for creative dramatics.

Teachers use other means to encourage children to engage in dramatic activity. Sometimes a bit of conversation or a picture is the stimulus. At Christmas time, one teacher heard an eleven-year-old telling about two small children looking at toys in a shop window. From this incident

[37] K. Methous, *The Egg Tree*, New York, Scribner, 1950.
[38] R. Sawyer, *The Christmas Anna Angel*, New York, Viking, 1944.

the members of the class developed a play depicting the meaning of Christmas for these children. In a similar way, teachers use pictures as a starting point. One teacher showed his class a painting of Mama and Papa Bear chasing Baby Bear in a forest. The teacher asked, "What happened?" One seven-year-old declared the little bear was about to be spanked for stealing candy. Another six-year-old announced that Baby Bear was very smart because he ran so fast that nobody, not even his mommy and daddy, could catch him. The group developed the story around the Baby Bear's ability to outrun everyone.

The same picture, used with a class of older children, brought forth this story: Mama Bear left Baby Bear home alone while she went shopping. As Mr. Mischief entered the room, he spied Mama Bear's knitting and asked Baby Bear whether he didn't want to have fun with the yarn. Baby Bear said "No." He tried coloring, drawing on his blackboard, repairing his cars; but he became bored with all these activities. Mr. Mischief kept pleading with Baby Bear to join him in the fun with the yarn. Finally, Baby Bear and Mr. Mischief unraveled the ball of yarn and wound it around the davenport, the chairs, the desk, and the tables. They had a wonderful time. But when Mama Bear came home, she couldn't quite believe it was all Mr. Mischief's fault. Baby Bear was running from Mama and Papa Bear as fast as he could, for they were going to spank him. Pictures make a good starting point for a story if they suggest an interesting set of circumstances or a definite mood.

Both the action and the mood of the story to be played are important. The teacher helps develop feeling through his own attitudes, gestures, and voice. As he reads the story aloud, he imparts its emotional content to his audience. When the children discuss a situation, he reacts to the children's suggestions in such a way as to help set the mood. Through skillful questions he brings forth discussion that establishes the feeling of the story.

ADAPTING THE STORY

After the children have decided on the feeling, they adapt the story for their play. They develop clear-cut characters, decide on the scenes in the play, introduce the story, move it forward, build its high point, and plan the essential costumes and scenery. The teacher and children work out these requirements of the play together. They attack the creation of character early.

FIG. 4. "Hansel and Gretel." (*University State Teachers College, Geneseo, N.Y.*)

FIG. 5. "Once upon a Clothes Line." (*University State Teachers College, Geneseo, N.Y.*)

PLAYING THE STORY

Creating Consistent and Imaginative Character. Children can create characters that are consistent and imaginative. Teachers guide them to delineate character with questions like What does he look like? What would he wear? How does he walk? Do you know anyone who is like him? Why is he always angry? Why does he treat the rabbit the way he does? What does he sound like? Who in the movies could play this part? After a child has performed as the character, the other children indicate what he did well and what he needs to improve. They suggest he twirl his mustache or push his hat back. They give him concrete suggestions on how to walk or talk. They examine the dialogue he has made up to see whether it is consistent with his character.

Telling the Story Clearly and Moving It Forward. In the second place, the story must be clear and must move forward. When the children and the teacher decide beforehand what scenes to include and what is to happen in each scene, the story is likely to be intelligible and to move smoothly. The teacher asks such questions as How should we begin our story? What happened first? What happened next? How will your dialogue tell that part of the story? After the children have played the story, they consider whether their classmates understood and were interested in what was happening. For example, in "The Tar Baby" the animals talked at such length about all the dreadful things they could do to the rabbit that they did not complete the play. The next time, they shortened their discussion of the punishment. Planning the scenes and the dialogue helps children tell the story clearly and smoothly.

Building the High Point. A story usually plays better when it has a high point, or climax. Usually, when the story, poem, or experience has a high point, children indicate it naturally. They get more excited or become very quiet, calm, and deliberate. They slow down or speed up the tempo. But when children do not build the high point naturally, the teacher asks such questions as What is the most exciting part of the story? How could the Duke make us feel he is having difficulty making his decision? How could Annie Lou help us realize that having a big china doll is the most wonderful happening in her life?

Where no high point exists in the original story or situation, the teacher may ask the children how they can make their story more exciting. She sometimes asks specific questions, such as "What could have happened to Johnny on the picnic?" A child may respond, "He got lost." The teacher may then ask, "While he is lost, when was he most frightened? What did he do?" The teacher may follow such questions by "How can he show us he was very scared before his mother found him?" By these queries the teacher encourages the children to include a high point on their story.

Properties, Costuming, and Scenery. After the children have decided how to play the story, they plan what costumes, properties, and scenery they want. They need very little. For example, in "The Tar Baby," the lion made himself a mane of brown paper and tied it on. The rabbit

FIG. 6. "Rumplestiltskin." (*East School, Long Beach, N.Y.*)

made herself a pair of big ears out of white cloth, slipped them over stiff pieces of cardboard, and fastened them on with string. The tar baby wore an old black coat brought from home. The well was a table turned upside down with gray paper pulled around three of its sides. They had no scenery. Costumes and properties were simple, but they were suggestive to the children. At times, children want to make more elaborate costumes, properties, or scenery. If they have the time and material available, they will find the designing and construction rewarding. However, good creative dramatics requires little equipment.

Discussing the Activity. Children discuss the process of the play in terms of its value to individuals and to the group. They ask themselves, Did we work together to make a good play? Did we stay friendly with each other? Were we willing to accept others' ideas? Did we cooperate to move the story forward? Did we offer suggestions to make the play better? How did those who were watching help us? Did each character do his very best?

After the children have talked over the merits of the play and the spirit of cooperation, they go on to discover how they can improve the play. They discuss the play in terms of whether or not their class-mates liked and understood it. They study the characterizations to make sure they were clear. When they use the names of the characters rather than those of the children, they tend to be more objective and constructive in their criticisms. They ask a question such as "Was the duck thinking and feeling like a duck?" They comment in this way: "You could tell the princess was lonesome. She seemed to be thinking she wished someone would come." The teacher may ask, "Did the ghost stay in character?" or "While Einstein wasn't talking, was he still the great scientist?" The teacher or a child may question one character's reaction to another. A comment like "I couldn't tell whether the giant was happy or provoked with the little man" points up the lack of interplay of characters.

The children also examine the action. "It was good to watch" means that the classmates enjoyed the play. "I lost the part of the story about the finding of the watch" shows that in one spot the actors did not make the story clear. "The story started off well, but it dragged in spots" indicates that it began well but did not move smoothly throughout. "The most exciting part of the story was the place where Johnny finally killed the lion" is a sign that the children built the highest point well.

Finally, they consider the voice and diction of the actors. They ask each other whether the audience heard and understood the lines. They find out whether the children spoke loudly enough and whether the diction was distinct. Furthermore, they examine the quality of voices to determine whether they were pleasant. The teacher helps those individuals whose diction is not clear or whose voices are unpleasant.

In the evaluation, the teacher and children must remember that the goal of creative dramatics is not a finished, polished performance but a cooperative endeavor where learning has taken place. Children will not do a play twice the same way, for the dialogue will be different and the action will vary or the plot will take a different turn. Through the skillful and subtle leadership of the teacher, the children should grow in many abilities: to portray character, to use language with facility, to understand the interplay of one character with another, to build a story effectively, to possess clear voice and diction, and, most important, to be a cooperative and resourceful unit of the whole. The teacher places emphasis on the growth of the talent and powers of all the children. Janey, the shy child, plays the part of an aunt well. Johnny, the aggressive child, no longer insists on being the star actor but is willing to help stage the performance or play a minor part. Each child in the class has gained from his participation in the dramatization.

PLAY PRODUCTION

Elementary school children engage in creative dramatics more frequently than they produce formal plays. Each of the activities serves different purposes. Creative dramatics gives all the children a chance to portray characters as they wish, to create their own dialogue, and to build stories in their own way. Play production gives the more able boys and girls opportunities to learn to act, to speak lines with literary value, to have pride and satisfaction in finishing and polishing a piece of work, and to perform before an audience other than their classmates. The artistic quality of the performance and the standards set for it establish goals for dramatics in the classroom. Both play production and creative dramatics have a place in the school program, although the average teacher will not put on many formal plays but will encourage a large amount of creative dramatics.

SELECTING THE PLAY

In the selection of a play, the director and the children consider four factors: (1) the story itself, (2) the staging limitations, (3) the actors, and (4) the audience.

The Story. The story should be one that will hold the interest of children through the rehearsals necessary for a finished production. The lines should be worth learning. In Percival Wilde's *The Dyspeptic Ogre,* a play which ten- and eleven-year-olds enjoy, the language is simple and spontaneous. "Six Who Pass While the Lentils Boil," with its universal appeal, is another good play for the same age group. Both of them possess literary value and remain fresh throughout rehearsals.

Staging Limitations. The second factor to take into consideration is the staging. The group must take into account the size of the stage, the lighting equipment, and the resources for designing and building scenery. Unless there is an active group of parents or a willing department of industrial arts, it is wiser to choose a play with simple or no settings. On the other hand, if the play is to be a cooperative endeavor of several departments, the art department may want the group to pick a play which challenges children to design and build effective scenery. For almost half a semester children in a fifth grade worked on the designing and construction of scenery for "Hansel and Gretel." Staging facilities influence the choice of a play.

Actors. The third factor is the abilities, number, and availability of the actors. A play may require a talented fairy who sings and dances or an emotional actress. If the story is dependent on either of these portrayals and if no such actress is available, the group should select another play. A role may demand genuine acting ability or certain physical characteristics on the part of the child who is to assume it. The director and children must take into account the number of potential actors. If they wish all twenty-five members of the class to be in a play, they select a play with a large cast. On the other hand, if only a few boys and girls are interested, they find a play with a small cast. They must consider the availability of their actors and actresses. Some boys and girls may not want to participate. Others, because of out-of-school activities, may not be able to take on another assignment. In selecting a play, they must consider carefully what kind of roles their members can play and how many members are available.

Audience. The fourth factor is the audience. Many times both adults and children comprise the audience. The play mentioned earlier, *The Dyspeptic Ogre*, appeals to both, but a play like "Aladdin" seems to be more popular with children than with adults.

The director and the children also consider the playgoing experience of their audience and what kind of theater they enjoy. Some audiences are more sophisticated and are ready for drama that depends on theater-going experiences. One fifth-grade group of boys and girls planned to do a take-off of *The King and I*. They decided the play would be meaningless to the audience, because a large part of the audience had not seen *The King and I*.

The author recently saw an original operetta written by children in the manner of Gilbert and Sullivan. The fairly sophisticated audience, with considerable playgoing experience, recognized its origin and enjoyed it the more. The director and children should deliberate on what kind of entertainment their audience enjoys and is capable of enjoying.

The director often utilizes the problem of choosing an appropriate play in group discussion since the selection vitally concerns the boys and girls. With the guidance of the teacher, they find, read, and evaluate plays for production. They criticize the intrinsic quality of the play and analyze it to see whether it is acceptable to the community, whether it is a suitable vehicle for their actors and actresses, and whether it is possible to stage it successfully with their equipment and personnel.

ORGANIZATION

From the time the play is chosen until the curtain call of the last performance, the director's responsibility is heavy. He must have an appreciation of the whole production and must be able to visualize it. He is the leader of the group of players who determine the meaning of the play, its interpretation, its movement, and its action. He should know what he wants the children to do but must allow them freedom of expression to develop their own interpretation and characterizations of the play. He acts as a guide to the players in developing appropriate interpretations of their parts. Part of the success of the performance depends on his organization of a staff to produce the play.

Director. The director organizes the class or club for the production of a play carefully and thoughtfully. In some cases, the organization will be complex, and in others, it will be fairly simple, depending on the magnitude of the production. When producing a play is a complicated affair, the director needs responsible and resourceful committees to plan and carry out the work. These usually include business, staging, prompting, lighting, costuming, properties, and ushering committees. Other teachers or parents may work with some of the groups. The director guides all of them and calls and presides at the meetings where the children plan the production.

The committee which begins to work when the play is chosen and does not finish until after the performance is the business committee.

Business Committee. One of the children or one of the teachers serves as the chairman of the business committee. He is responsible for the financial success of the play. He manages the printing and sale of tickets, the composition and printing of programs, the payment for costuming materials, make-up, and royalties, and any other expenses. He induces the community to come to the play. He keeps a record of all receipts and expenditures and gives a careful account to the class or club after the performance.

One of the tasks of this committee is to design, plan, and make available programs for the performance. Children can make good-looking and interesting programs. After they have studied the play, they plan a dummy copy of their program, which they frequently model after a Broadway or summer-stock playbill. They write in the copy the number of acts and scenes, the descriptions of the scenery, the time and place of the play, and the list of characters and actors and actresses. Sometimes they include a "Who's Who in the Cast" and an expression of appreciation to those who help with the production. Both of these add childlike and original notes to the program. In reproducing programs, the use of a ditto machine is practical, since children draw easily with the varicolored ditto pencils and when they make a mistake, they can erase readily. Sometimes the children provide covers with finger painting or block printing for the programs. The planning and composition of programs make an excellent learning experience for children.

Staging, Costuming, Make-up, Properties, and Lighting Committees. The committee on staging takes care that the scenery, where it exists, is set and that the properties are in the right place or in the hands of the character who is going to use them. A member of the committee also follows the script of the play to be certain each actor is at his right entrance. The costuming committee provides the necessary costumes and sees to it that they are in order the night of the performance; they also make certain the actors and actresses are properly dressed before going on the stage. The make-up committee makes up the actors and actresses. The property committee finds the necessary furniture for the stage and articles, such as guns and newspapers, for the characters to handle. Where the school has lighting equipment, the lighting committee, usually made up of one or two boys, handles the lights for the show. The work of these committees should be started when the play is in the early stages of rehearsal.

Prompters. The prompters, usually a boy and a girl, are present at all the rehearsals. One of their chief responsibilities is to see to it that the actors take their cues promptly. They also make certain that the designated member of the property committee produces the necessary sound effects on time. A teacher often asks a prompter to play a role if one of the cast becomes ill or gives up his part for some other reason. Because they have been at all rehearsals and because they understand the play, they will be able to fit in more readily than most other children.

Usher Committee. Finally, there is an usher committee. When the children in the director's own grade are producing the play, they invite members of another grade to be ushers. When a club is producing the play, members of the club serve. The director shows the ushers how to seat the audience. After an usher has led the guests to the end of the aisle, he presents the last one of the entering group with the necessary number of programs. He then goes back to escort the next group. The ushers reserve seats for those members of the class or club who can leave the production center. They also shut doors or open windows when necessary.

When the production is to be simple, groups of children take on several responsibilities, and single children handle others. In some plays, no scenery other than drapery, little or no costuming and make-up, and few properties are necessary. In such cases, the organization is usually an informal one of class committees. One committee acts as hosts and hostesses, another sets the stage, another furnishes the necessary costumes. The children may decide against using make-up or lights and against having programs. No prompters are necessary. The amount of organization needed depends on the type of production and the size and kind of audience.

CASTING

Having supervised the selection of the play and planned the organization for production with the children, the director's next task is to choose a cast. Probably the fairest way is through tryouts. A committee of the class or club, with the guidance of the director, casts the actors and actresses. Before the tryouts are held, the committee and the aspiring actors and actresses read and study the play so that they are well acquainted with its meaning and characters. Since the play is to be a formal experience, the tryouts may well be formal ones in which members of the class read or speak parts from the play and do a bit of necessary pantomime. Those trying out read alone and with others. The committee considers those boys and girls who are capable of interpreting the characters and the story well and who have pleasant voices and clear diction.

Besides the actual performance of those trying out, two other factors are important: (1) Those chosen to play parts should be reliable and cooperative. They must be responsible individuals, who will be at rehearsal on time, learn their lines promptly, and take their parts seriously. They should be willing to take criticism and make constructive use of it. They must be able to work well with the other members of the cast and the director, for if the play is to be successful, the actors and director must work together harmoniously. (2) The committee must think of each actor in the light of the other actors who are to play the roles. For example, the mother should be taller than the child; the voice of one actor should be distinct from that of another; the father's voice should sound older than the son's. After taking into consideration the competence of the students in acting, their ability to work well with others, and their characteristics in terms of their relationships in the play, the committee chooses a tentative cast, which is now ready to rehearse.

REHEARSALS

The Director's Preparation. The director studies the play carefully and plans the production in detail with his group. He makes sure that he himself understands the meaning of the play and the intent of its author before he starts rehearsals. He prepares for the discussion of the play with his cast. He investigates the historical and geographical background, the meaning of all the words, the explanations of allusions in the play, and the life of the author and the kinds of plays he writes. He knows the play completely and thoroughly.

Preliminary Planning of the Action. After his study of the play, he plans the details of movement and stage business. The actors and he may not follow these plans, but the preparation helps him to visualize the play and to lead discussions with the players. He decides when the actors may enter and leave the stage and where they may sit, stand, or move on the stage. He takes a large piece of stiff paper, such as an open manila folder, and draws in the floor plan, indicating doors, windows, and furniture. He uses buttons or small blocks of wood to represent the characters. If they are on the stage when the curtain opens, he places them on the plan to best advantage. He then moves them as he reads the lines. He keeps his picture balanced. He does not change the position of an actor unless the movement accomplishes a purpose, such as getting him to a particular place on the stage or indicating his feeling toward another character. For example, an actor's walking away from someone may indicate that he is disagreeing with that person or that a barrier is growing between the two. On the other hand, the actor may be giving the stage to someone else. The director indicates the movements, exits, and entrances of the characters.

Reading the Lines. After the director has discussed the play with the children, they begin work on the interpretation of lines and on acting. Actors must read lines so that they gain the desired responses from the audience. They should be fully aware of the meaning of the words as they speak them. They are re-creating the thought of the author. Furthermore, they should possess a lively sense of communication. In other words, they are interpreting the thought and feeling of the play to the audience.

After the actors have carefully discussed the play under the leadership of the director, they are likely to understand its meaning. However, an actor often needs help in determining the significance of a particular line or in deciding why a character speaks as he does. Children should not memorize lines until they arrive at a fairly acceptable interpretation. To change the interpretation of a line after it has been said in a singsong way many times is extremely difficult.

Emotional Understanding of the Play. The child must possess not only an intellectual understanding but also an emotional understanding of the character and the story. He should portray how the character feels to the audience. He makes the character a part of himself. If he is a king, he looks, walks, and feels like a king. He is making believe so well that the playing comes alive for the audience.

Teaching the Child to Read Lines and to Move Effectively. The director helps the child to read lines intelligently and to move effectively by asking questions about a small section of the play. The sections may be as small as four lines. He asks such questions as What happens in this one scene? What is the king's reason for saying "No"? Why does the daughter deny so strongly her real motives? Why do you move to the desk? What are you doing with the penknife? What can you do to make the story clear at this point? An actor indicates in his own script the movement he has found successful.

The Promptbook. The director or teacher notes in his promptbook the movements he and the children have agreed on. He also gives comments which clarify the interpretation he and the children have worked out. Besides the movement and interpretation, he places lists of properties, placement of furniture, lighting cues and special effects, such as the ringing of the telephone, in the book. The promptbook indicates in detail how the director and the children plan to produce the play.

A notebook considerably larger than the script contains each page of the script. The middle section of a page of the notebook, slightly smaller than a page of the script, is cut out and a page of script pasted in. The space around the script provides room to write the necessary details.

Guides for Acting. As the director is teaching acting to the children during the next rehearsals, he finds certain guides useful. When he has a reason for not following them, he ignores them. The guides are:

1. The child acts with all his body all the time. His posture and the movements of his arms, hands, legs, and feet should be part of his characterization, regardless of whether or not he is speaking.
2. As he listens, he reacts to the speaker.
3. He makes his turns toward the audience. As far as possible he stands or sits in a three-fourths position.
4. He keeps his gestures meaningful. He makes sure they belong to the character.
5. He walks his exit lines to the door.
6. He does not move needlessly. He stands and sits still.
7. He does not move while another actor is delivering an important line.
8. He keeps at least an arm's length away from the other actors unless he is purposefully moving close.
9. He looks in the direction he is to move and then moves there.
10. If several actors enter, the one who is to speak enters last.
11. All moves are in front of other actors.
12. In general, actors use the whole stage. They do not cramp their action in the center.

Finishing and Polishing the Performance. The last step of rehearsal is to finish and polish the performance. The director and children decide where the play needs to move more quickly and where it needs to move more slowly. To speed it, the actors do not speak faster; they pick up cues more quickly. The director may help a child pick up cues faster by suggesting that he start to speak before the preceding actor has finished. On the other hand, when he wants a child to slow down or pause before a line, he may ask him what he is thinking about, how long he would think about it, or how quickly he would respond. In this way, he gets the feel of the play as a whole. At this stage, the director helps his actors build the high point of the play. He concentrates on the unity and wholeness of the performance. He forgets that Mary is not walking right or that John is slapping his hat on too hard. He is ready for the dress rehearsal.

Dress Rehearsal. During the dress rehearsal, the play goes on exactly as it will the night of the performance. The director does not stop the actors although he may make some suggestions after the performance. He usually practices the curtain call.

While the director is conducting rehearsals, committees are working on scenery, costuming, make-up, and lighting. They are planning their part of the production to help tell the story of the play.

SCENERY

Scenery is the physical environment of the play providing the surroundings in which the actors move to tell the story. It indicates when and where the action takes place. It suggests to the audience the mood of the play. A simple unit with well-defined line and color rather than elaborate scenery creates feeling. In elementary schools, the most frequent scenery consists of simple draperies.

Line and color in scenery are important in elementary school plays, for they help set the mood. Wherever they occur, in screens placed before a cyclorama or in draperies hung at the windows, they suggest the emotions evoked by the play. Light colors suggest gaiety; drab colors, somberness. Red means danger; purple portrays nobility; black indicates tragedy; yellow signifies comedy; and soft green gives a feeling of peace and calm. Lines also suggest moods. Tall, vertical lines indicate majesty; horizontal, tragedy; and curved ones, comedy. One junior high school group carried out the spirit of their play by designing and making draperies. Their play was a gay story of how an underdog football team reached first place in its league. The use of yellow, orange, brown, and ovals and circles in the draperies gave the feeling of the season and of the fun of the play. The draperies were brown cambric on which the children painted large yellow ovals with orange curved lines across them. They carried out the color scheme in the furniture, pictures, and other accessories of the room. The setting added to the spirit of the play.

Designing scenery challenges boys and girls. This art must serve dramatic art and be subordinate to it. The essential aim is to express the mood and feeling of the play. In planning scenery, children ask such questions as What is the main idea of the story? What feeling does it evoke? When and where does the play take place? What is the ground plan that is necessary for the actors to play on? What color and lines best express the story? If children are interested in building sets or constructing scenery, the teacher may refer to the texts on scenery suggested in the Bibliography.

COSTUMING

Costuming, as well as scenery, sets the right kind of environment for the play and helps tell the story. Color and line are as important in costuming as in scenery. Fabrics, on the other hand, are of no consequence, except as they call attention to themselves or contrast too strongly with each other. Costumes help portray character and aid the audience in distinguishing one character from another or in thinking of a group as a unit. For example, since Janey is the tinkling, silvery fairy, her costume is trimmed with Christmas tinsel and silver buttons. Since Helen is the gay, frolicsome daisy fairy, her costume is yellow and her headdress is a chain of yellow daisies. Since the members of the chorus are simple fairies, they wear white fairy costumes exactly alike.

Children can make costumes such as those required by the fairies. But if the costumes need careful dressmaking, the parents or teachers assist the children. For example, in a school where the boys and girls were producing "Hansel and Gretel," one of the parents, with the help of the ideas and suggestions of the children, designed the costumes for the birds who ate the crumbs Hansel and Gretel dropped. These costumes consisted of a series of ruffles of crepe paper which she and the children made together. The experience was happy and rewarding for the children and the parent.

MAKE-UP

Besides costuming, make-up distinguishes characters. For children, little make-up is necessary except to transform a child into a character like a clown or an old man. Where the children are playing roles their own age, all the make-up they need is a small amount of rouge placed high on the cheeks and lines drawn around the eyes. Texts on play production give directions for make-up. Max Factor has published a number of pamphlets which explain the techniques of stage make-up.

PROPERTIES

Properties also help the audience to distinguish characters and to understand the story. They are the parts of a play other than the scenery or costumes. They include such articles as furniture, letters, the policeman's stick, clocks, and noises. Actors should handle the properties or substitutes for them early so that the handling becomes part of the characterization. Children can construct many properties from materials like tagboard, plywood, or colored paper. The author once saw a beautiful prow of a boat made from a huge corrugated box pulled apart, bent, painted with water paint, and lettered "Our Gal Sal."

LIGHTING

Lighting gives meaning to the play through its effects. It may indicate that night is approaching or that the sun is shining brightly. It may highlight certain parts of the play. It helps create atmosphere. Since most elementary schools have meager lighting equipment, the children in these schools do not present plays which depend on lighting effects. However, some elementary schools have fairly complete lighting equipment, and in these schools lighting helps tell the story of the play. Nine-year-old boys and girls can manage quite complicated lighting systems effectively if an adult trains them carefully.

DISCUSSING THE PERFORMANCE

After the performance, the children discuss what went well, what went badly, and what could be improved. They evaluate comments by adults. They discuss how they might work together better another time. They analyze the performance given by the actors and actresses. They talk over the effectiveness of the make-up, lighting, scenery, and costuming. They check expenditures. They make suggestions about points to watch for in their next production. Finally, they decide how to express their appreciation to those persons who helped in the production.

SUMMARY

In the elementary school, children participate in two types of dramatics: creative dramatics and play production. Creative dramatics is valuable in that children gain knowledge through a meaningful experience, learn to take and share responsibility for artistic work, and develop creatively and emotionally. In play production, the children also benefit from being part of a working group and, to some extent, develop emotionally; the distinct value in play production, however, is that children with ability are participating in a finished public performance.

In creative dramatics, children play their own experiences, poems, and stories, including folklore, fairy tales, and the stories of seasons and holidays; there is no set dialogue. In play production, they act in a play chosen on the basis of its story and of its requirements in terms of staging, actors, and audience.

The director in creative dramatics helps the children to create consistent, imaginative characters, to tell the story clearly, and to keep it moving. On the other hand, in play production, the director and the children plan the movement, the interpretation, and the action of the play; and the director helps the children to understand the lines, the characters, and the meaning of the play. He follows the traditional rules of acting. The direction and experience of the child is more formal than in creative dramatics.

Scenery, costuming, properties, and lighting help tell the story in both kinds of dramatics, although they are used more extensively in play production. In both costuming and scenery, color and line are important. A public performance demands more careful designing and construction. Creative dramatics requires no make-up or lighting. The production of a play needs enough lighting and make-up to project the action and the characters in the play to the back of the auditorium.

Both creative dramatics and play production have their place in elementary school education. Teachers use creative dramatics more frequently; but it is beneficial for elementary school children to see a finished, artistic performance produced by their peers, for it sets goals for dramatic activities in the classroom.

EXERCISES

1. Compare a book on play therapy with one on creative dramatics. Show where the philosophies of the two writers are alike and where they are different.

2. List a series of experiences children of a definite age level have that would dramatize well.

3. Make a list of stories and poems suitable for dramatic interpretation by the grade you intend to teach.

4. Plan a dramatization as it might be developed by children for a holiday or special event.

5. Make a promptbook for a children's play.

6. Indicate how a particular children's story could be adapted for creative dramatics.

7. Indicate how dramatics could be utilized in units of work of areas such as social studies or music.

BIBLIOGRAPHY
CREATIVE DRAMATICS

Axline, V., *Play Therapy*, Boston, Houghton Mifflin, 1943. Discusses the therapeutic value of play. Illustrated by examples of what dramatic play does for particular children.

Bowen, F. C., "Let's Play a Story," *Arts in Childhood*, Series 6, Bulletin 3, Fisk University, Nashville, Tenn., 1951. Shows how children play "The Three Bears" and "Cinderella."

Brown, C., *Creative Drama in the Lower School*, New York, Appleton-Century-Crofts, 1930. Gives the theory and practice of creative drama in the lower grades. Excellent suggestions for pantomime by children. Includes stories to play. Explains the use of excursions in dramatization.

Creative Schools, Washington, National Education Association, Department of Elementary School Principals, 1945. Tells of creative work in various schools throughout the country.

Hayden, E. (ed.), "Dramatic Play, a Way of Learning," *Arts in Childhood*, Series 6, Bulletin 4, Fisk University, Nashville, Tenn., 1951. Contains articles telling about dramatic play in the various grades.

Lease, R., and G. B. Siks, *Creative Dramatics in Home, School and Community*, New York, Harper, 1952. Shows the place of creative dramatics in school and community. Explains what creative dramatics is and how to use it. An unusually practical and helpful book.

Progressive Education Association, *Creative Expression*, Eau Claire, Wis., E. M. Hale and Co., 1939. Describes creative work done in such fields as music and art. Excellent illustrations of puppetry.

Seeds, C., "Dramatic Play As a Means to Democratic Social Living," *Childhood Education*, Vol. 19 (January, 1943), pp. 218–222.

Ward, W., "Dramatics—a Creative Force," *School Executive*, Vol. 69 (August, 1950), pp. 54–56. Describes creative play built around the story *The Japanese Twins* by Lucy Fitch Perkins.

———, *Playmaking with Children*, New York, Appleton-Century-Crofts, 1947. Explains the use of creative dramatics in the classroom.

———, *Creative Dramatics*, New York, Appleton-Century-Crofts, 1931. Discusses the theory and practice of creative dramatics for upper grades.

STORIES OF HOLIDAYS THAT DRAMATIZE WELL

Christmas

Association for Childhood Education, Literary Committee, *Told under the Christmas Tree*, New York, Macmillan, 1948. A collection of Christmas stories and poems. Intermediate.

Bernhard, J., *Lullaby*, New York, Roy, 1944. Folktale adapted from the Polish. Story of the Christ child. Primary grades.

Cavanah, F. (ed.), *Favorite Christmas Stories*, New York, Grosset & Dunlap, Inc., 1941. Includes Andersen, Dickens, Hugh Walpole for the older children, and Moore's " 'Twas the Night before Christmas" and Miriam Potter's "Mrs. Goose's Wild Christmas" for the younger children. All grade levels.

Chambers, M. C., *The Three Kings*, New York, Oxford, 1946. Tale of Spain, tender, gentle, humorous. Junior high school or upper grades.

Duvoisin, R., *The Christmas Whale*, New York, Knopf, 1945. An imaginative story of a whale's taking the place of the traditional reindeer. Primary.

Eaton, A. T. (compiler), *The Animals' Christmas*, New York, Viking, 1944. Traditional Christmas stories and poems. Intermediate grades.

Glover, F. R., *The First Christmas*, New York, Dutton, 1943. The Christmas story, simply and well told. All grades.

Hall, W., *Christmas Pony*, New York, Knopf, 1948. Delightful Christmas story of a black-and-white pony, a dancing turkey, and an air-minded rabbit. Primary.

Jones, J. O., *The Little Child*, New York, Viking, 1946. The Christmas story set between prophecies and expanded to include the episodes in the early life of Jesus. Lovely illustrations. Primary.

Lathrop, D., *An Angel in the Woods*, New York, Macmillan, 1947. Story of a little toy angel with a candle in her hand and how she brought Christmas to the woods. Nicely illustrated. Primary.

Meigs, C., *Mother Makes Christmas*, New York, Grosset & Dunlap, 1940. Good story. Primary.

Sawyer, R., *The Christmas Anna Angel*, New York, Viking, 1944. Delightful Hungarian folk tale of Christmas. Upper primary, middle, and upper grades.

Thoburn, J. (compiler), *Away in a Manger*, New York, Oxford, 1942. Well-selected familiar Christmas verse.

Tudor, T., *The Dolls House*, New York, Oxford, 1950. The story of two very old dolls who lived in a handsome doll house and who every Christmas gave a party for the dolls of the neighborhood. Primary.

Yates, E., *Once in the Year*, New York, Coward-McCann, 1947. The story of the flowers' blooming and the animals' talking at midnight on Christmas Eve. Upper grades.

Easter

Mariana, *Miss Flora McFlimsey's Easter Bonnet*, New York, Lothrop, 1951. Flora McFlimsey had nothing to wear, but Peterkins whisked away and returned with an Easter bonnet for her. Primary.

Methous, K., *The Egg Tree*, New York, Scribner, 1950. Katy and Carl spent Easter with their cousins and grandmother. When Katy went to the attic, she found eggs with pictures on them. Out of this adventure came the egg tree. Primary.

Price, O., *A Donkey for the King*, New York, Whittlesey, 1945. The story of young Joshua and his journey to the Golden City. Upper grades.

Tudor, T., *A Tale for Easter*, New York, Oxford, 1951. A tale of Easter's joy with the glimpse of life of woods and field. Primary.

Easter, Christmas, Thanksgiving, and Other Holidays.

Fenner, P. R. (compiler), *Feasts and Frolics*, New York, Knopf, 1949. Stories of Halloween, April Fool's Day, Easter, Fourth of July, Thanksgiving, Christmas, Washington's Birthday, Lincoln's Birthday. Intermediate and upper.

Lillie, A. M., *The Book of Three Festivals*, New York, Dutton, 1948. The story of Easter, Christmas, and Thanksgiving. Intermediate and junior high school.

Halloween

Linton, R., and A. Linton, *Hallowe'en through Twenty Centuries*, New York, Henry Schuman, 1950. Gives the mystic feeling of Halloween. This holiday traced through the centuries. Authors delve into the lore of witchcraft. A treasury of Halloween folklore, both religious and magical. Junior high school.

Sechrist, E. H., *Heigh-ho for Hallowe'en*, Philadelphia, Macrae Smith, 1948. Collection of stories, poems, plays, songs, and games for Halloween. Intermediate.

Tudor, T., *Pumpkin Moonshine*, New York, Oxford, 1938. The story of the adventures of Sylvie Ann who started out to find the biggest pumpkin she could. Primary.

Thanksgiving

Barksdale, L., *The First Thanksgiving*, New York, Knopf, 1942. Authentic story of the first Thanksgiving. Upper grades.

Patriotic Holidays

Brown, E., *Holidays and Everydays*, New York, Oxford, 1942. Holidays arranged according to calendar months. Includes Easter and Christmas.

Curtis, A., *Good Plays for Patriotic Holidays*, New York, T. S. Denison, 1932. Plays based on Lincoln's Birthday, Washington's Birthday, Memorial Day, Independence Day, Armistice Day. Intermediate.

Hertz, E. (ed.), *Lincoln Talks*, New York, Viking, 1939. Kaleidoscopic presentation of a multitude of living incidents in Lincoln's career. Emphasis on his ability as a storyteller and his unstudied humor. Excellent for dramatization. Junior high school, or upper grades.

Schauffler, R. H., *The Days We Celebrate*, New York, Dodd, Mead, 1946. Poems, plays, stories, and essays about Washington's Birthday, Lincoln's Birthday, Memorial Day, and Flag Day. Includes material by Eleanor Farjeon, Rose Fyleman, A. E. Houseman, Vachel Lindsay. All material not equally good.

Schauffler, R. H., and A. P. Sanford (eds.), *Plays for Our American Holidays*, New York, Dodd, Mead, 1945. Short plays that run about twenty minutes celebrating Lincoln's Birthday, Washington's Birthday, Flag Day, Memorial Day, Independence Day, and Armistice Day. Upper grades.

Religion

Pike, R., *Round the Year with the World's Religions*, New York, Henry
Schuman, 1950.   Facts and legends about the months and seasons that
have been invested with religious significance. Upper grades.

Fitch, F. M., *One God: The Ways We Worship Him*, New York, Lothrop, 1951.
Religious celebrations of the various sects. Well illustrated with photographs. Intermediate and upper grades.

Weilerstein, S. R., *What the Moon Brought*, Philadelphia, Jewish Publication
Society, 1942.   Stories of the significant occasions of the Jewish year.
Primary.

FOLKLORE FOR DRAMATIZATION

Association for Childhood Education, International, *Told under the Green
Umbrella*, New York, Macmillan, 1930.   Mostly folk tales, well chosen.
Primary.

Bowman, J. C., *Pecos Bill: The Greatest Cowboy of All Times*, New York,
Whitman, 1937.   Tall tales of the legendary cowboy. Intermediate and
higher grades.

Carmer, C. (compiler), *America Sings*, New York, Knopf, 1942.   Folk songs
with stories and illustrations for each song line.   Includes adventures of
Johnny Appleseed, Pecos Bill, and Stormalong.

Cornplanter, J. J., *Legends of the Longhouse*, Philadelphia, Lippincott, 1938.
Myths and legends of the Seneca Indians. Upper and intermediate grades.

Cunningham, C. (ed.), *Talking Stone*, New York, Knopf, 1939.   Indian and
Eskimo folk tales.

Field, R. (ed.), *American Folk and Fairy Tales*, New York, Scribner, 1939.
Indian legends, Uncle Remus stories, Paul Bunyan stories, mountain
tales, and other folk tales.

Harris, J. C., *Uncle Remus, His Songs and Sayings*, New York, Appleton-
Century-Crofts, 1940.   Collection of authentic folk tales of the Negroes.

Hatch, M. C., *Thirteen Danish Tales*, New York, Harcourt Brace, 1947.   All
grades.

Hogner, D., *Navajo Winter Nights*, New York, Nelson, 1938.   Collection of
tales of the Navajo Indians.

Jones, L. C., *Spooks of the Valley*, Boston, Houghton Mifflin, 1948.   Ghost
stories of the Hudson Valley. Upper grades.

Malcomson, A., *Yankee Doodle's Cousins*, Boston, Houghton Mifflin, 1948.
Collection of folk tales. Includes the story of Sal, the best cook on the
Erie Canal. Intermediate grades.

Malcomson, A., and D. J. McCormick, *Mister Stormalong*, Boston, Houghton
Mifflin, 1952.   Folk tales about the legendary New England sailor.
Upper grades.

Petersham, M., and M. Petersham, *Rooster Crows*, New York, Macmillan,
1945.   Nursery rhymes, finger games, skipping-rope songs, counting-out
rhymes. Primary or nursery school.

Shapiro, I., *Yankee Thunder: The Legendary Life of Davy Crockett*, New York, Messner, 1944. Upper grades.

Shephard, E., *Paul Bunyan*, New York, Harcourt Brace, 1941. Lively picture of the American frontier. Upper grades.

Wood, R. (compiler), *American Mother Goose*, Philadelphia, Stokes, 1940. Collection of American rhymes, riddles, games, and jingles. Primary.

Reference on Folklore for the Teacher

Barnes, R. A. (compiler), *I Hear America Singing: An Anthology of Folk Poetry*, Philadelphia, Winston, 1937.

Blair, W., *Native American Humour*, New York, American Book, 1937. A good collection of tall tales.

Botkin, B. A. (ed.), *Treasury of American Folklore: Stories, Ballads and Traditions of the People*, New York, Crown, 1944. Contains all types of American folklore including rhymes, tall tales, ballads, and even "nitwit" stories.

Carmer, C., *Hurricane's Children: Tales from Your Neck o' the Woods*, New York, Rinehart, 1937. Excellent regional tales.

———, *Listen for a Lonesome Drum: A York State Chronicle*, New York, Rinehart, 1936. An interpretation of upstate New York.

Daugherty, J. H. (ed.), *Their Weight in Wildcats: Tales of the Frontier*, Boston, Houghton Mifflin, 1936. Good pictures of pioneer life.

Drummond, A. M., and R. E. Gard (eds.), *Lake Guns of Seneca and Cayuga*, Ithaca, N.Y., Cornell University Press, 1942. A collection of plays based on folklore of New York State.

Lomax, J. A., and A. Lomax (compilers), *American Ballads and Folk Songs*, New York, Macmillan, 1934.

Sandburg, C., *American Songbag*, New York, Harcourt Brace, 1927.

Stewart, G. R., *Names on the Land: A Historical Account of Place-naming in the United States*, New York, Random House, 1945. Interesting tales and hypotheses of how towns and rivers were named.

Thompson, H. W., *Body, Boots and Britches*, Philadelphia, Lippincott, 1940. An excellent varied collection of folklore.

Tolman, B., and R. Page, *Country Dance Book*, New York, Rinehart, 1937. Contains directions for many folk dances.

PLAY PRODUCTION

Albright, H. D., *Working Up a Part*, Boston, Houghton Mifflin, 1947. Describes how to attack the interpretation of a role in a play.

Corson, R., *Stage Make-up*, rev. ed., New York, Appleton-Century-Crofts, 1947.

Chekhov, M., *To the Actor: On the Technique of Acting*, New York, Harper, 1952. Gives excellent advice on teaching acting.

Dolman, J., *The Art of Play Production*, rev. ed., New York, Harper, 1947.

Fuchs, T., *Stage Lighting*, Boston, Little, Brown, 1929.

Heffner, H. C., S. Selden, and H. D. Sellman, *Modern Theatre Practice*, rev.
ed., New York, Appleton-Century-Crofts, 1946. Describes the various
aspects of play production.

Smith, M., *Play Production for Little Theatres, Schools and Colleges*, New York,
Appleton-Century-Crofts, 1948.

PLAYS AND COLLECTIONS OF PLAYS

Collections of Plays

Field, R., *Patchwork Plays*, New York, Doubleday, 1930. Plays dealing
with a variety of subjects, such as history and animals. Primary grades.

Fyleman, R., *Eight Little Plays for Children*, New York, Doubleday, 1925.
Good collection, including "Cabbage and Kings." Intermediate grades.

Garnett, L. A., *Three to Make Ready*, Boston, W. H. Baker, 1923. Fairy,
Mother Goose plays. Primary grades.

Lutkenbau, A. M. (ed.), *Plays for School Children*, New York, Appleton-
Century-Crofts, 1915. Intermediate grades.

Moses, M., *A Treasury of Plays for Children*, Boston, Little, Brown, 1926.
Plays include classical stories and "Six Who Pass While the Lentils
Boil" and "Toymaker of Nuremburg." All grades.

Moses, M., *Ring Up the Curtain*, Boston, Little, Brown, 1932. Plays include
classical stories, of which "Aladdin" is one. All grades.

Plays

Henry, A., and D. Van Auken, *Boastful Benny*, New York, French. Good
story. Middle grades.

McFadden, E., *The Boy Who Discovered Easter*, New York, French. A play
for Easter. Upper grades.

————, *Why the Chimes Rang*, New York, French. A play based on the
Christmas story. Upper grades.

VanDerVeer, E., *The Boy on the Meadow*, New York, French. A delightful
Christmas story of a child who gives away his new shoes. Upper grades.

Wilde, P., *The Dyspeptic Ogre*, New York, French. Story of the ogre who
eats children. Excellent humor. Upper grades.

Index to Children's Plays

Hyatt, A. (compiler), *Index to Children's Plays*, Chicago, American Library
Association, 1931. Books about plays and play production, costuming,
puppetry—annotated. Index to plays listed according to subject matter
and special days.

3 Puppetry

The values of the puppet show for the participants are very like those of creative dramatics. Sharing in either activity gives children a chance to learn through a meaningful experience, to accept the responsibilities of membership in the group, and to express themselves creatively. Each experience benefits the children by releasing their tensions in the dramatization of their personal problems. An added value of puppetry is that children acquire skill in working with their hands through designing, making, and manipulating puppets. Some of the values are more evident in puppetry than in creative dramatics.

Children usually feel freer to express themselves through puppetry than through creative dramatics. Since they are manipulating dolls, they have little opportunity to think of their fear of the audience. They are thoroughly a part of the story. Because they enjoy the complete make-believe of the performance, children who do not talk much in a group speak more readily and fully when they use puppets. Furthermore, they make known fear, envy, anger, and sorrow through the dolls, while self-consciousness sometimes prevents the expression of the same emotions in dramatic play. In general, they will speak more naturally and fully and express their emotions more freely in puppetry than in creative dramatics.

MOTIVATION

One teacher encouraged her children to produce a puppet show with *Snow White and the Seven Dwarfs* by utilizing their interest in the tale and directing it to puppetry through the use of the illustrations of the story. Motivating children to produce a puppet show is in many ways like motivating children to participate in dramatic play. The teacher recognizes, stimulates, and guides the interests of the children; or he reads a story so vividly that the children want to hear it again and

finally to play it. But in puppetry, the teacher makes use of several
other devices, such as the use of motion pictures with puppets. *Little
Red Riding Hood*,[1] a colored film for kindergarten and primary children,
is entertaining and may suggest the activity of puppetry. Some of the
television shows, such as "Kukla, Fran and Ollie" or "In the Park,"
encourage children to make puppets and to produce a puppet show.

Professional puppet shows, music, and ballet sometimes attract children to puppetry. In large cities, the children may go to see a show put
on by the park department, health department, or one of the museums.
Some traveling shows play various towns. The Red Gate Players, a
group who produce Chinese plays, is an example of a traveling show.
Sometimes music helps to interest children in puppetry. While a recorded symphony orchestra played *Peter and the Wolf*, children interpreted it with puppets. Haydn's *Toy Symphony*, Tschaikowsky's *The
Nutcracker Suite*, *Mother Goose Suite*, by Ravel, or some of the folk songs
in the collections suggested in the Bibliography on folklore in the chapter on dramatics help to arouse an enthusiasm for puppetry. Some of
the modern ballets also inspire children to make and manipulate
puppets.

Most frequently, however, the teacher suggests play with puppets by
bringing them into the classroom to show children what fun playing
a role with a puppet is. In a first-grade class, a teacher brought in two
stick puppets, a dog and a cat. As the dog talked to the cat, he told him
he was a real "fraidy cat." Finally, one little six-year-old girl asked for
the cat, and a six-year-old boy for the dog. They meowed and barked
at each other. The angry cat spat at the dog and finally chased him
away. The children asked whether they could make their own puppets
so that all of them could play. A fifth-grade teacher brought in a com-
mercially made hand puppet. She explained to the children how they
could make puppets themselves. Because making the puppets fascinated the children, the construction itself was the inspiring force that
started their doing many puppet plays. Children enjoy making many
different kinds of puppets.

KINDS OF PUPPETS

Sometimes "puppets" is a general term which includes the following
two categories: hand puppets, dolls manipulated by hand, and string

---

[1] Encyclopaedia Britannica Films, *Little Red Riding Hood*, 1 reel, 16 mm, sound,
color. Wilmette, Ill.

puppets, dolls manipulated by strings. Usually, however, puppets are dolls worked by hand, and "marionettes" are those operated with strings. Boys and girls enjoy both types of doll. Children in the primary grades make and operate stick and shadow puppets of cardboard (Fig. 7) and hand puppets of paper bags, vegetables, and other common materials. Older children construct and manipulate hand puppets of socks and papier mâché and make and operate marionettes.

STICK PUPPETS

The materials needed for stick puppets are cardboard, staples, and long thin sticks. The children draw the fronts of the figures on cardboard. The next step is to cut them out and draw around them on second pieces of cardboard to make the backs. After they have cut out the backs, they color or paint the features, hair, and costumes on both sides of the figures. They are then ready to staple the backs and fronts to the sticks and to attach them to each other in several spots. In some instances, the children fasten a tail, an elephant's trunk, or a person's arm, also cut out of cardboard, to the figure with a piece of wire. As they move

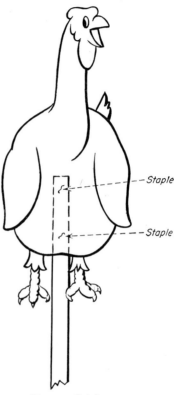

FIG. 7. Stick puppet.

the puppets about to tell the story, they manipulate the tail, arm, or trunk. Stories with plentiful action and quite different-appearing characters are suitable for play with stick puppets. Boys and girls in the primary grades make stick puppets for, and delight in playing, "The Three Billy Goats Gruff," "The Three Bears," "Christmas Stocking," by Dorothy Baruch, and "Little Chicken," by Margaret Wise Brown. The last two stories are in the anthology *Read Me Another Story*.[2] In these stories, the stick puppets represent readily distinguishable characters who are in motion most of the time.

[2] Child Study Association of America, *Read Me Another Story*, New York, Crowell, 1949.

SHADOW PUPPETS

Children play the same stories with shadow puppets. Shadow puppets are just like stick puppets except that they are not colored and they have holes in the faces of the figures for eyes. Children place them and figures of properties, such as tables and chairs, against a translucent screen with a light behind it so that only the shadows of the figures show. A white window shade with a 100-watt bulb and a reflector placed at the back of the shade in the center is an adequate lighted screen. The use of figures cut from black cardboard, attached to a stick and manipulated in front of a white sheet, achieves the same kind of effect.

HAND PUPPETS

Hand Puppets Made from Vegetables, and Other Solid Materials. Because young children sometimes prefer to construct and operate three-dimensional dolls, they fashion hand puppets from potatoes, top sections of carrots, apples, yams, Styrofoam, and Spongex. With an apple corer they scoop a hole in the center of the bottom, large and deep enough to hold their index fingers. Using a mixture of liquid glue and tempera paint about the consistency of heavy cream, they paint the features and hair on the doll; or they fashion them from various materials which they fasten on with glue or thumbtacks. The following are suggestions for materials to use as features and hair:

Eyes: push pins, upholstery buttons, buttons, marbles, cloves, or thumbtacks.
Nose: small pieces of potato, apple, or carrot, push pins, or a paper pyramid.
Nostrils: two cloves or two thumbtacks.
Mouth: red construction paper or a checker.
Hair: wood shavings, crepe hair, absorbent cotton, heavy rope, yarn, wool, pieces of old mops, strips of cut paper, foam rubber, or carrot curls.

Clothing this kind of puppet is simple (Fig. 8). A large piece of cloth, about a foot wide and a little longer, with a hole in the center big enough for the index finger, suffices as a costume. Since the child's thumb and middle finger serve as arms for the puppet, he drapes the material around them, fastening it with rubber bands. The accompanying diagram (Fig. 8) shows where to cut the hole and where to place the fingers and the thumb. Boys and girls may paint the cloth, crayon it, or decorate it with buttons, tinsel, braid, feathers, or bits of paper.

Hand Puppets Made from Paper Bags. In the primary grades, boys and girls make hand puppets from paper bags. They bring to school strong paper bags not wider than twice the width of their hands. The first step is to staple the corners of the bottoms of the bags so as to make them round (see Fig. 9). The next step is to turn the bags inside out and stuff them with pieces of soft newspaper or tissue paper in such a way as to shape them into heads. The children then insert round tubes of cardboard for their index fingers and secure them tightly at the necklines with a string. They now have round heads upon which to paint or crayon the hair, features, and costumes. Their final step is to

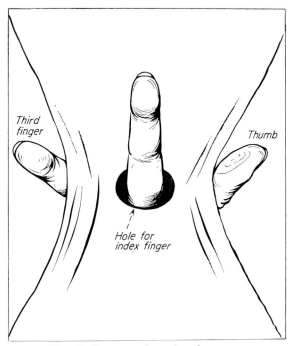

FIG. 8. Costume for a hand puppet.

cut holes at the sides of the bags for the thumbs and middle fingers and to paint dresses or suits on the bags.

Hand Puppets Made from Socks. Boys and girls in the middle and upper grades make puppets from socks or stockings. First, they cut off the foot of the sock as indicated in Fig. 10. Secondly, to make the head, they gather its top with a stiff thread or piece of string and pull it tight. Thirdly, they turn it inside out and stuff the top of the stocking with pieces of soft paper or cotton. After they have made a hole in the stuffing with their fingers, they insert a cardboard tube as indicated in Fig. 10. Fourthly, they gather the neck with an extra-strong thread and wind the thread around the neck securely to hold the tube in place. Fifthly, they sew the two pieces of material from the foot lengthwise and then insert them in the holes in the sock which were cut for the arms. Lastly, they paint the features on or sew them with wool. If the boys and girls sew them, they use French knots for the nose and an

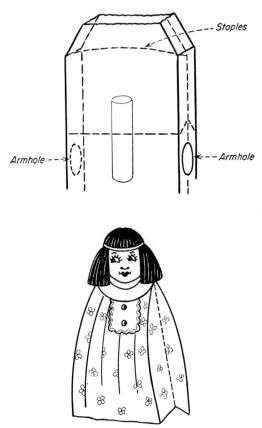

FIG. 9. Hand puppets made from paper bags.

outline stitch for the mouth and edges of the eyes. Sometimes they sew the eyes and mouth solidly. Buttons attached to the face also serve as features; they make particularly effective eyes. The hair may be wool or any of the materials suggested under Hand Puppets Made from Vegetables.

Hand Puppets Made from Papier Mâché. The desire to make puppets with more graphic or picturesque features challenges students to try modeling with papier mâché. Puppets made from papier mâché assure more accurate representation of character, although the construction is a slow process which requires care. The characters' habitual expressions are obvious because the children exaggerate the features in sculpturing them. There are three methods of making heads of puppets from papier mâché:

1. The materials necessary for this method are old newspapers, wallpaper paste, a light bulb, potato, or other object to model the head on, tempera paint, and shellac.

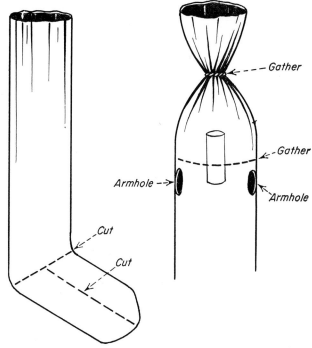

FIG. 10. Sock puppets.

Children soak newspapers in a large basin or pail with enough water to cover them long enough for them to disintegrate. They reduce the paper to pulp by stirring or squeezing it. To this pulp they add wallpaper paste made a little thicker than the directions on the box suggest and mixed thoroughly so that no dry particles or lumps remain. About two parts of pulp to one part of paste or enough paste to impregnate the paper thoroughly is an index of the amount of paste to use. To this mixture of pulp and paste the children add about two tablespoons of salt to prevent fermentation, and they may add whiting to give the mass a white look. After they have squeezed a handful of this between their hands hard enough to remove the excess paste, they place it over an object like a potato or discarded electric bulb, being sure to build out the papier mâché from the foot of the bulb or potato to form neck and shoulders. They then sculpture distinctive features. The character should have a sad, worried, or very happy look. Children show imagination in sculpturing dolls; for example, a ten-year-old boy made a head

FIG. 11. Papier mâché hand puppet.

of a gossip with five or six open mouths. A twelve-year-old girl sculptured a head of a mean old man with one eye squinting at an angle in the middle of his forehead. They cut the head in half when it is thoroughly dry, glue it together, place strips of paper dipped in paste on the underside of the doll, and reinforce the edges on the outside, where they pieced it together, with papier mâché.

2. The second method requires the same materials, but the head is solid papier mâché. As explained in the preceding paragraph, children

soak newspapers until they disintegrate. They then make wallpaper paste the consistency of thick cream in a No. 10 can or a pail. They put the newspaper pulp in the pail of paste, take out enough to hold between their hands, and push out the excess paste. They use a tube of cardboard big enough to hold the index finger and squeeze the papier mâché around it. Again they build the neck and shoulders. They then sculpture the features by pushing and squeezing the papier mâché. This method is somewhat simpler than the first since it eliminates cutting the head in half.

3. The materials needed for this method are Plasticine, about half a pound per doll, paste, newspaper, paste brushes, shellac, and sandpaper.

The children take pieces of Plasticine about as big as their fists and model from them heads, necks, and semblances of shoulders. They sculpture the expressive features broadly; for example, they push in eyes, forgetting about eyelids. In making dolls for *Snow White and the Seven Dwarfs*, they exaggerate the features of the witch, with her long pointed nose, and of Grumpy, with his scolding mien. After they have coated the model with a thin coat of petroleum jelly, they cover it with at least four layers of papier mâché. The children tear (*not* cut) newspapers into narrow strips, let them soak for a few minutes in wallpaper paste of the consistency of thick cream, and press them on the model over and into the contours. To be sure that they cover the heads completely each time, they alternate layers of plain newspaper with layers of colored newspaper (comic sheets). As they place the strips on the model, they must make sure that they overlap in a definite direction; for example, they put all the strips of the first layer on vertically, those of the second horizontally, those of the third in one diagonal direction, and those of the fourth in the opposite diagonal direction. They try to keep the papier mâché head as nearly like the model as possible. After each layer is dry, they sandpaper it to make it smooth. When the four layers are complete and dry, they cut apart the papier mâché on the model, remove the clay, and piece the two halves together with glue. They also use pieces of pasted paper on the underside of the head and reinforce the outside edges with more bits of torn paper.

Painting the Dolls. Whichever method has been used to make the heads of papier mâché, the children then paint them with tempera paint and finally give them two coats of white shellac. They often use color to reveal the personality of the character; for example, they may paint the villain's face gray or the witch's face green. The conventional flesh color is made of orange and white tempera paint with blue added to give it a lifelike appearance. The color of Negro flesh is made with orange and more blue; of Indian, with orange, red, and white.

After the children have manufactured the heads and painted them, they must still add hair, hands, and a costume. Each of these must be suitable to the character of the doll and complement its face.

Hair. Any number of materials serve as hair. Those used most frequently are crepe hair obtained from manufacturers of make-up like Miner (New York) or Max Factor (Los Angeles), dyed Turkish toweling, sponge rubber, yarn, steel wool, felt, or old pot cleaners.

Hands. Usually children fashion hands like mittens rather than show the four fingers. Sometimes they do not even indicate the thumb. Portions of stuffed old kid gloves or socks suffice as hands. Children also sculpture them from papier mâché or construct them from wire covered with cloth. The wire hands give a clawlike effect and are suggestive of an eerie character, such as a witch.

Costuming. The principles for designing costumes mentioned in the chapter on dramatics are equally important in dressing puppets. The costume should belong to the character, be expressive, and show the relationship of one character to another. Color and line help reveal the personality of the dolls, although the color should be appropriate and not drown out the expression of the dolls' features. Textures of material are important only in that they serve a purpose. For example, jersey drapes well; flannel or velvet gives a rich feeling; silk brocade is stiff and dignified. The patterns in the material should be scaled to the size of the doll.

The costume should be 6 inches or more wide and about 12 inches long. The body of the costume should be full enough to cover the hand of the manipulator and the sleeves wide enough for his fingers. It is often a kimonolike affair with its top gathered around the neck and tied with a heavy string. Boys and girls may trim it with buttons, braid, bits of paper, or feathers. It is kept simple, for it must not be a detriment to the child's manipulating the doll.

Manipulation of Hand Puppets. In the manipulation of hand puppets, the child places his thumb and middle fingers in the arms of the doll and his index finger in its head. When he wishes the puppet to talk, he moves his index finger up and down quickly. When he wants it to laugh, he moves it more vigorously; sometimes, in a very hearty laugh, he bends the whole figure forward. When he desires the puppet to clap, he brings his thumb and middle finger together; when he wishes the doll to gesture or to point to something, he raises his middle finger.

Some children become quite adept in using one puppet with the right hand and one with the left. They change their voice as each character talks and carry on a lively scene all by themselves. The longer children work with puppets, the more expert they become in their operation.

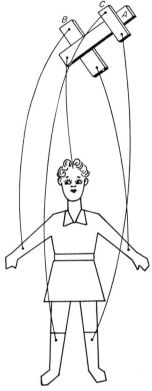

MARIONETTES

After children have constructed and manipulated hand puppets, they often become interested in marionettes. Marionettes are string-controlled dolls with head, body, legs, and arms worked from above. The legs usually consist of two pieces jointed at the hip and knee. The parts of the body are fastened together with joints made of heavy cord, leather, or screw eyes so that they can move. Four, five, six, or seven strings are attached to the marionette. If there are four, a string is fixed to either side of the head and to each forearm. If there are five, one is connected to the top of the head, one to each forearm, and one to each knee. When there are six strings, one is joined to each side of the head, one to each knee, and one to each forearm. Where seven strings are

FIG. 12. Stringing a marionette.

used, one more is secured to the back. The string is heavy gray linen thread or thin copper wire. The strings are all fastened to a board, usually a long board with two shorter ones across it, so that the children can manipulate them. The shorter horizontal boards, 6 inches long, hold four strings, one at each end of the boards; the longer vertical board holds one at its front end (see Figure 12).

CONSTRUCTION OF MARIONETTES

Children use different materials to make the heads, the two parts of the legs, the arms, and the bodies of marionettes. They may string pieces of cardboard together and fasten them with paper fasteners or heavy cord. The feet, however, should be weighted with fishing sinkers or similar material so that they are heavy enough to balance the doll. A second way to make marionettes is to carve the parts of the body from wood which is fairly soft and thick. A third way is to make the body like a rag doll and the head of papier mâché; or boys and girls can make an entire marionette from a pair of stockings. The same materials and technique to indicate features and hair are used for marionettes as for hand puppets. Costuming a marionette is like dressing a doll. The principles of costuming are discussed in Chapter 2.

MANIPULATION OF MARIONETTES

Manipulating marionettes is more complicated than manipulating puppets. Sometimes the child operates them for a while without speaking lines. If children remember that slackening a string lets the section to which it is attached move down, that tightening pulls the section up, that moving the string forward moves the section forward, and that moving it back moves the section back, they can develop all kinds of movements. The accompanying diagram (Fig. 12) shows how the strings are attached: the vertical board is labeled A; the longer horizontal board to the front, C; and the shorter horizontal board to the back, B. To make the figure bow, the operator moves A forward, to make it sit, he moves A backward. He can make it walk by moving B from side to side and slightly up and down. He can make it fall down by allowing the whole board to go down with the C section lowered first. He can cause it to kick by pulling one side of B up. With practice, children become proficient in working marionettes; they will experiment with the doll and find it can dance, hop on one leg, throw a ball, and weep. Children operate both marionettes and puppets on a stage.

STAGING

STAGES FOR HAND PUPPETS

The stage used most frequently in a puppet show in classrooms is a large table turned on its side so that the top of the table is toward the audience. Children sit in small chairs behind the table top and move their puppets just above it so that their arms do not show. They may place the table against a wall upon which they have attached scenery painted on paper.

The photograph (Fig. 13) shows the construction from lumber and plasterboard of one type of stage for puppets. This stage is placed on two horses or on two tables. If it is used on a school stage, the curtains are drawn to either side of it. Curtains are made to cover the front of the puppet stage from its floor to the floor of the room. If children use a stage like this, they paint the scenery on a continuous roll of gray exhibition paper which they thread through dowel rods at each corner of the back of the stage; two children stand at each side to help slide

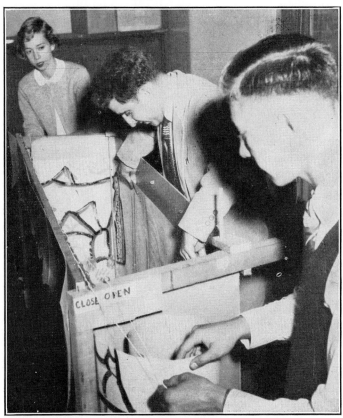

FIG. 13. Puppet stage.

the scenery through. In general, the same principles hold for designing and painting scenery for a puppet stage as for a real stage. The following two factors, however, need to be emphasized in making scenery for the smaller stage: (1) The scenery supplies the environment without calling attention to itself. The background is often a neutral one, since too much color and detail detract from the puppets and from their movement in the play. (2) The scenery in a puppet stage is small and must be in proportion; for example, a cottage is smaller than surrounding trees.

MARIONETTE STAGE

A marionette stage may be improvised from a card table set on
another; the top of the upper table is toward the audience, that of the
lower toward the performers. String tied around the legs on either side
holds the two tables together. The underside of the table and the sides
of the improvised stage are draped with material to make a cyclorama
for the marionettes. The top table hides the performers, who stand on
small chairs.

STAGE FOR PUPPETS AND MARIONETTES CONSTRUCTED FROM CARDBOARD BOXES

Cardboard boxes, such as those in which large television sets or refrig-
erators are packed, make good stages for either puppets or marionettes.
For a marionette stage, children cut the lower half of the front of the
box facing the audience and the upper half of the back of the box facing
the performer. For a puppet stage the box is reversed. When the children
operate marionettes, they stand on chairs or on boxes at the back of the
stage. If they use boxes, they must weight them with heavy stones, for
if the boxes are not weighted, they will tip over when the children move
toward the edge. They can decorate the interior of the sides and the
back of the box which make the stage for the performance.

LIGHTING THE STAGE

Christmas-tree lights light puppet stages in small rooms. If the stage
is to be used in a large room, however, these are not adequate unless
reinforced by spots. Desk lamps with 100-watt bulbs, one outside the
stage and one inside, make effective flood lamps. When the children
want colored light, they cover the lamps with gelatins purchased inex-
pensively from a lighting-supply house. Children can make tin reflectors
by cutting out a large section—almost half—of a tin can, or they may
use photoreflectors. Frequently, the small stage in the classroom is not
lighted at all.

DIRECTION OF PLAY WITH PUPPETRY OR MARIONETTES

SOURCES OF MATERIAL FOR PLAY WITH PUPPETS

Most of the sources suitable for dramatic play serve equally well for
puppetry. Children play experiences of the home and school and stories

and poetry. Sometimes they act in plays written especially for puppetry. But many educators feel a story composed by the children or adapted from one of their favorite stories is more valuable for the children than a script.

Four factors, which are not so important in the selection of a story for creative dramatics, are essential in the choice of a play for puppetry: (1) The story must be one with plenty of movement. (2) The story must be one whose characters challenge the ingenuity of the makers of the dolls. (3) The story must be one which requires only a limited number of characters on the stage at one time. (4) The story must be one which bears repetition.

First, if a puppet play is to hold the attention of the audience, the puppets must be active. In creative dramatics, the facial expressions of the children change to give meaning to the story. In puppetry, the expressions of the dolls remain constant. To be interesting to the audience, the characters must move about, run, chase each other, or even knock each other down. The story must be lively. In "The Three Bears," for example, the bears leave the house, come back, examine the chairs, the dishes of porridge, and the beds, and finally chase Goldilocks out of the house. Movement is an integral part of the story.

Secondly, the characters of the story must challenge the ingenuity of the children in representing them as puppets. Stories that involve animals or toys or distinctive personalities demand that children make expressive puppets. Inez Hogan,[3] in *Runaway Toys*, a gay tale of a boy's toys who run away, presents characters which are fun to design and make. *Snow White and the Seven Dwarfs* has distinctive personalities, although children may imitate Walt Disney's creations rather than be original. The story should inspire children to be creative and inventive in fashioning puppets.

Thirdly, in telling a story with puppets, the number of children who can perform at any one time is limited. The space backstage is small and usually holds no more than seven performers. Many stories with few characters are available. To illustrate, Ruth Sawyer's[4] *The Little Red Horse* tells of the adventures of Michael, Granny, and the little red horse on a Florida coastal island. Nevertheless, in spite of the limitation of the number of puppeteers who can use the stage at once, all members of the class can participate in the project. They may put on three or four short stories, prepare several stories around one theme, or make

[3] I. Hogan, *Runaway Toys*, New York, Dutton, 1951.
[4] R. Sawyer, *The Little Red Horse*, New York, Viking, 1950.

use of a double or triple cast. If several casts are to play the story, it is especially important that the story bear repetition.

Lastly, that the story bear repetition is usually important, for children tend to play a story with puppets oftener than the one played through creative dramatics. If they have spent time making the puppets, they will want to show them to their own group and to children in other grades. Younger children play stories like *Little Black Sambo*, *The Elves and the Shoemaker*, *Jack and the Beanstalk*, and older children act out parts of *Rip Van Winkle*, *Treasure Island*, *Tom Sawyer*, and *Aladdin* time after time without their becoming stale or dull.

ADAPTING THE STORY

Adapting such stories as these for puppetry is similar to adapting them for dramatics. Children create consistent and imaginative characters through their speaking and voice and manipulation of the dolls. They decide what scenes are necessary and what is to happen in each scene. Usually dialogue spoken extemporaneously for the particular scene is preferable to written dialogue. Occasionally, children write the dialogue. The following is an adaptation of the story *Snow White and the Seven Dwarfs* for the puppet stage. Children in the intermediate grades produce this play, or those in the upper grades present it for younger boys and girls.

SNOW WHITE AND THE SEVEN DWARFS

SCENE I: THE PALACE

READER. A long, long time ago, longer than anyone can possibly remember, a queen sat by her window sewing. As her needle flashed in and out of her work, her thoughts wandered. She was gazing at the snowflakes and pricked her finger and three little drops of blood fell on the snow. The red looked so beautiful on the snow that she thought, "If I only had a little child as white as snow, with cheeks as rosy red as blood, and with hair as black as the window frame."

Soon after this, a baby girl was born to her, a little princess with hair of black, cheeks and lips of rosy red, and a skin so fine and fair that she was called Snow White. But when the child was born, the Queen died.

After a year had passed, the King married a second time. His new wife, who was now Queen, was very beautiful but haughty, proud, and vain. Indeed, her only wish was to be the fairest in the land. She had a mirror, a magic one, and when she looked into it, she would say:

QUEEN. Mirror, mirror on the wall,
Who's the fairest one of all?

VOICE OF MIRROR. Oh, Queen, thou art the fairest in the land.

READER. With this the Queen was well content for she knew that her mirror always spoke the truth.

QUEEN. Mirror, mirror on the wall,
Who's the fairest one of all?

VOICE. Thou wert the fairest one of all.
But Snow White with lips of rosy red
Is now the fairest one of all.

QUEEN. (*Rises majestically and rings a bell. Huntsman enters.*)

HUNTSMAN. (*Bows*) Your Majesty.

QUEEN. (*Mutters*) Snow White—ugh! Lips of rosy red, more fair than I? She must die!

HUNTSMAN. You called—me?

QUEEN. Take Snow White into the forest—and return with her heart in this jeweled box.

Curtain

SCENE II: THE WOODS

HUNTSMAN. (*Alone, walking in the woods, thinking aloud.*) If I kill her, my soul will burn forevermore, and my shame will be so great that I shall hate myself and hang my head before all men. Yet if I fail the Queen, she will feed me to her panthers or shrink me to the size of a walnut. Yes, and Snow White? For the Queen will yet contrive some cruel death for her. Indeed it would be a mercy if I killed her myself.

SNOW WHITE. (*Enters*) Oh, please, dear hunter, have mercy! If you will let me go, I'll wander far, far away into the forest, and I'll never come back again.

HUNTSMAN. I cannot kill you even though the Queen has commanded it! She's mad—so mad! Quick child, run, run far, far away into the forest and hide. Never come back! (*Watches her until she is out of sight.*) I shall kill a wild boar and place its heart in the box.

Curtain

SCENE III: THE DWARFS' COTTAGE

SNOW WHITE. Oh! It's just like a doll's house! Oh, it's dark inside. Nobody's home. What a darling little chair. Why, there are seven little chairs. Must be seven little children. And from the looks of this table—seven untidy little children. Look! a pickax, a shovel. Such a mess! And a sink full of dishes. And cobwebs. Maybe they have no mother and need someone to look after them. I'll clean house and surprise them. What cunning little beds. Why, their names are carved on them, "Doc," "Happy," "Sneezy," "Dopey." Such funny names for children, "Grumpy," "Bashful," and "Sleepy." Oh— (*Yawns*) I'm a little sleepy myself. (*Lies down on bed and falls to sleep.*)

DWARFS. (*Enter singing.*)
>Hi-ho, Hi-ho,
>It's home from work we go,
>Da-da-da, da-da-da-da-da,
>De-do-do-do-do-do.

SNEEZY. Look! Someone's in our house!

SLEEPY. Maybe a ghost, or a goblin, or a demon, or a dragon!

GRUMPY. I knew it! There's trouble brewing. Felt it coming all day. I've been warning you for nigh two hundred years that something awful was about to happen.

DOC. This chair—it's been dusted.

BASHFUL. Cobwebs are missing.

GRUMPY. There's dirty work afoot. The place is clean.

DOC. Sink's empty! someone stole our dishes.

HAPPY. Hey, they're hidden in the cupboard. Huh, my cup's been washed. Sugar's gone.

SNEEZY. Psst. Look, it's full—ha, ha, ha.

GRUMPY. How do you think we can start this thing with you blowing like a cyclone?

DOC. It's here—in the bedroom. What will we do? Sneak peep! One of us has got to sneak up to it and chase it away. I'll stay here and butcher it. Who'll volunteer? (*Snow White stretches her arms. Dopey thinks it's a ghost and moves away.*)

HAPPY. Wha—wha—what is it?

SNEEZY. (*Sighs*) It's mighty purty.

BASHFUL. It's beautiful . . . like an angel.

HAPPY. But what is it?

DOC. Why bless my soul, I think, yes, that's what it is—a girl!

GRUMPY. (*Snapping and scowling.*) Girl, huh! It's a female and all females is pizen. What's more, they're full of wicked wiles!

BASHFUL. What's wicked wiles?

GRUMPY. I dunno, but they're mighty dangerous! (*Shakes head.*) Mark my word! We're in for a peck of trouble.

SNOW WHITE. (*Sits up, rubbing eyes.*) Why . . . why, you're not children. You're little men! How do you do!

GRUMPY. How do you do what?

SNOW WHITE. Oh, so you can talk! I'm so glad because now you can tell me about yourselves, who you are. But wait! Let me guess. . . . You must be Doc!

DOC. Wh—er—yes! So I am, my dear—er—er—my dear!

SNOW WHITE. And you are Bashful, aren't you?

BASHFUL. Ooooooooooooh! (*Sleepy's yawn gives him away, and Happy laughs.*)

SNOW WHITE. You are Happy!

HAPPY. That's me, ma'am. And this one's Dopey. He don't talk none. (*Dopey grins.*)

SNOW WHITE. You mean he can't talk?

SNEEZY. He dunno, he never tried. All he can do is ah-ah-ah-KER-CHOO!

SNOW WHITE. You're Sneezy! (*Turns with a frown.*) And you're Grumpy.

GRUMPY. Yeah. We know who we are. Ask her who she is and what she's doing in our house!

SNOW WHITE. Oh, I forgot to tell you. I'm Snow White.

DWARFS. (*All Together.*) THE PRINCESS!

GRUMPY. I'm warning you. If the wicked Queen finds out she's here, we'll wake up some morning and find ourselves dead!

SNOW WHITE. Nonsense, she doesn't even know where I am.

GRUMPY. Doesn't know. She knows everything! She can even make herself invisible. For all we know she may be in this very room right now! (*Dwarfs start looking and peering around.*)

SNOW WHITE. All right, I'll go. If you don't care whether the wild beasts eat me or the demons and goblins get me, I don't want to stay. Besides, why should I stay to clean house for seven little 'fraidy cats, and cook for them, and . . .

HAPPY. Did you say cook?

SNOW WHITE. I can cook everything. Apple dumplings, potato pancakes, gooseberry pies.

DWARFS. Gooseberry pies! Hurrah, she stays! She stays!

GRUMPY. Would you risk your necks for a piece of pie?

DWARFS. You bet! It'll taste mighty good. Melt in your mouth. You can eat 'til you bust!

GRUMPY. Well, she can stay till we get our pie. Then out she goes. (*Snow White dashes out gladly.*)

GRUMPY. Didn't I tell you? She's crazy. Bah!

SNOW WHITE. (*From offstage.*) Supper's ready! (Dwarfs *dash out, shouting gleefully.*)

Curtain

SCENE IV: CASTLE (SAME AS SCENE I)

QUEEN. Now, magic mirror on the wall, who is the fairest one of all?

VOICE. (*From behind the curtain.*)
Thou wert the fairest, Lady Queen.
Snow White is fairest now, I ween.
Amid the forest darkly green,
She lives with dwarfs—the hill between.

QUEEN. Dwarfs! How could she live with dwarfs?

VOICE. (*From behind curtain.*)
With the dwarfs will spend the night
The fairest in the land—Snow White!
The huntsman has tricked you! 'Tis the heart of a boar!

QUEEN. Oh-oh-oh-oh! Heh, heh, heh . . . The poisoned apple—the sleeping death . . . heh . . . heh, heh, heh . . . Perfect! (*Gloats*)

Curtain

SCENE V: WOODS (SAME AS SCENE II)

WITCH. Brew, poison brew. Brew, poison, brew. I take this apple and dip it into the poison, once, twice, three times! Heh, heh! This apple will tempt the princess. Heh, Heh. I'll put it with these other apples, and off I'll go! The sleeping death for you, Princess, for only love's first kiss can break it. Heh, heh, heh.

Ha! the dwarfs will think her dead and bury her alive. (*Shrieks with laughter.*) That must be the dwarfs' chimney! I'll be there by noon.

Curtain

SCENE VI: DWARFS' HOUSE

WITCH. All alone, my pet?

SNOW WHITE. Why, why . . . yes . . . I am.

WITCH. Smells good. But apple pies taste better! Delicious apples. Like to try one? (*Snow White hesitates and withdraws.*)

WITCH. I'll share a secret with you. This is a magic wishing apple! Take a bite as you make a wish, and your dream will come true.

SNOW WHITE, A wishing apple! Oh! (*Starts to take a bite.*) I wish . . . I wish . . .

WITCH. Quick. Bite the apple before your wish gets cold. (*Snow White lifts hand to apple and takes a bite, immediately sinks to the floor with a cry.*)

WITCH. *Now I . . . I am the fairest in the land!*

Curtain

SCENE VII: DWARFS' HOUSE

(*Dwarfs enter uttering sounds of dismay.*)

GRUMPY. I've been telling you for two hundred years something awful is about to happen. (*Dwarfs kneel around Snow White. Knock on door. Prince enters.*)

(*Prince kisses Snow White; she arises. Everyone rejoices.*)

(*Organ or phonograph record plays "Some Day My Prince Will Come."*)

Curtain

DISCUSSING THE ACTIVITY

As in creative dramatics, children discuss the activity. They talk over the appearance and effectiveness of the puppets and how well their operators handled them. They discuss the characterizations to see whether they were clear-cut and consistent. They examine the telling of the story to find out whether it moved smoothly and whether it was clear. They examine the voice and diction of the performers. They discuss the spirit of cooperation to determine whether the players were members of a cooperative working group. They remember that they are talking not just in terms of the play itself but about the growth of the abilities and talents of all the children.

SUMMARY

The values of puppetry for the participants are very like those of creative dramatics. Children, however, usually feel freer to express themselves through puppetry. An added value of puppetry is that boys and girls work with their hands in designing, making, and manipulating puppets.

The word puppets is sometimes used as a general term to include both dolls manipulated by hand and those manipulated by string. But, more commonly, puppets are dolls manipulated by hand, and marionettes are those manipulated by string.

Smaller children construct and operate shadow and stick puppets of cardboard and hand puppets made from paper bags, vegetables, rubber balls, Styrofoam, and Spongex. Older children make and manipulate marionettes and hand puppets made from papier mâché.

The stages for both puppets and marionettes are simple, such as tables turned on their sides. Stages may be constructed from cardboard boxes or from lumber and plasterboard. The lighting, scenery, and costuming, as in creative dramatics, help tell the story.

Most of the sources suitable for creative dramatics serve equally well for puppetry. They include experiences of the home and the school, stories, and poetry. The following four factors, which are not essential in the choice of a story for creative dramatics, are important in the selection of a play for puppetry: (1) The story must be one with plenty of movement. (2) The story must be one whose characters challenge the ingenuity of the makers of the dolls. (3) The story must be one which requires only a limited number of characters on the stage at one time. (4) The story must be one which bears repetition.

The same principles, important in creative dramatics, are also important in adapting the story, motivating it, and evaluating it. In motivating, however, other means are used to interest children in the use of puppetry: the use of motion pictures, television shows with puppetry, shows put on by various agencies within a community, and ballet. In discussing the activity, the children must further consider the appearance and effectiveness of the puppets.

EXERCISES

1. Make a hand puppet or a marionette according to one of the methods explained in this chapter.
2. Adapt a story for play with puppets.

3. By organizing into committees, play a story with puppets or marionettes.

4. Show how puppetry can be used with social studies in the elementary school.

5. Collect a list of stories or poems suitable for puppetry in the grade you plan to teach.

BIBLIOGRAPHY

TEXTS ON PUPPETRY AND COLLECTIONS OF PLAYS FOR PUPPETRY

Batchelder, M., *The Puppet Theatre Handbook*, New York, Harper, 1947. Excellent text on how to make the various kinds of puppets and marionettes. Includes material on staging, costuming, and lighting. Practical suggestions on where to buy materials.

Blackham, O., *Puppets into Actors*, New York, Macmillan, 1949. Chapters on construction, costuming, staging, and scenery. Excellent account of the construction of puppets from wood.

Board of Education of the City of New York, *Puppetry in the Curriculum*, Curriculum Bulletin 1, 1947–1948 Series. A comprehensive treatment of puppets, marionettes, shadow figures, and masks. Clear explanation of construction, staging, manipulation, and the place of puppetry in the educational program.

Bufano, R., *Magic Strings*, New York, Macmillan, 1939. Collection of nine plays for puppets. Includes "Hansel and Gretel," and "The Park is a Jungle."

Bussell, J., and A. Hogarth, *Marionettes: How to Make Them*, Ditchling, Sussex, St. Dominic's Press, 1934. Clear account of how to make puppets both from papier mâché and from wood.

Clark, G. M., "Creative Expression through Puppetry," *Elementary English*, Vol. 27 (February, 1950), pp. 88–90. A review of the objectives of puppetry. Suggestions for activities and stories that can be utilized in puppetry.

Dawson, M. A., and J. M. Miller, *Language for Daily Use: Grade 4*, Yonkers, N.Y., World, 1949, pp. 239–255. A discussion of planning a play, choosing a story, making puppets, and inviting guests. Middle grades.

Dreibelbis, J. F., "Total Learning via Paper Bags," *School Arts*, Vol. 48 (February, 1949), p. 210. A report of the use of 5-, 10-, 20-pound bags filled with crumpled newspapers and tied in place with heavy black carpet thread for puppetry.

Dunser, A., "Class Projects in Marionettes," *School Arts*, Vol. 48 (February, 1949), pp. 206–208. Exposition of how to make marionettes and to stage them. Illustrated.

Harding, M. E., "Active Dolls or Practical Puppets," *School Arts*, Vol. 47 (November, 1947), pp. 106–108. Instruction in making puppets from paper sacks and oak tag.

Hastings, S. and D. Ruthenburg, *How to Produce Puppet Plays*, New York, Harper, 1940. Chapters on choosing a play, making puppets, lighting the stage, music, and special effects. Good chapter on the making of animal puppets.

Liss, J. F., "How Puppets Helped John," *Childhood Education*, Vol. 26 (January, 1950), pp. 214–216. The use of puppetry to help in the adjustment of a child who was not accepted by his peers.

Lynett, H., "Fourth Graders Make Puppets," *School Arts*, Vol. 49 (December, 1949), p. 127. Explanation of how to make puppets and stages for them.

McCrea, L., *Puppets and Puppet Play*, London, Oxford, 1949. Kindergarten and nursery school stories, simply and easily produced. Includes "Jack and Jill," "Little Bo-Peep," "Mary, Mary Quite Contrary," "The Three Bears," "The Story of Christmas," and "Little Red Riding Hood."

Mills, W. H. and L. M. Dunn, *Shadow Plays and How to Produce Them*, New York, Doubleday, 1938.

Phillips, E. N., "Puppets Made from Newspapers," *Instructor*, Vol. 59 (January, 1950), p. 58. Information on how to make puppets from newspapers, paste, paint, and socks. Clearly and simply explained.

Sloan, M. D., "Let's Give a Puppet Show," *American Childhood*. Vol. 35 (November, 1949), pp. 1–13. Description of the performance of "Hansel and Gretel" with puppets.

Somers, P., "Hand Puppets from England," *School Arts*, Vol. 49 (December, 1949), p. 126. Clear, succinct explanation of how to make hand puppets.

Steiner, G., *Pete's Puppet*, New York, Doubleday, 1952. Story of Pete who makes puppets from eggs and vegetables. Gives excellent details on how to make simple puppets. Primary grades.

Stoddard, A., and T. Sarg, *A Book of Marionette Plays*, New York, Greenberg, 1927. Plays including "Little Red Riding Hood," "Rip Van Winkle," and "Hansel and Gretel." Plays for both primary and intermediate levels.

Taylor, D. R., "Puppet Play in the Kindergarten," *American Childhood*, Vol. 32 (June, 1947), pp. 14–15. Exposition of how to make puppets from stiff cardboard. Illustrated by the story of "Three Billy Goats Gruff."

Warner, F. L., *The Ragamuffin Marionettes*, Boston, Houghton Mifflin, 1932. A text written for children on how to make and produce marionettes. Intermediate grades.

STORIES ADAPTABLE TO THE PUPPET THEATRE

Andersen, H. C., *Andersen's Fairy Tales*, New York, Grosset & Dunlap, 1945. Many of these tales serve as a vehicle for plays with hand puppets, stick puppets, and shadow puppets. Intermediate grades.

Bannon, L., *Baby Roo*, Boston, Houghton Mifflin, 1943. The adventures of a kangaroo, a sailor, and some farm animals. Suitable for stick puppets. Primary grades.

————, *Billy and the Bear*, Boston, Houghton Mifflin, 1949. The story of how Billy saves the life of a trained bear. Suitable for hand puppets and marionettes. Intermediate grades.

Benét, W. R., *Mother Goose*, New York, Heritage, 1936. A collection of 400 verses. Illustrations will motivate children to make puppets. Primary grades.

Blair, W., *Tall Tale America*, New York, Coward-McCann, 1944. Many tall tales that can be adapted to puppetry. An excellent collection. Suitable for hand puppets and marionettes. Upper grades.

Bothwell, J., *Little Boat Boy*, New York, Harcourt Brace, 1945. The story of Hafiz, a little boat boy of Kashmir. Plays well with shadow puppets. Intermediate grades.

Brown, M. W., *The Runaway Bunny*, New York, Harper, 1942. A story of the little chicken and its friend, the big rabbit. Suitable for stick or hand puppets. Primary grades.

Defoe, D., *Robinson Crusoe*, New York, Grosset & Dunlap, 1946. Parts of this favorite story play well with hand puppets or marionettes. Upper grades.

Flack, M., *Angus and the Cat*, New York, Doubleday, 1931. Angus, the Scotty pup, gets in trouble with the cat. Suitable for stick puppets. Primary grades.

Gág, W., *Gone Is Gone*, New York, Coward-McCann 1935. An old peasant fairy tale of a man who exchanges work with his wife. Suitable for hand puppets or marionettes. Intermediate grades.

————, *Snippy and Snappy*, New York, Coward-McCann, 1931. The story of two little field mice who want to find a kitchen cupboard full of cheese. Suitable for stick puppets. Primary grades.

Garst, S., *Sitting Bull—Champion of His People*, New York, Messner, 1946. Real-life story of Sitting Bull of the Sioux Indians. Parts of this play well. Suitable for marionettes or hand puppets. Upper grades.

Gordon, P., *The Witch of Scrapfaggot*, New York, Viking, 1948. The adventures of the Bassett twins with the ghost of the old witch of Scrapfaggot Green. Suitable for marionettes or hand puppets.

Grimm Brothers, *Grimms' Fairy Tales*, New York, Grosset & Dunlap, 1945. Most of these tales can be used with any form of puppetry. Intermediate grades.

————, *Hansel and Gretel*, New York, Knopf, 1944. Well illustrated. A perennial favorite with children. Suitable for hand puppets or marionettes. Intermediate grades.

————, *Snow White*, New York, Coward-McCann, 1938. Another perennial favorite. Suitable for hand puppets or marionettes. Intermediate grades.

Harris, J. C., *Uncle Remus: His Songs and His Sayings*, New York, Appleton-Century-Crofts, 1908. Suitable for stick or hand puppets. Intermediate grades.

Kipling, R., *Just So Stories*, New York, Doubleday, 1912. Classics for children. Suitable for hand puppets and for shadow puppets. Intermediate grades.

Lathrop, D. P., *The Skittle-skattle Monkey*, New York, Macmillan, 1945. Story of Jasmine, the pet monkey, who had a wonderful time at home alone. Suitable for hand puppets or marionettes. Intermediate grades.

Leaf, M., *Story of Ferdinand*, New York, Viking, 1936. The story of a young bull who preferred smelling flowers to fighting and who sat on a bumble-bee. Suitable for paper-bag puppets, stick puppets, and shadow puppets. Primary grades.

Moore, C. C., *The Night before Christmas*, Philadelphia, Winston, 1942. Good format. Suggestive illustrations by Everett Shinn. Suitable for stick puppets or hand puppets. Primary grades.

Spyri, J. N., *Heidi*, New York, Grosset & Dunlap, 1945. Another favorite classic with children. Suitable for hand puppets or marionettes. Intermediate grades.

Stevenson, R. L., *Treasure Island*, New York, Scribner, 1924. The excitement and action of *Treasure Island* make its episodes a natural for puppetry. Upper grades.

Thurber, J., *Many Moons*, New York, Harcourt Brace, 1943. The story of the sick little princess who wanted the moon. Suitable for hand puppets or marionettes. Intermediate grades.

Williams, G., *Timothy Turtle*, New York, Scott, 1944. A simple, expressive story of Timothy Turtle. Plays well with stick puppets. Primary grades.

4 Oral Reading

Jane, an eight-year-old, was interested in what her daddy did when he went to work. She had heard him tell again and again how he boarded the bus, arrived at the building where he worked, took the elevator to the thirtieth floor, dictated letters to his secretary, had lunch, went back to his dictating, and returned home. She had seen him leave in the morning and come back at night. One summer day, when her mother was away, her father took her to work with him. They bought the morning paper, rode on the bus, and took the elevator up high in his building. The typewriter, reams of paper, rubber bands, and files in his office fascinated her. At noon when she went to a restaurant, she helped her father order lunch. In the afternoon, she drank at the water cooler, listened to her father dictate letters, and typewrote a letter herself. Her father's working day became meaningful to her.

When Jane returned to school in the fall, she told the teacher of her experience. The teacher suggested she read *At Daddy's Office*.[1] Jane, delighted with the story and with its illustrations, exclaimed, "Why, this office is almost exactly like my daddy's!" She read the story to herself first, then aloud to the teacher, and finally to her classmates.

DEFINITION

Jane's reading *At Daddy's Office* to her classmates was oral reading. She took the place of the writer and told what he had to say to an audience. As an oral reader, she understood the meaning and feeling of the story, and imparted them to her audience.

UNDERSTANDING THE MEANING AND FEELING OF THE STORY

Jane understood the story she was reading in terms of its intellectual content and its emotion. Before she read *At Daddy's Office*, she was

[1] R. J. Misch, *At Daddy's Office*, New York, Knopf, 1946.

familiar with the concepts in the story because of her trip. She grasped the main idea of the book clearly and knew the meanings of all the words. Furthermore, because of her own similar experience, she had a feeling of how exhilarating a trip to Daddy's office can be; she knew the thrill of riding an elevator high in a building, for she had done it.

IMPARTING THE MEANING AND FEELING OF THE STORY TO THE AUDIENCE

Not only did she understand the meaning and feeling of the story, but she also imparted them to her audience. As she read the story, the children saw the telephone, pen and pencil, tray for papers, many letters, and the picture of a girl and her mother that were on the father's desk. When she read the explanation of how a typewriter works, she made it clear to her listeners. In addition, by her voice, bodily action, and facial expression, she re-created the fascination of Daddy's office for the children. She communicated to her audience the noisiness and the hustle and bustle of the place where there were many typists at work. When she was reading about eating lunch in the restaurant, she showed, through her facial expression and her voice, how delighted the child was with her dessert of chocolate ice cream. In her reading she shared with her audience both the information and sensations of *At Daddy's Office*.

GUIDES TO SUCCESSFUL EXPERIENCES
IN ORAL READING

CONCEPTS IN MATERIAL TO BE READ ARE MEANINGFUL TO THE READER

Several reasons why this reading was satisfying to Jane and her listeners are apparent. First, the enjoyable excursion with her father to his office made the concepts in the book meaningful to Jane. Oral reading that is taking place in the classroom should always be meaningful to the reader. Trips, excursions, and parties broaden children's experiences and bring understanding to their reading of similar events. For example, because members of a third grade visited the zoo, William Bridges's[2] *Big Zoo* carried more import for the group. Just before Christmas, a seven-year-old read to her classmates *Christmas—This Way!*,[3] a tale describing the everyday preparations for Christmas. Since the children were counting the days until Christmas and were

[2] W. Bridges, *Big Zoo*, New York, Viking, 1941.
[3] C. Beebe, *Christmas—This Way!*, New York, Oxford, 1943.

planning for it, the reading of this book was important to the reader and to her listeners. The ideas to be read should carry significance for the reader.

A HAPPY CLASSROOM ATMOSPHERE ENCOURAGES CHILDREN TO READ ALOUD

Secondly, because the children in Jane's third grade lived happily together, they took pleasure in her enthusiasm for *At Daddy's Office.* A happy atmosphere in the classroom encourages children to read aloud. If children enjoy each other and their teacher in a healthy way and if they like to express their ideas, the audience is receptive to the reader. Whether the desire to communicate is the result of good human relationships or whether the good human relationships are the result of effective communication is difficult to discern, but, at least, they go along together. When children have planned their work together, attended parties with each other, gone on trips and excursions as a group, and have lived together successfully, they are interested in what each child has to say.

ORAL READING SHOULD BE PURPOSEFUL

Thirdly, Jane felt a genuine need to share with her classmates her excitement about her trip. Sharing her experience with them was the purpose in her reading. Oral reading should serve a definite purpose, for it is valuable only when the reader feels responsible for gaining and holding the attention of his listeners. Some of the reasons for reading aloud are: (1) A child wishes to share with others an enjoyable experience. (2) A child reads aloud a story or a poem, for the author's use of language makes the experience important. (3) A child reads the words of a writer who carries authority. (4) A child reads to impart information exactly to his classmates.

PURPOSES OF ORAL READING

SHARING AN EXPERIENCE WITH OTHERS

A child discovers a book or a poem he wants to share with his classmates. A seventh grader who became interested in "nit and nitwit stories," found a series of "little moron" stories. She wanted her audience to appreciate the story about the little moron getting up in the middle of the night to answer the phone and declaring that no, his

number wasn't one one one one; his was eleven, eleven.[4] As she read the tale seriously, after the manner of Jane Ace, it was delightfully humorous. When she unearthed the Little Audrey stories, she analyzed them, explaining to the class that Audrey was no hypocrite, that Audrey does what she wants to. She read them in such a way that the audience

FIG. 14. Getting ready to read aloud. (*Neil Croom, University State Teachers College, New Paltz, N.Y.*)

enjoyed their irony. After she outgrew these tales, she became interested in other folklore, such as the Paul Bunyan stories. Her classmates shared her enjoyment of them.

TELLING A STORY IN THE EXACT WORDS OF THE AUTHOR

Sometimes a story needs the flavor of the exact language of the author. Because the students in an eighth grade were studying the United Nations, they were reading and telling stories of various coun-

[4] B. A. Botkin, *The Pocket Treasury of American Folklore*, New York, Pocket Books, Inc., 1950, p. 194.

tries. A child read aloud rather than told "The Black Bull of Nor-roway," found in *Legends of the United Nations*, for this story needs the Scotch dialect of its author to be interesting to the audience. A short song

> Seven lang years I served for thee
> The glassy hill I clamb for thee
> The Bluidy socks I rang for thee
> And wilt thou no wauken and turn to me?[5]

gives Scotch flavor to the story when it is heard. Much of the humor and beauty of the A. A. Milne stories depend on Milne's use of language; they are the kind of stories that are better read than told.

The most striking illustration of this principle lies in poetry. Poetry is meant to be read aloud. The author of a good poem has made its mood and meaning more vivid through the imaginative use of language. For instance, a child might tell that a squirrel who had a curly tail ran up a tree, scampered to the ground, and ate his supper from a shell. But children can see the squirrel more vividly, can hear him eating his supper more clearly, when they listen to:

THE SQUIRREL

> Whisky, frisky
> Hippity hop,
> Up he goes
> To the tree top!
>
> Whirly, twirly
> Round and round
> Down he scampers
> To the ground.
>
> Furly, curly,
> What a tail!
> Tall as a feather,
> Broad as a sail!
>
> Where's his supper?
> In the shell
> Snappity, crackity
> Out it fell.
>   *Anonymous*

[5] From *Legends of the United Nations* by F. Frost. Copyright, 1943, by Whittlesey House, McGraw-Hill. Reprinted by permission of the publisher.

The author has made the idea vivid, for the poem's rhyme, rhythm, and marriage of sound and subject suggest the squirrel's activity, and its words stimulate the children to see and hear the squirrel. As children savor the rhyme and rhythm of

> Hippity hop
> Up he goes
> To the tree top!

they receive a lively impression of the squirrel's ascent. Furthermore, the sound of the language affects them. Phrases like "Whisky, frisky," "whirly, twirly," and "furly, curly" are rich in sensory meaning. The children receive lively pictures and sensations from this poem if the reader brings out its mood and meaning.

READING THE WORDS OF A WRITER WHO CARRIES AUTHORITY

A child may wish to quote an authority to support a point he is making. If he is speaking on the topic, "It Costs Too Much to Run for Office," he may wish to quote Senator Douglas's[6] statement that to run for the United States Senate in a fairly large state costs from $150,000 to $200,000. He may read the paragraph containing this statement of the cost and containing its breakdown into various items, such as expenses for advertising and for maintaining headquarters. Because Senator Douglas has run for office many times and has made a study of what it costs to run, quoting him would add weight to the speech.

IMPARTING INFORMATION EXACTLY

Readers impart exact information to their listeners for other reasons. Infantile paralysis struck one of the members of an eighth-grade class. Her group, therefore, decided to bake and sell cookies in order to make money for the March of Dimes fund. One of the members read the recipes aloud while the others put the right quantities and amounts of ingredients into their bowls. Another group of children was making puppets. One of its members read the directions for making papier mâché puppets while the rest followed her directions carefully. In both

[6] P. H. Douglas, "What It Costs to Run," *The Atlantic Monthly*, Vol. 190 (August, 1952), p. 43.

instances, the readers were giving their listeners exact and accurate information and directions.

MATERIALS FOR READING

INTERESTS OF THE CHILDREN

The choice of materials for reading is obviously related to the purpose the oral reading is serving. If a child is sharing his enjoyment of a piece of literature, his own interest has guided his choice, as in Jane's reading of *At Daddy's Office*. Different age groups have different interests. Preschool children like stories with rhythm and with funny rhyming words. First-grade youngsters want to hear of the world about them and what goes on in their street, school, or home. Second- and third-grade boys and girls become interested in fairy stories, in funny animals that talk. Those in the middle grades like factual material; later, enthusiasm develops for adventure, travel, biography, and inventions. All children enjoy material which is graphic, dramatic, and active. Furthermore, they all like to read of human experiences with which they are at least partially familiar.[7]

KINDS OF SHARING

Sharing through oral reading takes many forms. A child who reads unusually well may be interested in reading stories to younger children. If he is an effective oral reader and selects his stories for his audience well, the lower-grade children enjoy listening to him. Some boys and girls read aloud to their classmates parts of books they are reading at home. Others enjoy sharing a poem they like. Still others like to share their own creative efforts. In a fourth-grade class,[8] the teacher described the animals, flowers, and trees she saw on a walk through the woods. When the children entered the discussion, they told what they had seen as they played in the woods; in addition, they talked about using vivid words to describe in an imaginative way their experiences in the out of doors. After the group discussion, they wrote short essays or poems, which they later shared with each other. The members of the group indicated what they particularly liked about the writings and the readings. The experience was a learning one and a rewarding one for both the students and the teacher.

[7] W. S. Gray (ed.), *Promoting Personal and Social Development through Reading*, Chicago, University of Chicago Press, 1947.

[8] Miss Helen Trask, Manhasset Public Schools, Manhasset, N.Y.

CREATIVE EXPRESSION

Stories written by children often read aloud well. This activity motivates other children to try their hands at creative writing, because the group is proud of, and shows its enthusiasm for, the efforts of its members. The following are unedited stories written by third-grade children:[9]

THE LITTLE PIG WHO WENT OUT IN THE RAIN

Once there was a little pig who never liked to have an umbrella when it rained. One day it was raining very hard and his mother asked him to go to the market with an umbrella. But he said that he would not get wet. On the way to the market it rained so hard that his tail got as straight as a string. When he got home his mother said, "What happened to your tail?" She put it in some cloth and the little pig went to bed. In the morning the little pig woke up and his little tail was curly again.

Barby Bull

EILEEN WISH

Hey, Eileen Wish, why do your mother and father call you Eileen Wish? My mother and father call me Eileen Wish because I wish all the time. I wish for a ball and a dollar. I wish for a bicycle and a sewing kit. I wish for the moon and a basket full of stars. That's why they call me Eileen Wish.

Esther Fryer

THE MAN

Once upon a time there was a man who loved to work and work. When morning came he got up, ate his breakfast and went to work. One morning he got up and didn't want to work. He had always gone to work but this morning he didn't want to. He slept and slept and slept the whole day long. When he woke up he felt good and he always went to work after that.

Esther C.

These stories have a rhythm and a vividness of expression that contribute to their readability.

OTHER SOURCES RELATED TO CLASSROOM ACTIVITIES

Other sources for materials to read aloud are also related to purposes served by oral reading: reading notices to the group, reading reports written for a special occasion, reading a story about Halloween at Halloween time, reading minutes of a meeting, reading recipes as members of the class follow them, and reading a quotation from an authoritative

[9] Third grade of Miss Vivian McCullar, State Teachers College, Fredonia, N.Y.

source to support a point. A third-grade class prepared a television show to tell their parents about their study of Norway. An eight-year-old drew a picture showing Norway as a land of mountains, and a nine-year-old wrote the following script to go with the picture:

> This is a picture of Norway. It is called the Land of Mountains. Some of the mountains reach the sky. There are many water falls. They run into rivers, lakes, and streams.

Other children wrote about skiing, farming, and making cheese in Norway and about the market days and the reindeer of Norway; at the same time, still others illustrated the stories. As each picture appeared, the child who wrote the script to accompany the picture read it. Their reading served a definite purpose.

ORAL READING READINESS

Not all children are ready at the same time to share stories or to read to impart information exactly and authoritatively. A child should not read aloud for these purposes until he is ready, for he needs time to grow into this kind of sharing. Important factors in this growth are: (1) Before the child shares by reading aloud, he must speak in sentences. (2) He must be able to read silently so that he understands clearly the content of what he is to read aloud. (3) He must be secure in his relationship with the teacher and the other children. When the child meets these requirements and when he has a real interest and a purpose in what he is to read, he is ready to share his reading with his fellow classmates.

UNDERSTANDING THE MEANING INTENDED BY THE AUTHOR

The teacher should recognize that the one indispensable requirement in effective oral reading is that the reader understand the meaning intended by the author. The reader should comprehend the main idea of the story, essay, or poem. He should also know the meaning of the words in the selection, the allusions to names of people and places, and sometimes the historical and geographical background of the writing. Frequently, he must be aware of the author's purpose and the facts of his life. The teacher, in encouraging children to read aloud, takes into account these factors that influence meaning.

The teacher can make sure the child understands the meaning of the selection. One way of making sure that the child knows what he is reading is to guide his choice. For example, Janey was encouraged to read aloud *At Daddy's Office*, for she knew its meaning because of her own experience. In most instances, the teacher helps children select material that they readily and clearly understand. Through his guidance, children read aloud literature which they and their classmates enjoy.

Where the child selects material he is not prepared to read aloud, the teacher encourages preparation. The fun of sharing must remain paramount. Therefore, the analysis necessary for an understanding should be informal and indirect. By questioning, by discussion, and sometimes by supplying information, the teacher and the child together prepare for the reading. In the preparation for oral reading, the most significant step is arriving at the main idea of the selection.

STATING THE MAIN IDEA

The teacher encourages the child to state the main idea informally. He stimulates him to represent in a few words the theme of the story, the principal idea of the explanation, or the underlying thought of the poem. For example, because an eight-year-old girl liked Marcia Brown's[10] *The Little Carousel*, she asked to share it with her classmates. When the teacher asked her, "What makes Tony happiest?" she replied, "Tony loved riding the lion in the merry-go-round." Actually the little girl was telling the teacher the main idea of the story. Another teacher said to a ten-year-old boy who wanted to read aloud *Robbie, the Brown Little Collie*,[11] "Tell me in a few words what happened to Robbie." The child responded, "When Robbie was a puppy, he only wanted to play; but as he grew up, he liked taking care of his sheep." In both instances, the teacher was sure the child knew the main idea of the stories.

WORDS

The child must not only understand the main idea, but he must also know the meaning of the words in the selection. He understands these words better when he is reading material within the realm of his experience. Because he has taken a trip to the airport, the words in *The Little Airplane* mean more to him. In reading about experiences with which

[10] M. Brown, *The Little Carousel*, New York, Scribner, 1948.
[11] D. L'Hommedieu, *Robbie, the Brown Little Collie*, Philadelphia, Lippincott, 1948.

he is acquainted, such as a trip to the farm, to the beach, or to the zoo, a child is led to more significant reading. His interpretation reveals a more vivid realization of the meaning because of his direct experience. Where unfamiliar words occur in the selection, they exist in terms of a meaningful context. Since he is familiar with the main idea of the selection and the words around the new one, he is able in many instances to deduce the meaning of the strange words. For example, in Walter De la Mare's poem "The Cupboard," where the author talks about lollipops and the grandma who keeps the key to the cupboard, the main idea and most of the words are familiar. But the author mentions Banbury cakes, a new idea to almost all children. Inasmuch as the children know all the rest of the words, they are not too concerned; they are sure Banbury cakes are delicious. Sometimes they go home blithely to ask their mothers what Banbury cakes are, or they look them up in a dictionary. They are delighted to learn they are a kind of pie made with raisins and lemons.

Words and their meanings matter to some children. They like to look up words in the dictionary to discover which meaning fits into the context of what they are reading. Gesell says that boys and girls in the second grade begin to use to advantage dictionaries written for them.[12] When children are interested in what the poem or story is about, they will frequently want to know the meaning of the unfamiliar word to see what it adds to the selection as a whole. Some children have a greater interest in words and their meaning than others. The interest depends on their home background and their general ability in language. A delightful story[13] in the August, 1952, issue of *Harper's* draws a sharp contrast between the language usage of a bright child with a sophisticated literary background and a set of twins with an average middle-class background. Penelope, the child with the more sophisticated background, used the word "indubitably." Eva, one of the twins, doubled up with laughter, declared it was a wonderful word, and she was always going to say indubitably. The story contains many other examples of the verbal differences between the two children. Some children naturally look up words in a dictionary; the teacher encourages the others to follow suit.

[12] A. Gesell and others, *The Child from Five to Ten*, New York, Harper, 1946, p. 380.
[13] P. Frankau, "The Duchess and the Smugs," *Harper's Magazine*, Vol. 205 (August, 1952), p. 26.

ALLUSIONS TO NAMES OF PEOPLE AND PLACES

As far as possible, the teacher should encourage children to read material in which the names of people and places are familiar. As an eighth-grade group of children was studying the building of the Erie Canal, they were planning to read the "Ballad of the Erie" in choral speaking:

BALLAD OF THE ERIE

I've traveled all around the world and Tonawanda too,
Was cast on desert islands, was beaten black and blue
Was shot and cut at Bull's Run, I've wandered since a boy;
But I'll never forget the trip I drove from Buffalo to Troy.

CHORUS

For it was tramp, tramp and tighten up your lines
And watch the playful horse flies 'round the mules they climb.
For it was cuss, kick, and swish, forget it I never shall,
When I drove a team of sorrel mules on the Erie Canal.

The cook we had on board the boat stood six feet in her sock
Her hand was like an elephant's ear, her breath would open a lock
And when at night she'd go to sleep, phew!
Sufferin! How she'd snore!

Because the children were studying the Erie Canal, they had learned where Tonawanda, Buffalo, and Troy are in New York State. They were able to identify the allusion to "Bull's Run." They had found out about the early days of the Erie Canal so that the line "I drove a team of sorrel mules on the Erie Canal" created a specific picture in their minds. Since they had been studying this era of the history of New York State, they knew its historical background. Because they knew the allusions, they could read this ballad more vividly.

HISTORICAL OR GEOGRAPHICAL BACKGROUND

A knowledge of the historical or geographical background of a story or poem often makes the story or the poem clearer to the reader. For example, a discussion, based on research, of the history of the times of Dickens's *Christmas Carol* adds meaning to Scrooge and his activities. When the reader knows the kind of country the United States was during the invention of Johnny Appleseed and Davy Crockett, the tales gain interest. An understanding of American history in the period before the Civil War adds significance to *Uncle Tom's Cabin*.

Where students have sufficient interest, they should be encouraged to look up the necessary material. In instances where the students cannot be readily motivated to read for themselves, the teacher should supply the necessary background.

AUTHOR'S PURPOSE AND BACKGROUND

The teacher also often supplies information about the author's purpose and background, for only in rare instances can the teacher expect children to find them out for themselves. As children learn why the author wrote the selection and what his background is or was, its meaning frequently becomes plainer. Children are happy to know that Ruth Sawyer Durand is a woman particularly interested in telling stories and listening to them. They like to hear that, when she lived in a small college town, she sometimes told stories for the college students. They are glad to know she has traveled widely, talked to people in various lands, and learned the stories of these lands from the people themselves. The realization that her tales are true folk legends gathered from the lips of people who have lived in a country in the same spot for many, many years makes her stories more important to children.

After children have learned that Carl Sandburg tried his hand at being a truck driver, sceneshifter, and milkman, that he has had opportunities to know many kinds of people in many sections of the country, and that later he received some college education, they realize that his having lived and worked with all kinds of people gives him more intimate knowledge of them. As boys and girls read his *Rootabaga Stories*,[14] they recognize that he really knows the American people and their way of life. They will be aware that Sandburg's universal knowledge of people comes from his having worked as a truck driver, sceneshifter, and milkman.

UNDERSTANDING THE MOOD OR EMOTION
INTENDED BY THE AUTHOR

After a teacher has helped the child to determine the author's intended meaning, he helps him to determine his intended mood. The author uses language creatively and imaginatively to gain the desired response from his reader. The response may be one of many: sorrow,

[14] C. Sandburg, *Rootabaga Stories*, New York, Harcourt Brace, 1922.

anger, jealousy, gaiety, or serenity. To achieve these feelings, the writer uses various devices: colorful concrete words, images, repetition, rhyme, meter, and musical or unmusical sounds.

The teacher must recognize that words and their connotations help the reader feel the emotional intent of the author. In Elinor Wylie's "Velvet Shoes," words like "soundless space," "tranquil pace," "windless peace," and "velvet shoes" connote quietness, tranquility, and softness. The same feelings are made still stronger by her use of images, such as "under veils of white lace," "upon silver fleece," and "more beautiful than the breast of a gull." In contrast, the words and images may be stirring, as in Paul Edmond's "Look Out," in which he portrays a car coming quickly and then dashing down the road. The phrase "splashing and hooting and dashing" is exciting, and this excitement is intensified by the repetition mounting in admonition of the words "look out." The use of colorful words, images, and repetition evokes the desired atmosphere.

Rhyme, meter, and musical or unmusical sounds also heighten emotion. Both the rhyme and meter of "The Woodpecker" create the feeling of the woodpecker pecking. Elizabeth Roberts' use of "hole," "pole," "red," "head," "sky," and "by," all monosyllabic words, suggests the woodpecker in the pole. The rhythm of Robert Louis Stevenson's "The Swing" contributes to the effect of swinging inherent in the poem. The sound of words evokes feeling. Rachel Field's use of the phrase "tinkly bell hung over the door" suggests the sound of the bell in the general store. Again and again the attention of the child can be focused on the sounds which call forth feelings on the part of the reader.

The teacher will take advantage of opportunities to guide the children's selection of material to read aloud. The day after the big snow, he will bring to class *Katy and the Big Snow*, the story of what a huge snowstorm did to the city. He will make available poems like Wilkins's "Snow," which tells about the snow falling softly at night. With an older group, after a quiet spring rain, the teacher might have ready "There Will Come Soft Rains," by Sara Teasdale. He is showing the children the relationship of literature to current experience.

If the reader is to communicate fully to his audience this meaning and feeling intended by the author, he should strive to meet these requirements: (1) He needs to keep his mind on what he is reading. He should concentrate on conveying the ideas in the selection to his audience. To be free to communicate, he should be able to read the material easily. (2) He should be able, through his treatment of the material by effective use of voice and manner, to re-create the thought and feeling of the words for the audience. (3) He should be able to re-create the meaning of the words *as he reads them*. His attitude and manner indicate the following: I am talking with you or I am telling you what you need to know. Because he knows what he is reading, he can give his attention to communicating with his audience. (4) The reader should be able to reach his classmates who respond to the reading by thinking and feeling with him. They indicate their responses by smiling, frowning, or nodding agreement. The test of good reading is the amount of interaction between the reader and his listeners. If the reader is an integral part of his group and if he has a happy relationship with its members, the atmosphere of the class helps him to communicate. When the child is reading to share, when he asks to read aloud, when he is reading material well within his abilities, he usually communicates well.

The teacher must realize that the reader makes use of certain techniques in imparting thought and feeling to the audience. Phrasing, centering, subordination, emphasizing new ideas, building a series, indicating the climax, contrast, concession, and parallel attention help the listener to understand the selection. In addition, the skillful use of voice, of rate of reading, and of bodily and facial expression evokes responses from the audience. But the teacher does not teach centering, phrasing, and subordination as such to his children. When he realizes that attention is focused on the wrong word, he helps the child to pick out the key word. Through discussion, he encourages the child to keep his reading on the level of normal conversation. In the subsequent section, a definition of the technique appears first, followed by a brief explanation of how the teacher can help the child achieve the technique.

IMPARTING THOUGHT TO THE AUDIENCE

HIGHLIGHTING THE IMPORTANT IDEAS

The meaning of the selection the child wishes to convey to his audience determines which words are important. In reading, he gives attention to specific words so as to highlight certain ideas and to place others in shadow. Differences in degree of highlighting exist. Some ideas are very important, while others are only relatively so. Centering is the highlighting of some ideas and the placing of others in shadow. A center of a phrase is a word or words which must be highlighted to bring out the meaning.

In the verse

> "O Dandelion, yellow as gold,
> What do you do all day?"
> "I just wait here in the tall green grass
> Till the children come out to play."

the speaker admires the dandelion's being yellow as gold and asks him what he does all day. A reader might bring out the words "dandelion," "yellow," "gold," "what," "all," and "day." In all likelihood, "yellow" and "gold" will not be highlighted so sharply as the other words, because they do not bear the weight of the main idea. The dandelion, in reply, says that he just waits till the children come out to play. "Wait," "children," and "play," are the centers. One reader maintains that "in the tall green grass" explains "here" and does not need so much highlighting as do the other phrases of the verse. This reader will bring out "tall," "green," and "grass," but will not highlight them so brilliantly as the centers of the other phrases.

As one reader's interpretation differs from another's, he will use different words as centers. A second reader in interpreting the first stanza of "Dandelion" indicates that "in the tall green grass" is a desirable place to wait; he highlights the words "tall," "green," and "grass" as brilliantly as the centers in the other phrases.

When the child is interested in what he is reading, in communicating his thoughts to his classmates, and has a knowledge of the content of the material, the teacher will have to do little or no teaching of centering. But should a child not read this stanza well, the teacher may inquire, "What are you asking the dandelion?" The child responds with "What do you do all day?" The question will be conversational, meaningful. The teacher suggests that he read it the same way. The teacher may then ask what the dandelion's response is. The child may say, "He waits till the children come out to play," or, "He sits in the tall, green grass till the children come out." Again the teacher suggests that the child read the way he answered the question.

INDICATING UNITS OF THOUGHT

Some sentences are complete units of thought. Other sentences, more involved, present more than one unit of thought. The reader should be able to recognize these units and to show the relationship between them. These related units, each with at least one center of attention, are called phrases. Phrasing is dependent on centering and is made evident through pauses and changes in voice. In the first stanza of the same poem, "Dandelion,"

> "O Dandelion,/ yellow as gold,/
> What do you do all day?"/
> "I just wait here/ in the tall green grass/
> Till the children come out to play."

a reader may break the sentences into the indicated units of thought by means of pauses and changes in voice inflection. This particular reader feels the phrase "in the tall green grass" explains the word "here," and is not particularly important. Because the important idea is "I just wait here till the children come out to play," the reader will say "in the tall green grass" with a lower pitch and less intensity. The phrasing goes along with the centering which was dictated by the meaning.

As mentioned previously, all readers do not wish to highlight the same words; therefore, they will not pause in the same places. In the next to the last line, a different reader would not pause after "here." By not pausing and by highlighting the phrase, "the tall green grass," he is showing that to him the tall green grass is a very desirable place to wait. However, no matter where the pauses occur, they should add to the meaning of the poem. Again, if a child's reading is based on his interests, if he understands what he is reading and wants his classmates to understand, he is more likely to phrase correctly.

When the child does not phrase correctly, the teacher establishes the units of centering through questioning. Both phrasing and centering are dependent on meaning, and the child should convey meaning as clearly when he reads as when he converses. His reading should be conversational. When the child breaks the thoughts into too many units, the teacher sometimes reads the material back to him as he has read it. The teacher then asks him how he could improve the reading to make his classmates understand the meaning. Usually the child will be able to tell the teacher. For example, a child may read this way:

> Till the children/ come out/ to play.

He is using three units where he needs only one. After the teacher has repeated the line as he has read it, he realizes his frequent pauses interfere with the meaning. Or the teacher may ask, "How long does he wait?" The response will likely be:

> Till the children come out to play.

Again the teacher asks him to read it as he spoke it. Always the teacher stresses the idea that the child is conveying meaning to his classmates.

SUBORDINATING THE DEPENDENT THOUGHT

Subordination indicates the relationship of dependence of one idea upon another. It may be shown by lowering the intensity of voice, by the dropping of pitch, or by increasing speed on those thought units not dominant in the meaning; or it may be shown by separating units of thought by pauses. For example, in the first two lines of "Dandelion," the important idea is "O Dandelion, what do you do all day?" "Yellow as gold," used to describe the dandelion and dependent on it, is subordinated by pausing and by lowering pitch and intensity. In the last verse of "Long, Long Ago," which depicts the story of the birth of Christ,

> For in a manger bed,
> Cradled we know,
> Christ came to Bethlehem
> Long, long, ago.

readers subordinate the phrase, "cradled we know." The main idea is "for in a manger bed Christ came to Bethlehem long, long ago." The reader indicates by lowering the pitch and intensity of his voice that "cradled we know" is a detail, subordinate to the main idea.

When children have a full awareness of what they are reading, they ordinarily subordinate the necessary phrases without help. When they do not, the teacher asks leading questions. For example, he may ask, "What did Christ do?" The child answers, "He came to Bethlehem long, long ago." The teacher asks how. The child responds, "In a manger bed," or, "In a manger bed, cradled." In this conversation the necessary subordination will almost always occur in conversation. The teacher advises the child to read the line the way he said it.

HIGHLIGHTING NEW IDEAS

Subordination also indicates old ideas in contrast to new ideas. The reader highlights new thoughts and subordinates old ones except where they are repeated for emphasis or are restated. For example, again in the poem about the dandelion,

"O dandelion, yellow as gold,
What do you do all day?"
"I just wait here in the tall green grass
Till the children come out to play."

"O dandelion, yellow as gold,
What do you do all night?"
"I wait and wait till the cold dews fall
And blow my hair away."

the first two lines of the first and second verses are identical except for the words "day" and "night." In the second verse, the reader will subordinate all the words in the first two lines except "night," which he will highlight, for this word indicates a new important idea that is a center of attention. Core words which carry the new ideas are always highlighted.

When the child does not highlight "night" and subordinate the rest of the stanza to it, the teacher may ask, "How is the question in the second stanza different from the one in the first?" The child will say, "First, he's asking what the dandelion does in the *day*, then at *night*." The teacher then suggests that the child show the difference when he reads the two stanzas.

Increases or decreases in pitch and intensity are useful in indicating a series, building the climax, noting parallel attention, and showing concesson.

RELATING THOUGHTS IN A SERIES

The poem "Ambition," by Marchette Chute, tells of the exciting objects to be found on an island far away in the middle of the sea. She lists them: a friendly goat, a silver sword, a sailing boat, some purple grapes, and a breadfruit tree. Most children, as they read this verse, will keep the pitch up on the first four items and lower it on the last. This pattern is generally true of a series whether it consists of modified objects, as in this case, or of phrases like "bolts of calico," "balls of string," "jars of peppermint," "tins of tea" as found in Rachel Field's "General Store."

Again, children generally build the series, because they are usually interested in the wonderful objects on the island. When they do not, the teacher may say, "List what was on the island." As the children search their memories, they keep their voices up on the first four items and let

them fall on the last to indicate the series is completed. The teacher
advises that they read the items as they said them.

BUILDING IDEAS TO A CLIMAX

Each chicken in "The Chickens" wishes he could find a little worm, a
stone, a slug, some yellow meal, or a little green leaf. All the chickens
complain about finding food. The climax occurs in the last verse:

> "Now, see here," said the mother,
> From the green garden patch,
> "If you want any breakfast,
> Just come here and scratch."

Most children will naturally indicate this climax, the highest center of
attention. They will read the ultimatum of the mother chicken with
more force and vigor, as if to say, "This is the end to this talk, little
chickens!"

Usually, when children enjoy and understand what they are reading,
they will build the climax automatically. If they do not, the teacher asks
such a question as "What is the most exciting part of the poem?" or,
"How does the mother hen put an end to all the nonsense of the baby
chicks?" After the child has explained, the teacher says, "Then show us
it's exciting," or, "Sound like the mother laying down the law."

CONTRASTING OF OPPOSITE IDEAS

Christina Rossetti, in "Boats Sail on the Rivers," says,

> But clouds that sail across the sky
> Are prettier far than these.

This picture is in contrast to the boats that sail the rivers and the ships
that sail the seas. The reader achieves, through highlighting, the recognition of contrast between boats and ships on the one hand and clouds
on the other. He shows the differences between the two images. Words
in contrast are always centers of attention and are highlighted.

Sometimes a child will not indicate the necessary contrast. The
teacher asks, "In this poem how do the clouds differ from the boats and
the ships?" After the child has explained, the teacher asks him to let his
classmates know the difference. He shows his classmates that the boats
and ships sailing the rivers and seas are an idea in opposition to the
clouds sailing the sky.

INDICATING PARALLEL ATTENTION

The poem "I Saw a Ship" tells of the beauty of the ship itself and of the merchandise:

> There were comfits in the cabin,
> And apples in the hold;
> The sails were made of silk,
> And the masts were made of gold.

In these lines are two types of parallelism: that within the sentence, "comfits in the cabin" and "apples in the hold," and the parallelism of the sails made of silk and the masts made of gold. The reader achieves the recognition of the two parallel images through equal highlighting.

Occasionally, a child may not indicate the parallelism. When he does not, the teacher may ask, "What was in the cabin and what was in the hold?" or, "What were the sails made of and what were the masts made of?" After he has explained, the teacher asks him to let his classmates know that the one idea is as important as the other.

NOTING CONCESSION

In a play written by children, the little boy was complaining that he had had nothing to eat at the fair. His mother said, "But you did have two bananas, some ice cream, and a sandwich." The boy answered, "Yes, I guess I did." The mother then pointed out that he had also had two hot dogs, a candied apple, and a Popsicle. The boy replied, "I s'pose I did." Both times he was conceding that he had had food to eat.

Almost always the child will correctly read the lines indicating concession. If he doesn't, the teacher may ask, "When you say, 'Yes, I guess I did,' and, 'I s'pose I did,' what do you mean?" The child will respond, "I'm saying I really did have something to eat." The teacher may then advise that he sound as if he were admitting he had had a little something to eat.

IMPARTING MOOD TO THE AUDIENCE

In order to bring out the tranquility of "Velvet Shoes," readers read it rather slowly. On the other hand, Vachel Lindsay's "The Little Turtle" needs variation in speed to establish its mood of gaiety and to indicate the speaker's pride in being smarter than the turtle. As the child reads about the turtle and his living in a box, swimming in the puddle, and climbing on the rocks, he may get more excited and, consequently, speak each line more quickly. When he tells how the turtle snapped at a mosquito, a flea, and a minnow, he may for emphasis read each of the lines more slowly and then quickly say the last line, "And he snapped at me." He may well speed up as he tells about the turtle's catching the mosquito, flea, and the minnow and then emphasize the line "But he didn't catch me" with a slow rate. The poem can be read in many ways, but the use of time variation shows the action and excitement of the poem.

Variation in volume also helps to establish mood. A reader may say the lines of "Velvet Shoes" quietly and softly to bring out its serenity and quietness. In "The Little Turtle," a reader may speak the lines of the second verse progressively louder and the lines of the last verse progressively softer until he comes to the very last line, which he speaks very loudly. He uses intensity in many other ways in a poem. Changes of volume exemplify, in a simple way, one use.

Readers make use of rising and falling inflections and of those which both rise and fall. Usually a rising inflection indicates doubt, incredulity, or questioning. A falling inflection indicates the finish or completion of a statement or assertion. The use of rising and falling inflection together may indicate an attitude of not knowing quite what to believe, of indecision or sarcasm. For example, "Where are you going?" would be spoken with a rising inflection when the speaker is asking a simple question. "I'm going home" would be spoken with a falling inflection when the speaker is sure of his action. If the speaker is doubtful about where he is going, the inflection on home may be first rising and then falling.

As a child reads, his facial expression indicates mood. When he is excited, he will look excited. While he is reading a sad story, his faces indicates sadness. If the poem or story is gay, he looks particularly happy and bright. Furthermore, his posture and use of hands often help make the mood clear. He is communicating the feeling of the text with his whole body.

Through skillful leadership of discussion, the teacher can develop children's ability to get the feeling of poems and stories. After reading "Velvet Shoes," one teacher asked, "What does the poem make you think of?" The children replied differently: "A farmhouse almost hidden by snow; no noise, but complete quiet." "The woods with a hushed silence and animals moving quietly." "Somehow I think of the soft white wool of a toy lamb I had as a child." When the teacher finished reading "The Little Turtle," he questioned, "Who's talking?" One child said that it was a fish, and another, a little boy. The teacher asked, "How did each feel?" The one child said that the fish was a big fish and that he thought it funny that the turtle was scared of him. The other child replied that the boy felt smart because the turtle snapped at all the little things but not at him. In both instances, because the teacher helped the children establish mood, they reflected the understanding of mood in their use of volume, pitch, and animation in their reading.

The teacher may use other means to help children establish mood. He may ask what pictures they saw as they read the poem. Sometimes he may suggest they paint or draw the pictures. After the teacher had read John Drinkwater's "Tiptoe Night," which suggests the quietness of night, children drew or painted the following scenes: a long lane winding up a hill with flowers at its sides, a big tree with the moon shining through, a little boy looking out the window at the moon, and a garden gate with a house behind it. After another teacher read "The Squirrel," the children painted a squirrel with a big curly tail hopping over the ground, another eating his supper on the ground, and a third on the very top of a tree. When the children read these two poems themselves, they better understood the feelings and were able to convey them to their classmates.

SUMMARY

In oral reading, the reader takes the place of the writer and tells what he has to say to an audience. An oral reader understands the meaning and feeling and imparts them to the audience.

Guides to successful experiences in oral reading are: (1) The concepts in the material to be read are meaningful to the reader. (2) A happy classroom atmosphere encourages children to read aloud. (3) The oral reading is purposeful. The purposes of oral reading are: (1) A child wishes to share with others an enjoyable experience. (2) A child tells a story or a poem in the exact words of the author, for the author's use of language is what makes the experience a happy one. (3) The child reads the exact words of a writer who carries authority or who is giving information that must be imparted accurately.

To read aloud effectively, the child must understand both the meaning and feeling intended by the author. To understand the meaning, he must comprehend the main idea of the story, poem, or essay. He must also know the meaning of the words in the selection, the allusions to names of people and places, and often the historical or geographical background of the writing. He should usually be aware of the author's purpose and the facts of his life. He makes use of the relationship of words, phrases, and clauses as clues to the meaning of the selection. The teacher, through discussion, helps the child to understand meaning. His attack is an informal one.

The child must understand not only the meaning but also the mood intended by the author. The author establishes mood by his use of colorful words, of images, of repetition, of rhyme, of meter, and of musical or unmusical sounds. Through discussion, the teacher aids the child in understanding the mood of the selection.

Beyond understanding the meaning and the feeling of the poem, the reader must impart them to his classmates. He has a complete realization of the meaning of the words as he reads them and a vivid sense of communication. He uses certain techniques of oral reading to establish meaning for his audience: centering, phrasing, subordination, emphasis on new ideas, building a series, indicating climax, showing contrast, indicating parallel attention, and revealing concession. To impart feeling, he uses force and pitch of voice, rate of speaking and facial expression, posture and bodily gesture. If he understands what he is reading, wants his audience to comprehend, and is very interested in the material and in his audience's reacting to it, he is less likely to need instruction in these techniques. When he does need instruction, the teacher attacks the problem indirectly through discussion. The fun of reading aloud must remain paramount.

EXERCISES

1. Select three stories that children of the age you are to teach will enjoy reading aloud. Indicate reasons why they are suitable.

2. Select ten poems that children of the age you are to teach may enjoy. Justify your choice.

3. Show how you can interest children in poetry. Give specific examples.

4. Show how reading aloud can fit into a day's program in a particular grade in the elementary school.

5. Indicate how you will relate specific poems to the experiences of your children.

BIBLIOGRAPHY

SOURCES FOR FURTHER READING

Arbuthnot, M. H., *Children and Books*, Chicago, Scott, Foresman, 1947.
Considers how to select books for children and how to guide their reading.

Artley, H. S., "Teaching Word Meaning through Context," *Elementary
English Review*, Vol. 20 (February, 1943), pp. 68–74.

Arnstein, F. J., *Adventure into Poetry*, Stanford, Calif., Stanford University
Press, 1951. Analyzes Arnstein's own experience with youngsters who
read and write poetry. Contains examples of children's poetry.

Cohler, M. J., "The Uses and Abuses of Oral Reading," *Elementary English
Review*, Vol. 20 (December, 1943), pp. 327–329.

Duffy, G., and D. Durrell, "The Third Grade Difficulties in Oral Reading,"
Education, Vol. 56 (September, 1935), p. 37. Surveys the oral reading
difficulties of eighty-seven children in the third grade.

Evans, C., "On Reading Aloud," *Elementary English*, Vol. 28 (February,
1951), pp. 82–84. Lists books that read aloud well for younger children.

Gould, F. E., "Creative Expression through Poetry," *Elementary English*,
Vol. 26 (November, 1949), pp. 391–393. Tells how to encourage interest
in poetry. Includes poetry written by children.

Gray, W. S., *Promoting Personal and Social Development through Reading*,
Chicago, University of Chicago Press, October, 1947. Deals with the
promotion of personal and social development on various grade levels
through reading. Includes bibliographies of reading materials for children
at various grade levels.

Harbage, M., "Using Poetry with Young Children," *Elementary English
Review*, Vol. 26 (November, 1949), pp. 385–390.

Lee, C. I., *Oral Interpretation*, Boston, Houghton Mifflin, 1952. Explains the
basic principles of oral interpretation. Gives an account of the types of
prose. Tells how to interpret prose, poetry, and drama.

Parent, N., "Speech Techniques and Children's Literature," *Elementary
English*, Vol. 27 (November, 1950), pp. 450–453. Describes the use of
techniques of speech in furthering appreciation of children's literature.

Parrish, W. M., *Reading Aloud*, rev. ed., New York, Ronald, 1943. Discusses methods of learning to read aloud. Explains clearly the importance
and techniques of understanding the meaning and emotional intent of
writers.

Peins, M., "Speech Techniques for the Classroom," *Elementary English*,
Vol. 27 (November, 1950), pp. 446–449. Gives the results of a survey
which indicates what techniques are used by teachers in the classroom
teaching of speech. Poetry is used most frequently.

Smith, N. B., "Trends and Applications in Primary Reading," in *Reading,
a Tool for Learning*, Washington, American Childhood Education, 1938,
pp. 18–26. Shows the practical application of reading in the classroom
and the relationship of reading to classroom activities.

Stolper, J. R., *The Group Poem*, New York, Teachers College, Columbia
University, 1938. Explains the writing of poetry as a group classroom
activity.

Theman, V., "Techniques in Cultivating Effective Oral Interpretation, Appreciation and Tastes in Readings," in William S. Gray (compiler), *Basic Instruction in Reading in Elementary and High School*, Chicago, University of Chicago Press, 1948, pp. 188–191. Explains how to further good oral reading and an appreciation of it in children.

Westlake, H., "Understandings, Attitudes and Skills in Interpretative Oral Reading," in William S. Gray (compiler), *Basic Instruction and Reading in Elementary and High Schools*, Chicago, University of Chicago Press, 1948, pp. 179–182. Notes the criterion for good oral reading and describes how to improve oral reading.

Witty, P., A. Coomer, and D. McBean, "Children's Choices of Favorite Books," *Journal of Educational Psychology*, Vol. 37 (May, 1946), pp. 266–278. Shows favorite stories of children in ten elementary schools.

STORIES SUITABLE FOR READING ALOUD

Beim, J., and L. Beim, *Two Is a Team*, New York, Harcourt Brace, 1945. A delightful tale of Ted, a little Negro boy, and Paul, a little white boy, who play together every day and who work together making a wagon. Middle grades.

Brock, E. L., *Uncle Bennie Goes Visiting*, New York, Knopf, 1944. Uncle Bennie, a gay uncle, who has been a city grocery clerk, has come to spend the summer on his niece's farm. Middle grades.

Brown, M., *The Little Carousel*, New York, Scribner, 1948. Tony, who lives on a busy street in a large city, expresses his joy on finally being able to ride on the merry-go-round. Primary grades.

Burton, V. L., *Katy and the Big Snow*, Boston, Houghton Mifflin, 1943. The story of a huge snowstorm that blocks all life in the city. Katy is the beloved snowplow that gets the doctor to the patient. Primary grades.

———, *The Little House*, Boston, Houghton Mifflin, 1942. The city comes nearer and nearer to a little house that lives in the country until the house is surrounded with buildings; but the great-great-grandchildren of its former owners move it to the country where it is happy again. Primary.

Child Study Association of America, *Read-to-me Story Books*, New York, Crowell, 1943. Compilation of material to read aloud to the very young.

Dalgliesh, A., *America Begins*, New York, Scribner, 1938. The story of the finding of the New World. Middle grades.

———, *America Builds Homes*, New York, Scribner, 1938. The story of the first colonies. Middle grades.

du Bois, W. P., *The Twenty-one Balloons*, New York, Viking, 1947. A professor, tired of teaching arithmetic, builds a huge balloon and goes off on an adventure. Mixture of scientific fact and sheer nonsense. Upper grades.

Estes, E., *One Hundred Dresses*, New York, Harcourt Brace, 1944. The story of a little girl who tells her classmates that she has a hundred dresses at home but who wears an old faded-blue dress to school each day. Intermediate grades.

Fenner, P. R. (compiler), *Fools and Funny Fellows*, New York, Knopf, 1947. Anthology of humorous tales.

Flack, M., *Wait for William*, Boston, Houghton Mifflin, 1935. William can't keep up with the other children but triumphs when the elephant keeper asks him to ride the elephant. Primary grades.

Forbes, E., *Johnny Tremaine*, Boston, Houghton Mifflin, 1943. The role of Johnny Tremaine in the American Revolution. Upper grades.

Ford, E., *Jeff Roberts, Railroader*, Philadelphia, Macrae Smith, 1948. Jeff's climb from callboy to engineer on a freight train. Upper grades.

Gág, W., *Gone Is Gone*, New York, Coward McCann, 1934. The story of a man who wants to do housework. Primary grades.

Gerber, W., *Gooseberry Jones*, New York, Putnam, 1947. A small boy wants a dog despite the objections of his parents. Middle grades.

Gould, J., *Miss Emily*, Boston, Houghton Mifflin, 1946. Fictionized account of the life of Emily Dickinson. Upper grades.

Graham, A., *Timothy Turtle*, New York, Robert Welch, 1946. Timothy Turtle isn't satisfied with an easy life but longs for fame. After an exciting journey over Took-a-Look Hill, he is happy to return to his ferrying business. Primary grades.

Hader, B., and E. Hader, *Cat and the Kittens*, New York, Macmillan, 1940. The story of Minnie and her five kittens. Timmy, one of the kittens, wanders away from home and has many adventures. Primary grades.

Holberg, R. L., *Michael and the Captain*, New York, Crowell, 1944. The hero is Michael, the son of a Serbian farmer. Vivid picture of life on the farm. The Turks are struggling to conquer the Slavs. Michael meets with Capt. Smith, but decides to stay in his own land. Intermediate grades.

Hinkle, T. K., *Blaze Face*, New York, Morrow, 1947. Story of the adventures of the son of an outlaw mare who is captured, tamed, and stolen. Intermediate and upper grades.

Judson, C. J., *Michael's Victory*, Boston, Houghton Mifflin, 1947. An appealing story of an Irish immigrant family who settle in Defiance, Ohio. Upper grades.

Kipling, R., *Just So Stories*, New York, Doubleday, 1912. These stories read unusually well and are perennial favorites. Intermediate grades.

Lenski, L., *Cowboy Small*, New York, Oxford, 1949. Cowboy Small saddles his horse, rides ranges, cooks his supper, rounds up cattle, plays his banjo, and sings songs. Primary grades.

———, *Judy's Journey*, Philadelphia, Lippincott, 1947. The story of migrant workers from Florida to New Jersey. Intermediate grades.

———, *The Little Fire Engine*, New York, Oxford, 1946. The story of Fireman Small, who tells about fighting fires. Indicates all the equipment on a fire truck, like the pump, hose, and ladder. Primary grades.

———, *Blue Ridge Billy*, Philadelphia, Lippincott, 1946. A glimpse of the life of the mountaineers in the Blue Ridge section of North Carolina. Told through Billy, who wants a banjo. Intermediate and upper grades.

———, *Strawberry Girl*, Philadelphia, Lippincott, 1946. The raising of strawberries on a flatwood farm of Florida. Intermediate and upper grades.

Lindman, M., *Snipp, Snapp and Snurr, and the Red Shoes*, Racine, Wis., Whitman, 1932. A story of earning money to buy red shoes for Mother. Primary.

Lofting, H., *Dr. Dolittle and the Green Canary*, Philadelphia, Lippincott, 1950. Typical Dr. Dolittle story. Primary grades.

McGinley, P., *Most Wonderful Doll in the World*, Philadelphia, Lippincott, 1950. Angela is the most wonderful doll who is lost the same day she is received. Each time the story is told new details of her wonder are added. Intermediate grades.

McCloskey, R., *Make Way for Ducklings*, New York, Viking, 1941. Humorous story of ducks who travel through Boston to their new home. Primary.

Means, F. C., *Assorted Sisters*, Boston, Houghton Mifflin, 1947. Friendship of three girls of different backgrounds in a large city. Upper grades.

Milne, A. A., *Winnie the Pooh*, New York, Dutton, 1926. Typical Milne classic.

Mitchell, L. S., *Here and Now Story Book*, New York, Dutton, 1948. Contains many delightful stories for the young child.

Newberry, C. T., *Marshmallow*, New York, Harper, 1942. A story about the author's pet cat, Oliver, and her rabbit, Marshmallow. Primary grades.

———, *April's Kittens*, New York, Harper, 1940. Beautiful illustrations. Primary grades.

Nicolay, H., *Born to Command: The Story of General Eisenhower*, New York, Appleton-Century-Crofts, 1945. The story of Eisenhower written against the background of World War II. Upper grades.

Rey, H. A., *Curious George*, Boston, Houghton Mifflin, 1941. Delightful mischief of a monkey who is getting used to city life before he goes to the zoo. Primary.

Slobodkin, L., *Caps for Sale*, New York, Scott, 1947. The story of how the monkeys got the caps for sale. Primary.

———, *The Moffats*, New York, Harcourt Brace, 1941. Story of a rather poor family. Told from the viewpoint of Janey, a nine-year-old. Middle grades.

Stefanson, E., *Within the Circle*, New York, Scribner, 1945. Portrait of the Arctic. Upper grades.

Travers, P. L., *Mary Poppins*, New York, Harcourt Brace, 1940; *Mary Poppins Comes Back*, New York, Harcourt Brace, 1940; and *Mary Poppins Opens the Door*, New York, Harcourt Brace, 1943. Classics which read well. Mary Poppins, a lively and imaginative nursemaid, carries her charges through a series of adventures that delight children. Intermediate grades.

Seuss, Dr. (T. S. Geisel), *The Five Hundred Hats of Bartholomew Cubbins*, New York, Vanguard, 1938. Delightful humor. Middle grades.

Tresselt, Alvin, *White Snow, Bright Snow*, New York, Lothrop, 1947. Magical beauty of snow described for young children.

———, *Rain Drop Splash*, New York, Lothrop, 1946. Indicates what happens from the time the rain leaves the sky until it flows into the sea. Primary.

ANTHOLOGIES AND COLLECTIONS OF CHILDREN'S POETRY

Aldis, D., *Here, There and Everywhere*, New York, Putnam, 1928. Poems of the everyday in children's lives. Primary grades.

————, *Everything and Anything*, New York, Putnam, 1927. Poems that tell of the adventures of children. Primary grades.

Arbuthnot, M. H., *Time for Poetry*, Chicago, Scott, Foresman, 1951. Unusually good collection. Poems grouped under Animal Fair, Traveling We Go, Let's Play, Magic, and Make-believe.

Association for Childhood Education, *Sung under the Silver Umbrella*, New York, Macmillan, 1935. Excellent collection of children's poetry. Primary grades.

Benét, R., and S. V. Benét, *A Book of Americans*, New York, Rinehart, 1933. Poems about Columbus, Pocahontas, Miles Standish, Benjamin Franklin, and other American heroes. Intermediate and upper grades.

Brewton, S., and J. E. Brewton, *Bridled with Rainbows*, New York, Macmillan, 1949. Poems concerning the earth, sky, seasons, school, seas, ships, and water. Primary and intermediate grades.

Barrows, M., *Two Hundred Best Poems for Boys and Girls*, Racine, Wis., Whitman, 1938. Excellent collection; inexpensive.

Chute, M., *Rhymes about the City*, New York, Macmillan, 1947. Poems about New York City: its horses, drinking fountains, fish stores, skating, Radio City, doorman, and the zoo. Primary.

de la Mare, W., *Bells and Grass*, New York, Viking, 1942. Some of the poems tell of actual and personal memories. Others are concerned with the imagined and the imaginary. Intermediate.

Doane, P., *A Small Child's Book of Verses*, New York, Oxford, 1948. An excellent selection. Primary through upper grades.

Field, R., *Taxis and Toadstools*, New York, Doubleday, 1946. Everyday verses. Primary grades.

Frost, F., *The Little Whistler*, New York, Simon and Schuster, 1949. A collection of poems dealing with seasons, animals, the farm scene, and familiar holidays. Intermediate grades.

Fyleman, R., *Fairies and Chimneys*, New York, Doubleday, 1929. Primary grades.

————, *The Rose Fyleman Fairy Book*, New York, Doubleday, 1923. Primary grades.

Hubbard, A. and A. Babbitt (eds.), *The Golden Flute*, New York, John Day, 1932. Poems listed in terms of children's interests and activities, such as insects, home, Christmas, Arbor Day, Easter. Primary and intermediate grades.

Huffard, G. T., L. M. Carlisle, and H. J. Ferris, *My Poetry Book*, Philadelphia, Winston, 1934. A well-selected anthology. Primary grades.

Kissen, F., *Tales from the Four Winds*, Boston, Houghton Mifflin, 1948. Radio plays for children based on folklore. Intermediate grades.

Lenski, L., *Now It's Fall*, New York, Oxford, 1948; *Spring Is Here*, New York, Oxford, 1945; and *I Like Winter*, New York, Oxford, 1940. Primary grades.

Lindsay, V., *Johnny Appleseed*, New York, Macmillan, 1928. An introduction to folklore for primary children.

Milne, A. A., *Now We are Six*, New York, Dutton, 1927; *When We Were Very Young*, New York, Dutton, 1924. Delightful whimsical poetry. Primary grades.

Petersham, M., and M. Petersham, *The Rooster Crows*, New York, Macmillan, 1945. Collection of jingles, rhymes, and bits about weather. Primary, intermediate, and upper grades.

Roberts, E. M., *Under the Tree*, New York, Viking, 1930. Vivid description of child life in country and village. Artistic writing. Primary grades.

Sechrist, E. H., *One Thousand Poems for Children*, Philadelphia, Macrae Smith, 1946. Part I for younger children. Part II for older children. Well indexed.

Thompson, B., *Silver Pennies*, New York, Macmillan, 1925. A useful anthology. Primary grades.

Tibbett, J. S., *I Spend the Summer*, New York, Harper, 1930. The story of a summer spent at a mountain lake. Primary grades.

———, *I Live in a City*, New York, Harper, 1927. Poems describing apartment house, zoo, park, elevator boy, and telephone girl. Primary grades.

5   Choral Speaking

"Verse speaking," "choral reading," "choral speaking," "unison speaking," "choric speech" are terms used to denote the art of speaking in unison. Most teachers call it choral speaking. Choral speaking is the speaking together of a poem or a piece of prose by a group that imparts the meaning and spirit of the selection with clarity and spontaneity. The group chooses a selection appropriate for speaking in unison and decides on an interpretation which will make its thought and feeling clear to the listeners. The teacher helps the members of the group to speak the lines so that they share their interpretation with their listeners.

THE DEVELOPMENT OF CHORAL SPEAKING

The advent of choral speaking as a technique in the classroom is relatively recent, although Greek drama made use of it in 500 B.C. and the psalms from the Old Testament were read with a choral response. John Masefield, in modern times, suggested the idea of group interpretation to Marjorie Gullan, who carried it out. She first experimented with the art form in the Glasgow Music Festival of 1922, when she trained a group of speakers in Greek drama choruses. Because of her successful performances with choral speaking groups, John Masefield established the Oxford Recitations, where speech choirs spoke, heard each other, and received criticism from Miss Gullan. Miss Gullan was also a decided influence in the growth of the movement in the United States. When she lectured here in the 1930's, she demonstrated the techniques of choral speaking. Many copies of her books on how to teach choral speaking have found their way into the hands of classroom teachers; her records of choral speaking of children and adults have been widely played and heard. Her performances are polished and artistic. Poetry-speaking assemblies, similar to the music festivals in this country, motivate teachers in England to produce artistic work. In spite of Miss Gullan's influence, the standards in the United States generally are not high, and teachers here use choral speaking more as a motivating device to interest children in poetry than as an art form.

VALUES OF CHORAL SPEAKING

Writers have attributed many values to choral speaking but three are paramount: (1) Participation in choral speaking furthers an appreciation of poetry in children. (2) Participation in it makes children more able to interpret poetry. (3) It provides an opportunity for speech work in which the timid participate readily and in which the excessively loquacious child is submerged.

APPRECIATION OF POETRY

Poetry is meant to be read aloud. Admittedly, many children think it dull and wordy, avoid it, and pass on to the narrative forms of literature. But they are more likely to enjoy it if they have experienced the excitement of hearing it read well and of participating in effective choral speaking of it. Members of the group stimulate each other; the rhythm, the contrasts in groups of voices and in individual voices, and the sound of the full quality of voices skillfully blended impress children. Furthermore, the students and teacher interpret the poem in a meaningful way, because they have planned the reading. Through group reading, children develop an appreciation for poetry.

INTERPRETATION OF POETRY

Participation in choral speaking motivates children to interpret poetry well. As they discuss the mood and thought of the selection, as they agree and disagree on whether light or heavy voices are better suited to a line, they find more meaning and beauty in poetry. They are interpreting poetry when they declare that a chorus of light voices must speak the refrain in Christina Rossetti's "Lullaby" to establish its mood. When they set up a pattern for interpretation, through trying out and talking about different ways of reading lines, they are learning to read aloud. If the teacher asks the children to reproduce the lines as he has read them, they are merely parroting him with no thinking on their own. Little or no real learning has taken place. The interpretation of a selection can take many forms besides the teacher's. Children learn to read poetry aloud as they try out a variety of forms and decide logically on the pattern they like best.

DEVELOPMENT OF GOOD ATTITUDES TOWARD SPEAKING

Beyond encouraging children to appreciate and interpret poetry, participation in choral speaking helps develop in children a good attitude toward speaking. Even some young children are self-conscious about talking before an audience. In group speaking, these children lose their self-consciousness. Through sharing in choral speaking and through the speaking of solo parts, the child gains confidence in his ability to speak. He discovers that he likes to speak with the group, that he can speak well, and that he is encouraged to speak alone. On the other hand, the aggressive individual benefits by being submerged in the group reading. He finds himself sharing in the sense of achievement and being proud of his participation. The attitude of both types of children toward speaking changes.

Most teachers use a form of choral speaking even in kindergarten, for the children repeat parts of stories or poems with the teacher. For example, they will spontaneously speak together their favorite nursery rhyme. They speak together for the sheer enjoyment of the sounds, rhyme, and rhythm of the poetry. When the children are ready, the teacher will help them to speak together more effectively. The first efforts will likely be informal speaking together of simple poems, phrases, or refrains. When they have shared the fun of choral speaking as a group and have become fairly skillful, the teacher may divide the members of his class into groups of different types of voices in order to make use of the various forms of choral speaking in the interpretation of poetry. He shows the children how a division of voices into light and heavy helps interpret some lines. He does not impose any particular type on the group, for the materials to be read and the children themselves are the determining factors in the selection of a type of choral speaking.

ARRANGEMENT OF THE SPEAKING GROUP

DIVISION OF VOICES

Voices in the elementary school are divided into two groups, light and heavy; or into three groups, light, heavy, and medium. Light voices are those which are higher-pitched, finer, and more delicate.

Heavy voices are those which are lower-pitched, heavier, and fuller. To hear the range of voices and to get the feel of which are heavy and which are light in the class, the teacher listens to ten or fifteen voices. Medium voices are those falling between the two extremes. When he is judging the pitch and quality of a voice, he asks the child to give his name and address or some other piece of information which requires thought, for if the child repeats a phrase after another youngster, he is likely to imitate his pitch and quality. Children enjoy judging the light and heavy quality of voices along with the teacher. Where the teacher is in doubt about a particular voice, he assigns the child to a group and changes him later if he finds it necessary. He will quickly discern that a child's voice does not belong in a particular group.

PHYSICAL ARRANGEMENT

Those children with heavy voices, those with light voices, and those with medium ones must stand or sit with their own group to blend their voices. They must be close enough together to speak as a unit. While children discuss the meaning of the poem and rehearse, they sit on the

FIG. 15. Speaking together. (*University State Teachers College, Geneseo, N.Y.*)

floor or on chairs placed fairly close together. When they are to perform for an audience, they stand in a more formal arrangement. They usually stand in groups somewhat triangular in shape. Students who have a good sense of pitch and an ability to remember the pattern of interpretation stand at the apex of the triangles. They serve as leaders of groups much like the first violinist of the violin section of the symphony orchestra.

TYPES OF CHORAL SPEAKING

The voices of heavy and light groups and of individuals bring color and contrast to the interpretation of a poem. Sometimes individuals speak different lines of a poem; sometimes all the members speak in unison. The interpretation of poems responds to other forms: antiphonal speaking, in which one group answers another; cumulative speaking, in which groups are added until all the choir speaks one part of the poem; refrain speaking, in which a group of children, an individual, or several individuals read the narrative and all the children repeat the chorus; and part speaking, in which several groups speak different portions of the selection. High voices read lines which suggest lightness and delicacy; low voices read those which suggest gloom, majesty, or solemnity. Medium voices often given the necessary explanations. An individual's voice may supply moods. For example, in "Hollyhocks," by Lew Sarett, a sharp voice portrays "onions acrimonious," a light voice, "lettuce frivolous," and a deep, heavy voice, "beets apoplectic."

Children take part in the decision to divide a poem. After the children have had considerable experience speaking as a group for the fun of it, the teacher suggests divisions. He does not teach all of the divisions at once but advises a particular type for a specific poem. After children have had experience with a particular type, they will frequently suggest it for the interpretation of another poem. They learn informally that divisions should add to the sense and emotional intent of the poem, that they should make it richer and clearer, and that they should not merely give variety.

Line-a-child. Individual children speak different lines. The entire class speaks the first and eighth lines of "Solomon Grundy," whereas six individuals read the second, third, fourth, fifth, sixth, and seventh lines. Children with light, bright voices speak the first three lines, whereas children with rich, heavy voices speak the last three lines.

Children are unusually discerning in selecting voices for a particular line. One seven-year-old said, "Let Kay say 'Married on Wednesday'; she'll make it gay!" She quickly judged the kind of voice that interpreted a particular mood. Children must learn, in this type of reading, to pick up the lines in the tempo and rhythm of the poem. Line-a-child reading adapts well to poems in which different lines express quite different moods.

Antiphonal. The heavy and light voices talk to each other; for example, one group asks, "Witch, witch, where do you live?"; and the other group answers, "Under the clouds and over the sky." Which group speaks which lines depends on the interpretation of the poem agreed on by the children. The Mother Goose rhyme "Little Tommy Tucker's Dog" is another dialogue poem which is often spoken with antiphonal choral speaking. Children read poems which contain dialogue between two persons or two groups of persons in this way.

Cumulative. Choral reading achieves a cumulative effect with a small group reading one section, the original group and an additional one reading the second section, and the original group and two others reading the third section. Usually no more than five groups build the cumulative effect. "African Dance" adapts well to cumulative speaking. A small group reads the first line, "The low beating of the tom-toms"; group one and group two read "The slow beating of the tom-toms"; and groups one, two, and three read the phrase "low, slow"; groups one, two, three, and four read "slow-low"; and, finally, five groups read the last line, "Stirs your blood." The emphasis grows more forceful; the poem becomes louder and faster in each line. The cumulative effect indicates the increasing intensity in the beating of the tom-toms. In the second verse, a night-veiled girl whirls softly in a dance; light voices read these lines lightly and melodically to suggest the grace and flow of the dance in contrast to the growing intensity of the beating of the tom-toms in the first verse. Cumulative reading is usually used to indicate an increasing intensity of feeling.

Refrain Speaking. In refrain speaking, the members of the class speak the refrain while one child, or several speaking one at a time, tells the story. For example, a soloist reads "This is the song of the bees" and "A jolly good fellow is he," while the class repeats the refrain, "buzz, buzz, buzz," after each line. The chorus carries out the mood of the preceding line. For example, in this poem, the children speak gaily, approvingly, "buzz, buzz, buzz," after the reader has declared the bee to be a good fellow, but where the reader indicates he is making his honey on a sunny day, the group speaks "buzz, buzz, buzz" in a busy, workmanlike way.

Part Speaking. Part speaking refers to the type of choral speaking in which each group of the class speaks a portion of the selection and in which all the groups maintain the continuity and sequence of ideas expressed in the poem. Two, three, or more groups may participate. For example, in Walter De la Mare's "Bunch of Grapes," three children, quite different, speak in the three verses. Timothy is a kindly, dreamy boy. Elaine is dainty and fairylike. Jane is down-to-earth, gay, and practical. The heavy voices might speak Timothy's lines; the light voices, Elaine's; and the medium voices, Jane's. Hillyer's "Lullaby" is often spoken with a heavy and a light group. The heavy voices read the "one . . . two . . . three . . . four" which are repeated to indicate the paddle's movement. Light voices read the rest of the poem, which describes the canoe's quiet movements.

Unison Speaking. The group reads the entire poem together where it maintains one mood and one theme throughout. Both heavy and light voices should speak with rhythm, with control of tone, pitch, and volume. Children should articulate clearly, pronounce accurately, and blend their voices well. In a girl's school, the eighth-grade girls read Elinor Wylie's "Velvet Shoes" together. They spoke the words slowly and quietly and portrayed for their audience the hushed peace of walking in the snow. In contrast, a group of third-grade children created the fun of skipping in its reading of Paul Edmond's "Skipping."

Whatever division the children decide upon should add meaning to the poem. They should not use the division for dramatic effect alone but should use it to make the sense and emotional intent of the poem clear to their listeners. At first, children may suggest too many divisions, but they quickly learn that some divisions interfere with meaning. In the beginning, they also tend to want to break lines too frequently. As soon as they realize that too frequent breaking detracts from meaning, they assign longer units to individuals and to groups. Divisions should help make a selection clear to the listeners.

After the teacher and children have decided to try speaking together, the selection of material is very important, for if it is selected carefully, the activity will be more successful. After it is chosen, the teacher leads a discussion on the interpretation of the selection so that the children understand it. Furthermore, he helps them set the pattern for the group interpretation. After this preliminary work, he conducts the group in such a way as to make the meaning and feeling of the poem clear to the listeners.

SELECTION OF MATERIAL

The careful selection of material may mean the success of the reading of the poem or piece of prose. It further means that choral speaking is more likely to achieve some of the values ascribed to it. The material should meet the following requirements: (1) It should interest the children. (2) It should be within their intellectual and emotional understanding. (3) It should possess literary value. (4) It should possess thought that is universal. (5) Its form should be adaptable to choral speaking.

MATERIAL SHOULD INTEREST THE CHILDREN

A committee of children, with the guidance of the teacher, chooses the poems to be read. A group of eighth-grade students became interested in America's being made up of all kinds of people who belong to different trades and professions. They had first listened to, and later sung, the "Ballad for Americans." When one twelve-year-old boy found Walt Whitman's "Song of America," he suggested the group read it together. The group, with individuals portraying the different vocations, read the poem in a sincere, simple, meaningful manner. It was an excellent choice, because the students were already interested in America's composition.

MATERIAL SHOULD BE WITHIN CHILDREN'S INTELLECTUAL AND EMOTIONAL UNDERSTANDING

Closely related to the first is the second principle: that the children understand the material. They might better read a nursery rhyme within their understanding than a Shakespearean sonnet beyond their intellectual level. When they do not understand the poem, they will not be interested in it, nor will they read it well, no matter how great it is. They should thoroughly understand the concepts, ideas, and experiences in the poems; this understanding involves emotional as well as intellectual comprehension. The unusual words in poetry sometimes discourage children; but if the poem is within their general intellectual grasp, they can deduce their meaning. Sometimes the mood of a poem is too subtle for them. Provided the teacher can prepare them for it, all may be well. If not, he had better encourage them to select another poem.

MATERIAL SHOULD HAVE LITERARY VALUE

The third principle is that the material should have literary value; it should not be elocutionary material that will draw tears or be cheaply sentimental. It should be material worth learning, imaginative, poetical. May Arbuthnot[1] gives the following advice in choosing poetry for children:

> First, does it sing—with good rhythm, true unforced rhymes, and a happy compatability of sound and subject—whether it is nonsense verse or narrative or lyric poetry? Second, is the diction distinguished— with words that are rich in sensory and associative meanings, words that are unhackneyed, precise and memorable? Third, does the subject matter of the poem invest the strange or the everyday experiences of life with new importance and richer meaning?

If the poem meets these requisites, it will be one that is worth learning.

MATERIAL SHOULD POSSESS THOUGHT THAT IS UNIVERSAL

That the teacher and children select material with universal thought is the fourth principle. A single voice gives more color, more meaning, to some poems than does a choir. Such poetry draws forth different feelings in different individuals; it is too subtle and too highly imaginative for group interpretation. Individuals can interpret Robert Frost's "Birches" better than a choir can, for each individual views the effect of the birches and the boy's swinging on them somewhat differently. It is a poem that is highly personal. Material for choral speaking should not be too delicate or subtle.

FORM OF POEM ADAPTABLE TO CHORAL SPEAKING

The last principle is that the form of a poem must be adaptable to choral speaking. Choral speaking needs strongly rhythmical poetry,

---

[1] From *Children and Books* by May Hill Arbuthnot, p. 160. Copyright, 1947, by Scott, Foresman and Company. Reprinted by permission of Scott, Foresman and Company.

poetry where variety in tempo and volume can express its different moods. Variation in intensity, pitch, and timing indicates a variety of moods, differences in ideas, and changes in persons speaking. Poetry in which the change and contrast in use of voices can indicate different ideas, moods, and feelings is suitable for choral speaking.

TEACHING CHILDREN TO SPEAK TOGETHER

The teacher has already laid the foundation for children's appreciation of poetry. He has read poetry to them, recited it to them, and encouraged them to speak parts of it with him. As he introduces choral speaking, he explains to them that they have already spoken together. Sometimes he plays recordings of choral speaking. As children begin to participate in choral speaking, they want to learn more about it and do more of it.

USE OF NURSERY RHYMES

The teacher and children begin with a simple piece of poetry, usually a nursery rhyme. "Solomon Grundy," which was used earlier as illustrative of line-a-child speaking, is good for the first choral speaking attempt. Six individuals speak the lines, "Born on Monday, etc."; the whole group speaks the first line, "Solomon Grundy," and the last line, "And that was the end of Solomon Grundy." The teacher and children decide how they want to read the rhyme. They almost always agree on the individual children's voices getting progressively gayer and gayer and then sadder and sadder. But they differ on the last line. Some will want to say it slowly and sadly; others will want to make it very gay, as if stating "What difference does it make?" The teacher will then help the children to speak together so that their speaking sounds like records that they have heard earlier.

USING LIGHT AND HEAVY VOICES TO SPEAK SIMPLE PHRASES TOGETHER

After the children have spoken simple rhymes and poems together. the teacher shows the children how a division of voices into light and heavy helps interpret some selections. For example, he may talk over with the children the tones of different kinds of bells: those that have heavy, deep tones, such as church bells, fire bells, or the Liberty Bell; those that have light, tinkling tones, such as the small dinner bell or the doorbell. He then tells the children that the heavy bell says "ding-ding-a-dong," and the light bell says "ting-a-ling-ling." He asks the boys and girls how they can make the heavy bell sound like a church bell and the light bell like a dinner bell. Together, he and the children decide how to speak the phrases. The heavy voices speak "ding-ding-a-dong" usually in a slow, measured tone; and the light voices speak "ting-a-ling-ling" lightly and quickly. Children distinguish between heavy rain, "pat-pat," and a light gentle rain, "pit-a-pat." The heavy rain may be falling fast and the light gentle rain slowly. A high-pitched wind, "whee-whee-whee," comes down the chimney, or a low-pitched wind, "whoo-whoo-whoooooo-oo" goes around the corner of the house. Frequently children will make up lines to go with the sounds. For example, after the heavy bell, a child may contribute "Says the heavy church bell in the tower"; after the light bell, another child may suggest "Says the tiny little bell on the table."

SETTING THE PATTERN FOR INTERPRETATION OF THE POEM

Finally, children are ready to prepare for speaking more difficult poems of their choice. They must first understand the thought and feeling of the poem and then decide on how they are going to impart these to an audience. This need for understanding the poem, discussed in Chapter 4, is just as important for group reading as for individual reading. Therefore, the members of the class discuss the meaning of the poem and its mood carefully and thoroughly. Individuals try reading lines in different ways, citing their reasons for their readings. The group decides on how to read the poem effectively. The teacher must lead the discussion skillfully so that the children do not accept a reading because it is bizarre or unusual. In a children's discussion of the poem mentioned earlier,

> Witch, witch where do you fly?
> Up in the clouds and over the sky.

some of the children wanted the light voices to speak the first line to give the effect of a small child naïvely and gaily asking the question. The heavy voices were to answer in an eerie manner. Another group wanted the heavy voices to say "Witch, witch . . . " in a scared, frightened fashion and the light voices to answer flippantly with wide pitch variation, "Up in the clouds and over the sky." Both groups gave excellent reasons for their interpretations. The teacher brought forth the discussion of the different ways of interpreting the lines by asking, "What kind of person is the witch?" "What does she look like?" "What does she sound like?" "Does she have fun?" After the children have once set the pattern, they do not change it unless a real and obvious need for change becomes evident. This need exists only if they discover that they are failing to impart the thought and feeling intended by the author to their audience.

Boys and girls of an eighth grade became interested in ballads when they sang some folk ballads. As they discovered that the early settlers had brought some of the ballads over from Scotland and England, they studied the possible sources of the ballads. In their study they came across "The Raggle, Taggle Gypsies":

> There were three gypsies come to my door,
> And downstairs ran this lady, O.
> One sang high and another sang low,
> And the other sang "Bonnie,
> Bonnie Biskay, O."
>
> Then she pulled off her silken gown,
> And put on hose of leather, O.
> With the ragged, ragged rags about her door
> She's off with the Raggle, Taggle Gypsies, O.
>
> 'Twas late last night when my lord came home.
> Inquiring for his lady, O.
> The servants said on every hand,
> "She's gone with the Raggle,
> Taggle Gypsies, O."
>
> "Oh, saddle for me my milk-white steed,
> Oh, saddle for me my pony, O,
> That I may ride and seek my bride
> Who's gone with the Raggle
> Taggle Gypsies, O."
>
> Oh, he rode high and he rode low,
> He rode through woods and copses, O,
> Until he came to an open field,
> And there he espied his lady, O.
>
> "What makes you leave your house and lands?
> What makes you leave your money, O?
> What makes you leave your new-wedded lord
> To go with the Raggle, Taggle Gypsies, O?"

"What care I for my house and lands?
What care I for money, O?
What care I for my new-wedded lord?
I'm off with the Raggle Taggle Gypsies, O."

"Last night you slept on a goose-feather bed,
With the sheet turned down so bravely, O.
Tonight you will sleep in the cold open field,
Along with the Raggle, Taggle Gypsies, O."

"What care I for your goose-feather bed,
With the sheet turned down so bravely, O,
For tonight I shall sleep in a cold, open field,
Along with the Raggle, Taggle Gypsies, O."

They discussed the poem before they spoke it: they talked about the woman who had left her lord; they examined her motives. Some children thought she was just plain faithless. Some thought she had married the lord for his money and now regretted her decision, since it hadn't brought her happiness. Others guessed that she had originally been a free gypsy girl who had been fascinated by a rich husband and a beautiful home; but, when the gypsies came to her home, she couldn't resist them and ran off with them.

They determined the division and interpretation of the poem. They chose to have the medium voices read the explanations, the heavy voices interpret the lord's lines, and the light voices the lady's lines. But they also tried using individual voices for the lord and the lady. They talked over how they could interpret the narrative. In the first verse, one child wanted one voice to say "one sang high," a second voice, "and another sang low," and a third voice, "And the other sang Bonnie, Bonnie Biskay, O." The teacher pointed out that, while the division was logical, it would break the reading too much. But they created the picture of the three gypsies at the door. They also indicated the excitement of the lady's pulling off her silken gown and dashing off with the raggle, taggle gypsies. They showed the dismay of the lord and of the servants who explained where she had gone. The heavy voices revealed the determination of the lord to seek his bride and his anger when he found her. Some of the children asked to add a pleading note to the anger. They finally agreed to have her turn him down with a flippant, light quality, although some of the children wanted her to renounce him in a determined yet sad way. Their reading of the lines was based on their discussion of the motive of the lady in leaving her lord.

SELECTING THE FORM OF CHORAL SPEAKING

As indicated in the preceding paragraphs, the teacher and children decide how to interpret the mood and thought of the poem to their listeners through the type of choral speaking best suited to the poem. They try out and evaluate the various forms. Where there are solo parts, different children read them. The group chooses whom it wants to do the reading. The teacher must be careful that gifted pupils are not consistently starred as soloists.

KEEPING VOICES LIGHT

In the first reading of the poem, the teacher encourages children to speak softly and lightly. They are likely to show their enthusiasm through an increase in volume, speaking louder and louder until they are fairly shouting. When they are sure of the interpretation, they increase volume where necessary, but their early readings should be kept light.

THE TEACHER'S DIRECTION

Direction involves having the students start together and stay together and speak with approximately the same interpretation. The director gives the signal to start and to end and indicates the rhythm of the poem. He reveals the rhythm of the poem through onward flowing motions of his hand. He responds not to the beat of the poem but to its sense and meaning. In his direction, he leads lightly so that the children respond first to the meaning of the poem and then to the rhythm. The teacher also designates the pauses which he and the children have agreed on beforehand. He reveals an increase or decrease in tempo and shows increases and decreases of volume sometimes by the use of his other hand. The children learn to watch for these signals and to follow them. The direction should not call attention to itself. After members of a group have worked with the teacher, they need very little direction except indications of where to begin and to stop. Children can then take over whatever direction is necessary.

GUIDES TO CHILDREN

After the children have listened to the recordings of choral speaking, they discuss what it is like and what they must do to make their speaking together effective. They make a list, much like the one below, to serve as a guidepost in the discussion of their own performance:

1. We must start together.
2. We must stay together.
3. We must follow the leader.
4. We must blend out pitches so that we sound like one voice.
5. We must move along.
6. We must make ourselves understood.
7. We must sound as if we were talking to other children.

A child checks on any one of these seven requisites. As a critic, he indicates if the group started together, stayed together, or followed the leader. But his criticisms must be specific. He must indicate which particular words weren't spoken clearly, what line and what words didn't sound like one voice, where the reading dragged, and on what line the group didn't start together. A device used to help the children judge their own choral reading is recording. They listen to their own reading and point out how they can improve it.

LEARNING THE LINES

As the children work on setting the pattern for the poem, they automatically begin to learn the lines. When they speak the lines with the teacher, they begin almost unconsciously to remember. Children learn them from saying them over and over again.

When the teacher and children choose the poem carefully, when the meaning and mood of the poem to be imparted are the results of group interpretation, and when the direction is clear and meaningful, choral speaking provides a valuable and significant experience for children. But if the teacher imposes his pattern of reading, if his direction is mechanical, if he allows children to read in a heavy, labored, dull way, the experience will have little value. Choral speaking should fit into the pattern of the school day. The teacher should not decide that between 10 and 10:30 the children will do choral speaking. A reason for speaking together should exist.

USES FOR CHORAL SPEAKING IN THE CLASSROOM

Teachers use choral speaking in the classroom for its own sake. For example, the first fall of snow may motivate a first-grade class of children to speak together "Snow," with its "The fence posts wear marshmallow hats"; or popping popcorn may arouse the third graders' enthusiasm for "A Popcorn Song"; or a very windy day may remind the fifth-grade boys and girls of "The North Wind." Children occasionally participate in choral speaking as a performance for an audience. Where they use it as a performance, it is most valuable when it is an integral part of a larger program involving dramatics and music. The Christmas story told through pantomime, choral reading, and choral singing is most effective. Each section of the story of the birth of Christ as taken from the Bible is interpreted first in choral speaking and is repeated in song and in pantomime on the stage.

A far different type of program is one which an eighth grade did. They produced an operetta based on the story of the Erie Canal. The story showed the forces that worked against the building of the Canal, the overcoming of these forces, and its final successful opening. The folklore and language of the time provided the color and set the atmosphere. The first scene opened with children dressed in the costumes of the era singing "Itiskit, Itaskit." Some of them then spoke a ditty common in that time:

> Tobacco is a nasty weed.
> It's the Devil that sows the seed.
> It soils your pockets,
> Scents your clothes,
> And makes a chimney of your nose.

After the children had helped create the atmosphere of the period, some of the eighth-grade boys, dressed in overalls and carrying picks and shovels, entered. They spoke in chorus:

> We are digging the ditch through the mire,
> Through the mud and the slime and the mire, by Heck,
> And the mud is our principle hire.
> Up our pants, in our shirts, down our neck, by Heck,
> We are digging through the gravel
> So the people and freight can travel.

This old ballad effectively told the story of the digging of the Erie Canal. After they had spoken the chorus, they talked about the advantages and disadvantages of working on the Canal, the chances of its being completed, and some of the problems of building a canal, such as the mosquitoes that infested the area.

An example of the use in a much simpler way of choral speaking for a program is that of a third grade who decided to celebrate Halloween. On Halloween, when they came to school in their costumes, they visited the other grades in the school and spoke poems about Halloween. They read Vachel Lindsay's "The Mysterious Cat." They brought along a couple of hand puppets made like black cats that acted along with the speakers. When they spoke the line "Too proud to catch a mouse or rat," the children turned the two cats' heads to one side and held them high. When they said, "But catnip she would eat and purr," they held the puppets' heads down as if they were nibbling. Their second poem was about goblins:

> A goblin lives in our house, in our house, in our house,
> A goblin lives in our house all the year round.
> He bumps
> And he jumps
> And he thumps
> And he stumps.
>
> He knocks
> And he rocks
> And he rattles at the locks.
> A goblin lives in our house, in our house, in our house,
> A goblin lives in our house all the year round.

They concluded their program with "The North Wind." Both they and the children in the other grades took delight in the program.

SUMMARY

Choral speaking is the speaking together of a poem or a piece of prose by a group who have been trained to impart the meaning and spirit of the selection with clarity and spontaneity. Choral speaking as a technique in the classroom is relatively recent, although the Greek drama made use of it in 500 B.C. Marjorie Gullan has been a decided influence in the growth of the movement in this country and in England.

Writers have attributed many values to choral speaking, but three are paramount: (1) Participation in choral speaking furthers in children an appreciation of poetry. (2) Participation in it makes children more able to interpret poetry. (3) It provides an opportunity for speech work where the timid participate readily and where the overly loquacious child is submerged.

Voices in the elementary school are divided into two groups, light and heavy, or three groups, light, heavy, and medium. Children participate in the following types of choral speaking: line-a-child, antiphonal, cumulative, refrain speaking, part speaking, and unison speaking.

The teacher and children select material carefully for choral speaking. Materials selected should meet five requirements: (1) It should interest the children. (2) It should be within the intellectual and emotional understanding of the children. (3) It should possess literary value. (4) It should possess thought that is universal. (5) Its form should be adaptable to choral speaking.

In helping children prepare for choral speaking, the teacher first encourages them to speak together simple poems for the sheer fun they provide. After they have experienced the enjoyment of speaking together, he shows them how a division into different types of voices makes the interpretation of some selections more vivid. He and the children set the pattern for interpretation of the poem after they have tried out and discussed various interpretations. The teacher indicates the rhythmic pattern, keeps the voices light, and directs the children. In directing, he helps the students to start together, stay together, and to speak with approximately the same interpretation. He and the children discuss their work. They find out whether they started together, stayed together, and followed direction. They also analyze their articulation, pronunciation, interpretation, and blending of voices. They make sure they move along and speak with a lively sense of communication.

Choral speaking is used largely for its own sake. Occasionally it is part of a program. Where it is to be part of a program, it is usually used with dramatics, music, or dance.

EXERCISES

1. Make a collection of children's poems for choral speaking. Indicate the division of voices, rhythm of the poem, and a possible interpretation.

2. Work out with a group the interpretation of a poem. Record how you arrived at the interpretation decided on by the group.

3. Find six poems suitable for choral speaking based on a particular theme, such as Thanksgiving, Halloween, or birds.

4. Indicate how choral speaking of specific poems could be related to the experiences of children in a particular grade.

5. Show how choral speaking could be used as part of an assembly program involving other arts, such as music, dance, and dramatics.

BIBLIOGRAPHY

SOURCES FOR FURTHER READING

Abney, L., *Choral Speaking Arrangements for the Junior High School*, Boston, Expression Co., 1939. Gives the educational values of choral speaking, the types of choral speaking, and suggestions as to procedures. Contains many selections.

————, *Choral Speaking Arrangements for the Upper Grades*, Boston, Expression Co., n.d. Contains selections for use in grades 4 to 8. Includes old chanties, ballads, and lullabies.

Abney, L., and G. Rowe, *Choral Speaking Arrangements for the Lower Grades*, Boston, Expression Co., 1937. A similar book for the teacher of the lower grades.

Adams, H., and A. Croasdell, *A Poetry Speaking Anthology*, Boston, Expression Co., n.d. An English collection divided into three books: Book I, infant work, Book II, junior work, Book III, senior work. Contains many selections for both lower and upper grades. Many of the primary poems are unusual and delightful.

Berry, K. R., "Rhythms in the School Program," *Elementary English*, Vol. 25 (April, 1948), pp. 221–227. Explains the five types of choral speaking and discusses the values of choral speaking.

Brown, H., and H. Heltman, *Let's-read-together: Poems*, Evanston, Ill., Row, Peterson, 1950. Includes poems carefully selected for children. One of the best, comprehensive, and usable collections of poetry for choral speaking.

Gode, M., "What Makes Spring," *American Childhood*, Vol. 35 (March, 1950), p. 29. Presents a poem about spring arranged for choral speaking.

Gullan, M., *The Speech Choir*, New York, Harper, 1937. Presents the history and theory of choral speaking.

Gullan, M., and P. Gurrey, *Poetry Speaking for Children*, Boston, Expression Co., 1941. Discusses techniques of choral speaking.

Hamm, A., *Choral Speaking Techniques*, Milwaukee, Wis., Tower Press, 1946.

McCauley, L., "Little Children Love Poetry," *Elementary English*, Vol. 25 (October, 1948), pp. 353–358. Describes use of poetry in the classroom and tells how to include it in the work of the day.

Newton, M. B., *Unit Plan for Choral Reading*, Boston, Expression Co., 1938. Includes values of choral speaking, suggestions for its teaching, and material for the upper grades.

Partridge, D. C., "Verse Speaking As a Creative Art," *Elementary English*, Vol. 25 (November, 1948), pp. 442–445. Reviews the history of choral speaking and its values.

Swann, M., *Many Voices*, London, General Howe, 1934. Suggests poems for older children.

Thone, B. C., "Choral Reading Selection," *Elementary English*, Vol. 25 (March, 1948), pp. 177–179. Contains a selection for choral speaking, a poem representing America, its freedom, its kinds of workers, and its land.

SOURCES FOR READING FOR CHILDREN

Dawson, M. A., and J. M. Miller, *Language for Daily Use: Grade 5*, Yonkers,
N.Y., World, 1948, pp. 308–312. Explains how to participate in choral
speaking.

Patton, D., and A. Beery, *Using Our Language*, St. Louis, Mo., Webster
Publishing Co., 1953. Grade 4, pp. 148–150; grade 5, pp. 136–137;
grade 6, pp. 172–174. Explains how to speak as a group. Gives selections for choral speaking. Suggests others.

POEMS FOR CHORAL SPEAKING FOR THE LOWER GRADES

Title	Author	First line	Source
		ANIMALS	
"Bees"	Unknown	"This is the song of the bees"	Hamm, A., *Choral Speaking Techniques*, Milwaukee, Wis., Tower Press, 1946.
"The Chickens"	Unknown	"Said the first little chicken"	Hubbard, A., and A. Babbitt, *The Golden Flute*, New York, John Day, 1932.
"The Goldfish"	Aldis, D.	"My darling little goldfish"	Aldis, D., *Everything and Anything*, New York, Putnam, 1927.
"Jiggety, Jiggety, Jog"	Konrad, J.	"Jiggety, jiggety, jog"	Hubbard, A., and A. Babbitt, *The Golden Flute*, New York, John Day, 1932.
"Mice"	Fyleman, R.	"I think mice are rather nice"	Fyleman, R., *Fifty-one New Nursery Rhymes*, New York, Doubleday, 1932.
"Robin, Robin Red-breast"	Mother Goose	"Little Robin red-breast"	Tileston, M. W., *Sugar and Spice*, Boston, Little, Brown, 1928.
"Tu-whit, Tu-whoo"	Barrows, S. T.	"The owl by day can't see 'tis said"	Barrows, S. T., and K. Hall, *Games and Jingles for Speech Development*, Boston, Expression Co., 1936.

POEMS FOR CHORAL SPEAKING FOR THE LOWER GRADES—(Continued)

Title	Author	First line	Source
"The Little Kittens"	Follen, E. L.	"Where are you going, my little kittens?"	Hubbard, A., and A. Babbitt, *The Golden Flute*, New York, John Day, 1932.
"The Squirrel"	Unknown	"Whisky, frisky, Hippity, hop"	Brown, H., and H. Heltman, *Let's-read-together: Poems*, Evanston, Ill., Row, Peterson, 1950.
"The Little Turtle"	Unknown	"There was a little turtle"	Rasmussen, C., *Choral Speaking for Speech Improvement*, Boston, Expression Co., 1939.
"Two Little Kittens"	Unknown	"Two little kittens one stormy night"	Brewton, J., *Under the Tent of the Sky*, New York, Macmillan, 1937.

CARS

"Look Out!"	Edmonds, P.	"Look out! Look out!"	Hamm, A., *Choral Speaking Techniques*, Milwaukee, Wis., Tower Press, 1946.
"The Light Hearted Fairy"	Unknown	"Oh, who is so merry, so merry, heigh-ho!"	Sechrist, E. H., *1000 Poems for Children*, Philadelphia, Macrae Smith, 1946.

FAMILY AND HOME

"Bad"	Aldis, D.	"I've been bad and I'm in bed"	Aldis, D., *Here, There and Everywhere*, New York, Putnam, 1936.
"The Coffee Pot Face"	Fisher, A.	"I saw my face in the coffee pot"	Huffard, G. T., and L. M. Carlisle, *My Poetry Book*, Philadelphia, Winston, 1934.
"The Cupboard"	de la Mare, W.	"I know a little cupboard with a teeny, tiny key."	de la Mare, W., *Peacock Pie*, New York, Holt, 1936.

POEMS FOR CHORAL SPEAKING FOR THE LOWER GRADES—(Continued)

Title	Author	First line	Source
"Hiding"	Aldis, D.	"I'm hiding, I'm hiding"	Aldis, D., *Everything and Anything*, New York, Putnam, 1936.
"My Zipper Suit"	Allen, M. L.	"My zipper suit is bunny brown"	Association for Childhood Education, *Sung under the Silver Umbrella*, New York, Macmillan, 1935.
"Sh"	Tippett, J. S.	" 'Sh!' says Mother"	Tippett, J., *I Live in the City*, New York, Harper, 1927.
"Smells"	Morley, C.	"My Daddy smells like tobacco and books"	Morley, C., *Rocking Horse*, Philadelphia, Lippincott, 1946.
"The Pancake"	Rossetti, O.	"Mix a pancake"	Hutchinson, U. S., *Chimney Corner Poems*, New York, Minton, 1929.
"Walking"	Glaubitz, G.	"When Daddy walks with Jean and me"	Hubbard, A., and H. Babbitt, *The Golden Flute*, New York, John Day, 1932.

CHRISTMAS

Title	Author	First line	Source
"Santa Claus"	Unknown	"Little fairy snowflakes dancing in the flue"	Sechrist, E. H., *1000 Poems for Children*, Philadelphia, Macrae Smith, 1946.
"Black and Gold"	Turner, N. B.	"Everything is black and gold"	Huffard, G. T., and L. M. Carlisle, *My Poetry Book*, Philadelphia, Winston, 1934.
"A Goblin Lives in Our House"	French origin	"A goblin lives in our house, in our house, in our house"	Abney, L., *Choral Speaking Arrangements for the Junior High School*, Boston, Expression Co., 1939.

POEMS FOR CHORAL SPEAKING FOR THE LOWER GRADES—(Continued)

Title	Author	First line	Source
		PLAY	
"A Popcorn Song"	Turner, N. B.	"Sing a song of popcorn"	Rasmussen, C., *Choral Speaking for Speech Improvement*, Boston, Expression Co., 1939.
"Hoppity"	Milne, A. A.	"Christopher Robin goes hoppity, hop"	Milne, A. A., *When We Were Very Young*, New York, Dutton, 1921.
"Skipping Song"	Edmonds, P.	"Skipping is fun, skipping is fun"	Hamm, A., *Choral Speaking Technique*, Milwaukee, Wis., Tower Press, 1946.
		WEATHER	
"Help One Another"	Hunting, G. F.	"Help one another, the snowflake said"	Bouton, J., *Poems for the Children's Hour*, Springfield, Mass., Bradley, 1927.
"The North Wind Blew"	Mother Goose	"The north wind blew"	Rasmussen, C., *Choral Speaking for Speech Improvement*, Boston, Expression Co., 1939.
"Snow"	Aldis, D.	"The fence posts wear marshmallow hats"	Aldis, D., *Everything and Anything*, New York, Putnam, 1936.
"Who Has Seen the Wind?"	Rossetti, C.	"Who has seen the wind?"	Sechrist, E. H., *1000 Poems for Children*, Philadelphia, Macrae Smith, 1946.

POEMS FOR CHORAL SPEAKING FOR THE UPPER GRADES

Title	Author	First line	Source
		CHRISTMAS	
"A Christmas Folk Song"	Reese, L.	"The little Jesus comes to town"	Sechrist, E. H., *1000 Poems for Children*, Philadelphia, Macrae Smith, 1946.

POEMS FOR CHORAL SPEAKING FOR THE UPPER GRADES—(Continued)

Title	Author	First line	Source
"Christmas Bells"	Longfellow, H. W.	"I heard the bells on Christmas Day"	Schauffler, R., *Christmas*, New York, Dodd, Mead, 1927.
"I Saw Three Ships"	English carol	"I saw three ships come sailing in"	Gullan, M., *The Speech Choir*, New York, Harper, 1937.
"Long, Long Ago"	Unknown	"Winds through the olive trees softly did blow"	Dalgleish, A., *Christmas*, New York, Scribner, 1950.
"The Shepherd and the King"	Farjeon, E.	"The shepherd and the king"	Gullan, M., *The Speech Choir*, New York, Harper, 1937.
"Why Do the Bells of Christmas Ring?"	Field, E.	"Why do the bells of Christmas ring?"	Brown, A., and H. Heltman, *Let's-read-together: Poems*, Evanston, Ill., Row, Peterson, 1950.

FOLK TALES, BALLADS

Title	Author	First line	Source
"In Come de Animals"	Negro rhyme	"In come de animals two by two"	Gullan, M., *The Speech Choir*, New York, Harper, 1937.
"Johnny at the Fair"	Traditional	"Oh dear, what can the matter be?"	Rasmussen, C., *Choral Speaking for Speech Improvement*, Boston, Expression Co., 1939.
"The Hangman's Tree"	Unknown	"Slack your rope, hangman,"	Botkin, B. A., *The Pocket Treasury of American Folklore*, New York, Pocket Books, 1949.
"The Raggle, Taggle Gypsies"	Unknown	"There were three gypsies come to my door"	Untermeyer, L., *The Book of Living Verse*, New York, Harcourt Brace, 1945.
"Robin-a-Thrush"	English ballad	"Old Robin-a-Thrush has married a wife,"	Gullan, M., *The Speech Choir*, New York, Harper, 1937.

POEMS FOR CHORAL SPEAKING FOR THE UPPER GRADES—(Continued)

Title	Author	First line	Source
		HALLOWEEN	
"The Mysterious Cat"	Lindsay, V.	"I saw a proud, mysterious cat"	Abney, L., *Choral Speaking Arrangements for the Junior High School*, Boston, Expression Co., 1939.
"The North Wind"	Unknown	"Whoo-oo-ooooo"	Abney, L., *Choral Speaking Arrangements for the Junior High School*, Boston, Expression Co., 1939.
		HUMOROUS VERSE	
"Elizabeth O'Grady"	Edmonds, P.	"Elizabeth O'Grady"	Hamm, A. C., *Choral Speaking Techniques*, Milwaukee, Wis., Tower Press, 1946.
"Little Charlie Chipmunk"	LeCron, H. C.	"Little Charlie Chipmunk was a talker"	Hubbard, A., and A. Babbitt, *The Golden Flute*, New York, John Day, 1932.
"My Pretty Maid"	Unknown	"Where are you going, my pretty maid?"	Hamm, A. C., *Choral Speaking Techniques*, Milwaukee, Wis., Tower Press, 1946.
"Pirate Don Durk of Dowdee"	Merryman, M.	"Ho for the Pirate Don Durk of Dowdee"	Gullan, M., *The Speech Choir*, New York, Harper, 1937.
"The Camel's Hump"	Kipling, R.	"The camel's hump is an ugly lump"	Kipling, R., *Just So Stories*, New York, Doubleday, 1912.
"The Owl and the Pussy-cat"	Lear, E.	"The owl and the pussy-cat went to sea"	Hubbard, A., and A. Babbitt, *The Golden Flute*, New York, John Day, 1932.
"There Was an Old Woman"	Unknown	"There was an old woman tossed up in a basket"	Hamm, A. C., *Choral Speaking Techniques*, Milwaukee, Wis., Tower Press, 1946.

POEMS FOR CHORAL SPEAKING FOR THE UPPER GRADES—(Continued)

Title	Author	First line	Source
"Whistle, Whistle Old Wife and You'll Get a Hen"	Unknown	"Whistle, whistle old wife and you'll get a hen."	Gullan, M., *The Speech Choir*, New York, Harper, 1937.

MISCELLANEOUS

Title	Author	First line	Source
"The Chain of Princess Street"	Fleming, E.	"If I were queen of all the land"	Richards, Mrs. W., *Magic Carpet*, Boston, Houghton Mifflin, 1924.
"Danse Africaine"	Hughes, L.	"The low beating of the tom-toms"	Thompson, B., *More Silver Pennies*, New York, Macmillan, 1948.
"Four Little Foxes"	Sarett, L.	"Speak gently, Spring, and make no sudden sound"	Gullan, M., *The Speech Choir*, New York, Harper, 1937.
"Hollyhocks"	Sarett, L.	"I have a garden but oh dear me"	Griffith, W., and Mrs. J. W. Paris, *Garden Book of Verse*, New York, Morrow, 1932.
"Lullaby"	Hillyer, R.	"The long canoe toward the shadowy shore"	Thurston, R., *Poetry Arranged for the Speaking Choir*, Boston, Expression Co., n.d.
"Men"	Reid, D.	"I like men"	Bowlin, W. R., *Book of Fireside Poems*, Chicago, A. Whitman, 1937.
"Old Love"	Bates, K. L.	"New love is passion"	Gullan, M., *The Speech Choir*, New York, Harper, 1937.
"Prairies"	Sandburg, C.	"I was born on the prairie."	Gullan, M., *The Speech Choir*, New York, Harper, 1937.
"Swing Song"	Allingham, W.	"Swing, swing, sing, sing"	Sechrist, E. H., *1000 Poems for Children*, Philadelphia, Macrae Smith, 1946.
"The Table and the Chair"	Unknown	"Said the table to the chair"	Rasmussen, C., *Choral Speaking for Speech Improvement*, Boston, Expression Co., 1937.

POEMS FOR CHORAL SPEAKING FOR THE UPPER GRADES—(Continued)

Title	Author	First line	Source
		OUT OF DOORS	
"April Rain Song"	Hughes, L.	"Let the rain kiss you"	Association for Childhood Education, *Sung under the Silver Umbrella*, New York, Macmillan, 1935.
"Autumn Fairies"	Unknown	"The maple is a dainty leaf"	Huber, M. B., *Story and Verse for Children*, New York, Macmillan, 1930.
"Autumn Mood"	Abney, L.	"A golden leaf is falling to the ground"	Abney, L., *Choral Speaking Arrangements for the Junior High School*, Boston, Expression Co., 1939.
"The Chirrupy Cricket"	Thomas, M. B.	"There's a chirrupy cricket as guest in my room"	Hubbard, A., and A. Babbitt, *The Golden Flute*, New York, John Day, 1932.
"Fragment"	Wordsworth, W.	"Up! Up! My friend, and quit your books"	Hamm, A., *Selections for Choral Reading*, Boston, Expression Co., 1941.
"Sea Fever"	Masefield, J.	"I must go down to the seas again, to the lonely sea and the sky."	Hicks, H., *The Reading Choir*, New York, Noble, 1939.
"Snow"	Wilkins, A.	"The snow fell softly on the night."	Hubbard, A., and A. Babbitt, *The Golden Flute*, New York, John Day, 1932.
"Snowflakes"	Cleveland, E.	"Snowflakes falling through the air"	Brown, A., and H. Heltman, *Let's-read-together: Poems*, Evanston, Ill., Row, Peterson, 1950.

POEMS FOR CHORAL SPEAKING FOR THE UPPER GRADES—(Continued)

Title	Author	First line	Source
"Song at Dusk"	Gregory, S.	"The flowers nod, the shadows creep"	Moult, T., *Best Poems of 1935*, New York, Harcourt Brace, 1936.
"The Captain's Daughter"	Fields, J. T.	"We were crowded in the cabin"	Burt, M., *Poems Every Child Should Know*, New York, Grosset & Dunlap, Inc., 1904.
"The Mist and All"	Willson, D.	"I like the fall, The mist and all."	Huffard, G. T., and L. Carlisle, *My Poetry Book*, Philadelphia, Winston, 1934.
"The North Wind"	Unknown	"Whoo-oo-ooooo"	Abney, L., *Choral Speaking Arrangements for the Junior High School*, Boston, Expression Co., 1939.
"The Year's at the Spring" (from *Pippa Passes*)	Browning, R.	"The year's at the spring"	Braddy, N., *Standard Book of American Verse*, Garden City, N.Y., Garden City Publishing Company, 1932.
"There Will Come Soft Rains"	Teasdale, S.	"There will come soft rains and the smell of the ground"	Gullan, M., *The Speech Choir*, New York, Harper, 1937.
"Velvet Shoes"	Wylie, E.	"Let us walk in the white snow"	Teasdale, S., *Answering Voices*, New York, Macmillan, 1917.
"White Butterflies"	Swinburne, A. C.	"Fly, white butterflies, out to sea"	Untermeyer, L., *Modern British Poetry*, New York, Harcourt Brace, 1936.

6 Informal Speaking Situations

Life today emphasizes the informal speaking situation. Adults chat with the milkman about the weather. They proffer and accept invitations over the telephone. After they saw and heard the Republican and Democratic national conventions, they talked about the procedures of the conventions with their family and friends. They go to school to interview the teacher to see how they can help son John. In an evening visit with friends, they tell a tall tale or a good story. Children also speak informally. They answer the telephone for their mothers. They discuss the relative merits of the Ford and the Plymouth with the corner garage man. They sympathize with each other over the replacement of all good television programs with stupid conventions. They laugh uproariously over each other's riddles. Both adults and children spend a large part of the day speaking informally.

Since most teachers realize the need for this type of communication, they promote it in the classroom. In most classrooms, speaking is an all-day activity. When children arrive in the morning, they greet each other and the teacher. Shortly, some of them share yesterday's exciting experiences. A child tells a story he has read the night before. They plan their work for the day together. After they have worked in groups, they explain to the others what they have done. They telephone the forest ranger to ask for an interview. They interview him. All day long they talk; and a large part of the talk is informal.

The teacher and the children can promote an atmosphere in the classroom which stimulates informal speaking. Their bulletin board contains the latest news events. Copies of children's books and magazines lie on the table in one corner. Maps and dictionaries are evident. Materials for a new bookcase are stacked in another corner. The children themselves are happy in planning their program, for their plans result in many worthwhile experiences. Trips to the fish market, to the farm, to the grocery store invite conversation. The boys and girls are engaging in many interesting activities which call for oral expression. Minnie

Glantz[1] says that teachers attempt to lay a foundation for interesting and effective expression by enriching, enlarging, and utilizing those activities which involve speech and by directing children in the use of the language forms necessary in performing their normal activities. She is pointing up the importance of a rich program in the elementary school which affords opportunity for many contacts with objects and experiences in the community. Furthermore, she indicates that these experiences demand better communication, for which children should be trained. While the rest of this book has to do with more organized speech situations, this chapter deals with the more informal ones: conversation, using the telephone, the speaking necessary in social activities, and storytelling.

CONVERSATION

DEFINITION

Conversation is derived from words which mean "living together." Conversation is a means by which people live together successfully. They exchange information or opinions in a profitable way, and they think and talk together on a subject in which they are interested. As children converse, they influence each other subtly: they gain more information; their opinions modify or change, and they alter their modes of conduct; they learn to give in to another or to influence him to accept their way of thinking. The child who is learning to converse successfully is also learning to be a better citizen of his group. Conversation includes not only the spoken words but also the facial and body gestures. A person may utter the words "It is nice to meet you" but communicate "I'm utterly bored with this whole party." Before verbal expression, the welcome occurs: the smile, the friendly attitude, and the air of being interested in the other person. To the degree a person sincerely desires to share his ideas, he is participating in conversation. The sharing is evident in his whole being.

TOPICS FOR CONVERSATION

Children's topics depend to some extent on what is happening in the classroom. Their field trips, their newspaper, the activity of their

[1] M. Glantz, "Oral Language in the Primary Grades," in *Language Arts in the Elementary Schools*, Twentieth Yearbook of the Department of Elementary School Principals, Washington, National Education Association, 1941, p. 259.

group, books they've liked, pictures they've seen, and music they've listened to all influence their conversation. They also discuss their out-of-school experiences, such as their family excursions, the queer bird they saw on the way to school, or their favorite television show. Small children talk about persons or objects close to themselves; they converse about pets, holidays, picnics, parties, birthdays, and their daddies and their mommies. Elise Hahn[2] reports that apparently the desire to impart other than personal experiences does not occur until the third grade. She finds that younger children talk mostly about play at home, then about objects displayed, and finally about family activities. Older children talk about their school work and about concrete experiences, such as gardening, Christmas activities, raising plants, finding antiques, holidays, and excursions. But they also converse about ideas. Sometimes they talk about the platforms of candidates in state and national elections. They begin to make judgments on such problems as graft in city government. They talk over the causes of juvenile delinquency. As they mature, they display a growing interest in ideas; they begin to talk less about people and more about ideas. Along with this increasing concern with beliefs grows regard for the other person's point of view. An interplay of minds is an index of maturity. The school, home, and community environment and the degree of maturity of children affect their conversation.

TEACHING CONVERSATION

The teacher helps children to participate effectively in conversation in four ways: (1) He takes advantage during the school day of opportunities to practice conversation. (2) He helps individual children become part of a conversational group. (3) He helps the children develop skills in conversational procedure. (4) He encourages them to evaluate their own assets and liabilities.

Taking Advantage of Opportunities to Practice Conversation. The teacher takes advantage of opportunities to practice conversation. He encourages it in the early moments of the school day, in the snack period, and at other times, such as the planning period. As he greets the children in the morning, he inspires easy and natural talk: he asks about Janey's baby sister, about Bob's big brother in college; he tells about the Rolls-Royce he saw on his way to school; he helps to gather a group

[2] E. Hahn, "Speech Habits of First Grade Children," *Elementary English*, Vol. 25 (January, 1948), p. 42.

around the aquarium in the corner of the room to look at, and talk about, their newly acquired goldfish. After school, one teacher shakes hands with, and bids good night to, each of his fourth graders. The conversation is brief, but it is lively. The good nights are not per-functory, for each child eagerly awaits his turn. Two of the boys, who obviously have something important to say, may remain behind so that they are the last to say good night. Inherent in the teacher's taking

FIG. 16. Inviting conversation. (*Neil Croom, University State Teachers College, New Paltz, N.Y.*)

advantage of opportunities is the principle that he approves the class-room as a place conducive to communication.

Aiding the Child in Participation. Secondly, he encourages individual children to become part of a conversational group. He draws out the timid child and helps the more aggressive realize he must take his turn. He assists all of them in seeing how certain attitudes hinder con-versation; he helps the members participate fully and freely. Part of the encouragement comes from the classroom atmosphere. When it is friendly, when a good relationship exists among members of the class-room, conversation thrives. By his drawing out the timid child and by his furtherance of the right kind of atmosphere, he is promoting participation.

Developing Skills in Conversation. Thirdly, he helps the boys and girls be effective members of a conversational group. He motivates them to find interesting topics to talk about. In the upper grades, the teacher and children attack the problem directly. They ask the following questions:

1. What makes for good conversation?
2. How do you start a conversation?
3. How do you change the subject?
4. What subjects do you avoid?
5. How do you find a topic to interest the other person?
6. How do you show consideration for the other person?
7. When do you keep still?
8. How do you encourage others to enter a conversation?

As the children work directly on conversation, they stress these items and what they involve. They talk about the interplay of ideas, listening intelligently, not monopolizing, keeping on the subject, handling conflict in the group, and differing tactfully.

In the intermediate grades, children frequently talk about conversation in relation to a specific activity. One fifth-grade group invited the children from the fifth grade of another school to one of their programs. They planned a social hour after the program. The children agreed they should be friendly to the other fifth graders and make them feel comfortable and at home. They discussed how they could accomplish their goal. They agreed on several ways to achieve it: most important was that they sound and look friendly; they said that they should try to share their friendliness with each one of the fifth graders and that they would try to include all of them in conversation. Furthermore, they were to listen attentively and talk only about topics that would interest the fifth-grade children. They would be polite, not interrupt, or talk too much. The way they talked was to help make friends of the other fifth graders. As they participated in several similar situations, they became quite good conversationalists.

Children in the lower grades also learn to converse from participating in a social situation. One teacher asked a group of second graders to share with each other what they would do if some fairy godmother gave each of them a hundred dollars. Before the talk began, the teacher mentioned several requirements of good conversation. She suggested that, if one child interrupted another, he should say, "I'm sorry." She reminded them to make sure that others heard, for they were all listening to hear how each would spend the money. After the conversation began, she encouraged all to participate. Their talk was unusually interesting. When they finished, they talked over why it was good conversation. They said: "Everyone talked; each took his turn." "We listened well." "The ways we spent the money were fun." "Nobody talked too much." "We said, 'I'm sorry,' when we broke in." "We stopped before it got boring." In this instance, the children were evaluating their own conversation.

Evaluating Conversation. Frequently the teacher and the children talk over their own assets and liabilities in conversation. They bring out how many times they participate, find out the worth of their contributions, examine the effect of their contributions on others, and discover whether the contributions promote successful group living. They determine how well they listen and what they have gained from others. They analyze their actions and the listener's reactions to make sure they have been kind to, and considerate of, the members of the group.

TELEPHONING

Much conversation occurs over the telephone. Adults chat with their friends, order groceries, call to make appointments for an interview about a job, and ask the doctor to call. Some use it skillfully; others antagonize their listeners. Children also use the telephone frequently. They receive calls for other members of the family and extend and receive invitations. They use it to say "thank you" for a favor. They give an order over the telephone. The teacher can promote successful and gracious telephone conversations in children.

He talks over with the children when and how to use the telephone. They plan how to call or dial a number and how to identify themselves at the beginning of the conversation. They discuss the manner in which to speak over the telephone, although almost all boys and girls realize they must speak clearly and distinctly. They talk about what to say and how to close the conversation. They also talk about using their telephones at home, how they can be considerate of their family and those on their lines, and how they can take messages for members of their family. They consider ways of being courteous and gracious in the use of the telephone.

Teachers take advantage of opportunities for children to use the telephone. Children, in planning trips, call to ask permission of the manager for the class to go through his plant. They call again to make the necessary arrangements concerning the time they are to come and what they are to see. Sometimes they order refreshments for their parties over the telephone. The children in one class take turns calling the homes of absent children. When a child is not in school, one of them calls to ask tactfully if the child is ill. When he finds out that Jimmy has chicken pox, the members of the group write him letters and send him cards. The call has helped to promote a friendly feeling among the children and the parents. In each case, the children plan what they are going to say; sometimes they practice in the classroom. They take turns actually using the telephone for different purposes during the year.

SOCIAL FORMS

When social forms are taught as they are needed in the classroom, the children learn them readily. As the third graders plan a party, they decide what is expected of them as hosts and hostesses. They learn how to extend invitations and how to make and acknowledge introductions. They learn the basic principles of being considerate of others. When they are having a program, they talk about how they will modestly and graciously accept the congratulations of those in attendance. The actual participation in a social activity and the use of the social forms makes the learning meaningful.

INTERVIEWING

Interviewing is another speech technique that the teacher teaches as the need for it arises. When children are studying about the village government, they may want to interview one of the trustees of the village. Children realize they do not have the right to waste his time, and, therefore, they plan the interview beforehand. They formulate its purpose carefully; they decide what questions will bring forth the most fruitful answers. They work out the arrangements for the time and place of the interview and what to tell the trustee concerning its purpose. They learn to be gracious and courteous during the interview and to show their appreciation of his having given them his time.

STORYTELLING

A child usually enjoys sharing a story with his classmates, and because of his enjoyment, he communicates well. He uses his hands, body, and facial expression freely. Because he is able to watch his audience, he adapts his story to them. When members of his audience become bored, he knows. Both the teacher and the child can contribute to their group through telling a story artistically and effectively; all the members benefit through the listening.

Before a child tells a story, he must have some preparation. He must have listened to stories that have been told well. He must have already taken part in storytelling by repeating parts of a story with the teacher or by telling parts alone. He must belong to his group and feel the response of his audience. He must have guidance in the selection of his material and, in some cases, in the preparation of his story.

CHOICE OF MATERIAL

Folk and fairy tales tell well, for they are stories that have been handed down by mouth from generation to generation. Most of their action is exciting. Their form is clear-cut and definite; the introduction, development, and conclusion do exactly what they are intended to do. The plots are vigorous, full of suspense and action. The characters are clear-cut. In *The Three Little Pigs*, the audience listens carefully as the third pig tries to find security in a world of wolves. The activities of Cinderella's sisters make the listeners sympathetic to Cinderella; they rejoice with her when the prince finds her.

Many of the modern stories tell very well. Dr. Seuss's *The Five Hundred Hats of Bartholomew Cubbins* is a delightfully humorous story. Mary Justus's *Here Comes Mary Ellen* has stories that picture life in the Tennessee mountains. They are fun to tell and fun to listen to. Cornelia Meig's *The Willow Whistle* has plenty of action and an exciting plot. Mary Ellen is a very real little girl whom a friendly Indian takes visiting; when his tribe is attacked by enemy raiders, Mary Ellen is stolen. The story has to do with the search for her. Because all of these stories have clear-cut characters and original plots with plenty of action, they tell particularly well.

Some stories, however, need illustrations to help tell their plots. For example, part of the fun of Lois Lenski's *The Little Auto* lies in its pictures. They tell that Mr. Small takes his car out of the garage, drives downtown, obeys all the traffic signals, parks it, and brings it safely home. Children enjoy its illustrations. Marjorie Flack's stories belong with their illustrations, which show delightful action with few details and bright, gay colors. The stories about Angus are well told, but their excellent plots and pictures go together. The first of the series, *Angus and the Ducks*, is typical: Angus, a curious small Scottish terrier, runs out through the open door and encounters ducks. He is very happy when they run away as he barks. He chases them, but they turn on him: He comes home quickly to his own sofa. A teacher or a child can tell the story, but its pictures make it live. Claire Turlay Newberry's stories have exquisite illustrations. Her cats are fluffy, furry creatures that invite a child to stroke them. Because her stories have little action, they need the pictures to make them meaningful for children.

Some stories, as mentioned in the chapter on oral reading, need the language of the author. Both the poems of A. A. Milne and the *Just So Stories* of Rudyard Kipling depend on the language of the authors to give charm and meaning to them.

THE STORYTELLER'S REQUIREMENTS

The storyteller must have a good voice and clear diction. His voice must be audible, pleasant, and free from qualities that distract the listener. His articulation, while not overly precise, must be so distinct that his listeners understand what he is saying without effort. Neither the child nor the teacher should have a voice and diction that he assumes as he tells a story. The voice and diction should be the same used in daily conversation.

The storyteller must be able to re-create the story for his audience; he must gain a response from them. If he enjoys the story in a genuine way, if he responds to its characters, action, and changing moods, he is likely to tell the story well. He must be sincerely sorry for, entertained with, or happy for, the characters. He reacts to the story and conveys this reaction to his audience. He need not be dramatic and act out the story; this ability belongs on the stage. He should tell the story simply, sincerely, and not artificially. Some tales, however, need more dramatic telling than others; in such cases, the teller suggests rather than acts out the dramatic elements. Always, he helps the characters live for his listeners.

ORGANIZATION OF A STORY FOR TELLING

Introduction. In the beginning, the storyteller indicates who is involved, where and when the story is taking place, and the preliminary action. He gives the general feeling of the story. When he tells a ghost story, he makes his audience realize its mystery and awe. When he relates a gay story, he portrays for his audience a lighthearted, happy attitude. He puts his audience in the right mood to help them anticipate what is coming. In the introduction, he gives them the necessary information to aid them in understanding what is to follow and predicts the mood of the story. In teaching a child to make his beginning effective, the teacher may suggest that he start with the story right away or that he interest his listeners immediately. When the child tells a ghost story as he would a fairy tale, the teacher asks him how it feels to be a ghost and how he can make his listeners afraid of the ghost.

Body. In telling the story, the teller memorizes the incidents and their relationships. He decides beforehand what the main and subordinate ideas are. He builds them to the climax, the most exciting part of the story. He makes sure that he has included all the essential details of the plot, so that his listeners are able to follow him. The teacher helps the child make clear the "what is happening" part of the story to his classmates. The teacher suggests that he think through the story several times in order to be sure that he remembers the events in the right order. The child plans to place the details in the correct order and to omit all unnecessary ones. In the early grades, the teacher may ask, What happened first? What happened next? and, finally, What is the surprise of the story? When the child does not build the climax of the story, the teacher asks, What is the most exciting part? What is the surprise? or What is the most important happening in the story? He advises the child to let his listeners know that this part is the exciting part, the surprise, or the most important happening in the story.

Conclusion. The storyteller leaves the members of the audience satisfied and with a sense of completion. They are happy for Cinderella and quite contented with her fate with the prince. They feel triumphant with Little Black Sambo, since he has outwitted the tigers. They have enjoyed living with Beatrix Potter's *Peter Rabbit* in a world of scampering creatures. They laugh at, and recall with laughter, Hugh Lofting's *The Story of Dr. Dolittle.* Children frequently do not end a story soon enough. When they do not, the teacher suggests that their story will be more interesting if they end it right after the surprise or the most exciting part. He reminds them that the story must sound finished and that their listeners must feel satisfied with the ending.

DISCUSSION OF THE STORYTELLING

Finally, after the child has told the story, the boys and girls talk about his telling. They ask such questions as:

1. Did he interest you right away?
2. Did his voice help tell the story?
3. Could you understand him?
4. Could you follow the story?
5. Did you respond to this telling the story?
6. Did he make you live with the characters?
7. Did he enjoy the story himself?
8. Did his dramatic telling get in the way of the story or did he subtly suggest moods?
9. Did he end the story in a satisfying way?

LISTENING

In all these informal speaking activities, listening is very important. Young children do little conscious listening; they tend to listen passively with little reaction. Then, as they begin to react to what they hear, they ask questions. Next, they begin to have a genuine intellectual understanding and to participate emotionally. Finally, a real meeting of minds occurs. The teacher can help the child to progress from one step to another.

FACTORS THAT INFLUENCE LISTENING

Physical Arrangement. The teacher can make sure that his students are arranged in such a way that listening is easy. When children all face the front of the room, the child in the right front seat has very little contact with the child in the left rear seat. The space between them and the fact that the child in front must turn around in an uncomfortable position are barriers to communication. Children placed quite close together in groups invite talk and listening to talk.

Motivation to Listen. Secondly, the atmosphere of the classroom must motivate listening. The teacher gives weight to the opinions of the students; he helps them to feel that what they have to contribute is important to him and to the group. He encourages the other children to feel what a member of the group has to say needs a response. He takes advantage of listening opportunities for the children. For example, when the class agreed to have one child interview the trustee, they helped prepare the questions he was going to ask. He knew he had to listen to the trustee carefully, for he had to report to the class. When he did report, the children listened, for they were eager to find out the answers to their questions.

Purpose of Listening. Thirdly, he recognizes that children listen for different purposes. Some of it is a casual kind of listening, such as the kind that occurs in chatting about the weather. Children learn that a place exists for listening to "small talk." Some listening is appreciative; for example, the children listen to *The Nutcracker Suite* or *The Dyspeptic Ogre.* Some is thoughtful listening; children listen carefully that they may understand a process like making papier mâché or that they may learn how the trustees of the village campaign. Lastly, some listening is a questioning kind, where the children listen intently and analyze what the speaker is saying. They are thinking and listening critically. It is the kind of listening that should occur throughout a group discussion.

Ability to Listen. Fourthly, the teacher takes into account the children's ability to listen. Youngsters in the first grade have limited attention spans. They cannot be expected to listen for a long period. Listening is also related to interests. As a child is interested, he listens more carefully; therefore, the teacher takes into account his interests. He sets up the standards for effective listening, according to the children's abilities to listen.

In all these experiences, children are talking and listening all day long. They talk about what they've done, plan their activities, interview, telephone. Their talk centers around what they know best. It is tied directly to meaningful experiences. As the need arises in the classroom, they learn to talk more effectively.

SUMMARY

Life today emphasizes participation in many informal speaking situations such as conversation, telephoning, interviewing, speaking in social activities, and storytelling.

In conversation, children think and talk together about a subject in which they are interested. Topics grow out of the environment of the school, home, and community. The degree of the children's maturity affects their conversation. Younger children tend to talk about people; older children about ideas. The teacher helps boys and girls participate in conversation effectively: (1) He takes advantage during the school day of opportunities to practice conversation. (2) He helps individual children become part of a conversational group. (3) He helps the children develop conversational skills. (4) He encourages them to evaluate their own conversational assets and liabilities.

The teacher encourages the children to use the telephone efficiently and courteously, to learn the necessary social forms, and to participate in an interview effectively.

In storytelling, the teacher and children choose the story to tell on the basis of plot, characterization, and listeners. The storyteller re-creates the story for the members of his audience; he gains a response from them. He makes sure his introduction puts them into the right mood and prepares them for what is to follow. In the body, he includes all essential details in their correct order. His conclusion leaves the listeners satisfied.

All these informal speaking activities involve listening. The teacher makes sure that his students are arranged so that they can listen easily and is certain that the atmosphere of the room motivates listening. He recognizes the purposes of listening. He takes into account different abilities to listen.

Children talk and listen all day long. When the talk is tied to a meaningful experience and takes place as it is needed, children learn to talk effectively.

EXERCISES

1. List ten stories that children of the age level you plan to teach might tell.

2. Visit a classroom for one hour. Indicate the various kinds of listening experiences which the children participate in.

3. Analyze the factors that helped or hindered the children's listening in a particular situation.

4. Tell a children's story to a group of children.

5. Indicate experiences that children may have in interviewing.

6. Indicate specific ways in which a teacher can encourage interesting conversation.

BIBLIOGRAPHY

SUGGESTED SOURCES FOR FURTHER READING

Informal Speaking Activities

Anderson, J. E., *Child Development and the Curriculum*, Thirty-eighth Year-book of the National Society for the Study of Education, Part 1, Bloom-ington, Ill., Public School Publishing Co., 1939, p. 211. Studies language growth as correlated with intelligence, motor ability, and socio-economic levels.

Baker, H. V., "Discussion in Separate Class Periods," in *Language Arts in the Elementary Schools*, Twentieth Yearbook of the Department of Elementary School Principals, Washington, National Education Association, 1941, pp. 278–286. Discusses conversation periods in classrooms.

Bowden, F., "Conversation and Discussion in the Elementary School," *Elementary English*, Vol. 24 (May, 1947), pp. 293–302.

Coyner, N. I., "Criteria for Evaluating Programs of Oral and Written Language," *Elementary English*, Vol. 28 (March, 1950), pp. 323–329. Discusses individual differences, techniques teachers use to motivate language development, and the kind of atmosphere conducive to language development.

Dawson, M. A., *Teaching Language in the Grades*, Yonkers, N.Y., World, 1951, pp. 160–161. Tells about conversation.

Eginton, D. P., "Conversation: Queen of Speech Arts," *The Journal of Education*, Vol. 27 (May, 1944), pp. 163–164. Shows the importance of conversation and lists ten rules for the friendly art of good talk.

Glantz, M. H., and M. C. Cohee, "Oral Language in the Primary Grades," in *Language Arts in the Elementary Schools*, Twentieth Yearbook of the Department of Elementary School Principals, Washington, National Education Association, 1941, pp. 259–268. Includes sections on telephoning, telling stories, and other informal speaking activities.

Hahn, E., "An Analysis of the Content and Form of the Speech of First Grade Children," *Quarterly Journal of Speech*, Vol. 34 (October, 1948), pp. 361–366. Includes an analysis of conversational speaking of children based on length of responses, sentence structure, and topics.

Harris, D., "Child Development and the Language Arts," *Elementary English*, Vol. 23 (December, 1946), pp. 367–369. Shows what a study of child development offers the teacher of language arts. Based on research.

Hatfield, W. W., *An Experience Curriculum in English*, Report of the Curriculum Commission of the National Council of Teachers of English, New York, Appleton-Century-Crofts, 1935, pp. 138–142, 159–163, discusses conversation; pp. 142–144, 163–165, talks about telephoning; pp. 147–150, gives the objectives of storytelling; pp. 167–169, shows the place of interviews in teaching English.

McCowen, A., "Opportunity to Develop Skill in Communicating Ideas," *Elementary English*, Vol. 19 (March, 1942), pp. 99–104.

Murphy, G., "Conversation—A Lost Art," *Childhood Education*, Vol. 27 (February, 1951), pp. 256–260. Discusses conversation of children at home and at school. Stresses the fun of good conversation.

Murphy, G., "We Also Learn by Listening," *Elementary English*, Vol. 26 (March, 1949), pp. 127–128. Considers purposeful, accurate, critical, and responsive listening.

Niles, D., "Conversation and Discussion," in *Language Arts in the Elementary Schools*, Twentieth Yearbook of the Department of Elementary School Principals, Washington, National Education Association, 1941, pp. 287–296. Explains how to teach conversation. Includes topics children discuss.

Parkes, M. B., "Children's Ways of Talking and Listening," *Childhood Education*, Vol. 29 (January, 1953), pp. 223–230. Includes characteristics of children's development in oral language, needs of children for expression, and a description of classroom situations which make use of needs in meaningful situations.

Rasmussen, C., *Speech Methods in the Elementary School*, New York, Ronald, 1949, Chap. 8.   Deals with storytelling, talks, and conversation.

Smith, D. V., "The English Curriculum in Perspective," *Elementary English*, Vol. 23 (February, 1946), pp. 45–53.   Suggests kind of program that furthers language development.

Strickland, R. G., *The Language Arts in the Elementary School*, Boston, Heath, 1951, pp. 101–105, explains the purposes of oral language in the school; pp. 122–123, 154–156, gives the kinds of listening and their values; pp. 31–33, 146–147, discusses conversation.

Weber, J., "Speaking and Writing in the Elementary School," *Elementary English*, Vol. 24 (April, 1947), pp. 230–239.   Tells the story of the growth in language of three children under the guidance of the teacher.

How to Tell Stories

Arbuthnot, M. H., *Children and Books*, Chicago, Scott, Foresman, 1947, pp. 239–248.   Discusses when to read and when to tell stories. Explains how to tell stories.

Betzner, J., *Exploring Literature with Children*, Practical Suggestions for Teaching, No. 7., New York, Teachers College, Columbia University, 1943.   Suggests how to select materials, advises how to tell stories and to encourage children's participation in storytelling.

Bryant, S. C., *How to Tell Stories to Children*, Boston, Houghton Mifflin, 1905.

Sawyer, R., *The Way of the Storyteller*, New York, Viking, 1942.   Gives advice on how to tell stories. Contains several unusual stories.

Storytelling, Washington, Association for Childhood Education, 1945.   Gives advice on how to tell stories to children.

Collections of Stories That Are Adaptable to Telling

Association for Childhood Education, *Told under the Green Umbrella*, New York, Macmillan, 1933.   Carefully selected folk tales. Primary grades.

Belpré, P., *The Tiger and the Rabbit and Other Tales*, Boston, Houghton Mifflin, 1946.   Folk tales of Puerto Rico. Intermediate grades.

Bleeker, M. N., *Big Music or Twenty Merry Tales to Tell*, New York, Viking, 1946.   Well-chosen old and new stories. Intermediate and upper grades.

Canfield, D., *Tell Me a Story*, Lincoln, Neb., University Publishing Co., 1940.   Stories to tell to small children.

Dalgliesh, A., *The Blue Teapot and Other Sandy Cove Stories*, New York, Macmillan, 1934.   The adventures of children in Nova Scotia. Primary grades.

de la Mare, W., *Told Again*, New York, Knopf, 1927.   Old tales. Primary grades.

Fenner, P. R., *Time to Laugh*, New York, Knopf, 1942.   Old folk tales and modern nonsense tales. Intermediate and upper grades.

Grimm Brothers, *Tales from Grimm*, New York, Coward-McCann, 1936. Illustrated by Wanda Gág. Primary and intermediate grades.

Undset, S., *True and Untrue and Other Norse Tales*, New York, Knopf, 1945. Upper grades.

Stories That Children Enjoy Telling and Hearing

Beskow, E., *Pelle's New Suit*, New York, Harper, 1929. Story of a little boy, Pelle, who needs a new suit. He watches the shearing of the sheep, sees the wool made into yarn. He helps with the dyeing and weaving. Finally he helps the tailor make it into his own suit. Primary grades.

Brock, D. L., *The Greedy Goat*, New York, Knopf, 1931. Story of the naughtiness of a Tirolese goat. Primary grades.

Brooks, W. R., *Freddy and the Popinjay*, New York, Knopf, 1945. The story of Freddy's sadness about his lack of a tail to wag. Amusing. Intermediate grades.

Credle, E., *Down, Down the Mountain*, New York, Nelson, 1934. Story of Hetty and Hank, two Southern mountaineer children, who want a pair of squeaky shoes. They raise turnips, most of which they give away, but they save the biggest one, which wins a prize. With this money they buy shoes. Primary and intermediate grades.

Field, R., *Hitty: Her First Hundred Years*, New York, Macmillan, 1929. Adventures of an antique doll, Hitty, who is shipwrecked. Upper grades.

Gág, W., *Snippy and Snappy*, New York, Coward-McCann, 1931. An amusing story of two little field mice who want to find a cupboard full of cheese. Primary grades.

Lathrop, D. D., *Who Goes There*, New York, Macmillan, 1935. Story of the animals' picnic in the woods. Primary grades.

Lofting, H., *The Story of Dr. Dolittle*, Philadelphia, Lippincott, 1920. Humorous adventures of a famous animal doctor. Primary and intermediate grades.

Seredy, K., *A Tree for Peter*, New York, Viking, 1941. A child's initiative turns a slum into a beauty spot. Upper grades.

7 Giving Talks

A quiet, friendly young man presided over an eighth grade. After he had greeted his new group in an easy, casual way, he told its members that he had enjoyed their minstrel show of the year before. When the teacher mentioned the show, Joe announced he would like the class to give another minstrel show. Mary, another eighth grader, responded quietly with "Oh, some of us were sick of that before we finished it." Helen quickly said, "We don't want to be known as the minstrel show class, do we?" At that point, the teacher assured them that they would find something they were all interested in doing as they planned their work and carried it out together. Because his own friendly attitude invited comments, he heard plenty of conversation even the first day. He not only promoted communication in the classroom but he also was able to help the students build upon the abilities they already possessed and to hold them to certain standards.

John was a member of this class. He had spent six years in a rural school where there were only ten pupils, representing three families. From this small, intimate school, he had been catapulted the previous year into a classroom with thirty students. He did excellent written work but rarely participated in class discussion. His oral reports were brief and obviously memorized. When, in the course of his class work, he was called on to make a short speech, he prepared it with minute care and delivered it in a rather dull fashion. His material was accurate and complete, but he awakened little response in his classmates.

The eighth-grade teacher came to know John well; he helped him to share his interests with his classmates. One day, John told him a Paul Bunyan story. The teacher laughed heartily and asked John to tell it to the class. John's reticent manner and his serious demeanor enriched his portrayal of Paul Bunyan. Because his interest in this type of story was high, he told it quietly but effectively. The members of the class were intrigued. In fact, they decided to find more tall stories and proceeded to read about Johnny Appleseed, Davy Crockett, and Paul Bunyan. Tall tales became as popular for that group as the Little

Audrey stories were for the adolescent of a decade ago. Furthermore, John's enthusiasm for the out of doors and his accounts of his fishing and hunting expeditions aroused the interest of the members of the class in conservation. Since the topic was near to John's heart, he was eloquent on it. Being a naturally curious person and having already read in this area, he was glad to get the teacher's help in finding more material on the subject. He always organized and planned well; because of the appreciation of his classmates in his contributions and because of his interest in what he was saying, he was becoming a more communicative speaker. His natural reticence, his interest in the out of doors, and a curiosity about national affairs and many other areas made him the kind of speaker he was. His assets were his knowledge based on his readings, his careful planning, his sincerity, and a growing desire to communicate with his audience. His liabilities were his fear of saying the wrong thing, his nervousness, and a tendency to monotony.

Joe, on the other hand, was different. He was the boy who quickly announced that he would like to repeat the minstrel show. He himself said "I personally like to talk about almost anything. Once I'm started and know where I'm going, I like to talk. You know, I do like to make people laugh. I sincerely hope I'll always be able to do it." He had a definite flair for telling an experience and a flexible voice that he used expressively. His account of having been a porter for a week at his uncle's hotel was a work of art. Unlike John, he did not wait to weigh or to consider what he was going to say. He talked first and thought afterward. John's logic was seldom faulty; Joe's, often. The teacher helped Joe plan his speeches more carefully and weigh his evidence. One day, he grinned and groaned, "How do I know it? I heard it somewhere." The teacher pointed out to him the necessity of accuracy in speaking. Each week, he supported his statements better.

No teacher will ever make Joe into John or John into Joe. Joe will never do the necessary reading, will never have a deep interest in current affairs or a curiosity that will motivate him to do research. But a teacher can encourage him to do some research, to build an outline, and to check his faulty logic. John will never speak so easily as Joe; he will probably never hold an audience entranced. But John learned to speak to an audience more effectively through experience in communicating and through the discovery that his listeners were interested in what he was saying. John will keep his audience thinking: Joe will make them laugh.

THE CLASSROOM ENVIRONMENT
AND CONVERSATIONAL SPEAKING

The environment of this classroom was conducive to conversational speaking. First, the atmosphere was a free and friendly one. The situation was not tense nor filled with a dread of speaking but was easy and natural. Secondly, the children broadened their horizons. They were motivated to learn more in certain areas through activities of the classroom, through the interests of individual children, and through visits to factories, stores, and newspaper plants. The children used speech not as an end in itself but as a means at their disposal for communication with their classmates. The teacher was aware of opportunities that promoted successful communication. Lastly, the teacher took cognizance of the level of the group and of the individual children within it. He knew their interests, weaknesses, and strengths in speaking.

FREE, FRIENDLY ATMOSPHERE

The atmosphere in this classroom was free and friendly; the teacher stimulated and encouraged the children to talk of what they had done and seen. They shared with their classmates their trips, experiences with music and books, and other happenings they enjoyed. John, the reticent member, was motivated to speak. The teacher utilized his ability to tell a tall story to motivate the rest of the class to learn more about tall stories and their inventors. Furthermore, the happy relationships among students and between the teacher and students promoted communication.

BROADENING THE INTERESTS OF CHILDREN

The teacher's recognition of John's interest in conservation set the class off on the trail of learning more about it. John's experiences were meaningful, and the class shared vicariously in these. The teacher and the group planned activities which made conservation still more significant to them. They visited the reservoir and an oil field; they invited the local forest ranger to visit their class. These activities stimulated their interest in conservation. Teachers need to emphasize the kinds of vital and meaningful experiences which demand that the children plan together and talk with each other and with other people.

COGNIZANCE OF THE LEVEL OF THE GROUP AND OF INDIVIDUALS IN THE GROUP

The teacher took cognizance of the level of the group and of the individuals within the group. He recognized John's intellectual prowess and his tendency to withdraw from the group. He praised John's abilities to organize and to prepare and helped him to communicate with his audience. He also evaluated carefully Joe's strengths and weaknesses and encouraged him to think before he spoke, to read more widely, to collect facts, and to organize what he had to say. Each child was given a chance to build on his natural assets to become a successful speaker in his own way.

DIFFERENCES AND LIKENESSES BETWEEN PUBLIC SPEAKING AND CONVERSATION

From the discussion of this class, it is apparent that these particular eighth-grade students were encouraged to talk freely of what they had done and seen. Joe described his activities of being a porter at his uncle's hotel. After he had explained his uncle's instructions, he pictured his taking his place in the lobby of the hotel. Then he told how he approached each patron. Finally, he related the story of his encounters with the patrons. He spoke about five minutes, seated with his group.

LIKENESSES

This performance was very like a public speech. Joe had a purpose: to entertain his audience. In addition, the speech was adapted to his classmates; for example, when telling how very pleasant and amiable one patron was, he compared him with the school janitor, whom the class particularly liked. Although the planning was probably limited, his material was fairly well organized. Even though he had not told the story before, he had thought about it and from the thinking had brought order to it. The humor in the story was delightful; in fact, his bit of conversation was quite similar to an after-dinner speech.

DIFFERENCES

In a public speech, he would have had the same kind of conversational quality, and he would have re-created the thoughts of his work as a porter for his classmates. Differences do exist, however. In a public speech, he probably would have stood. He probably would have spoken more loudly so that all his classmates could hear him without strain. He would have organized his material more carefully, and would have given more thought to gaining the attention of the audience in his introduction; he would have concluded his speech a bit more formally. Differences are, however, of degree and not of kind.

PURPOSES OF SPEAKING

Like the purposes of conversation, the purposes of speaking before a group are four: (1) entertaining, (2) impressing, (3) informing, and (4) persuading. In some instances, a single speech will accomplish more than one purpose; for example, it may, at the same time, be informative and entertaining. These four types of speech should not be taught separately and for themselves but as they fit into the classroom experiences. As opportunity arises, however, students will give each type of speech in the classroom, and the teacher will help each student to make the speech more effective in terms of his interests, the requirements of the occasion, and the expectations of his listeners.

ENTERTAINING

In the eighth-grade group mentioned earlier, the purpose of many of the short talks was entertainment. During the first week of school, several of the children related some of their unusual summer experiences. Jack told about his first lessons on the violin and about the agony of his sister, brother, and mother during his practice periods. Helen, interested in symphonic music, explained her delight in *The Nutcracker Suite* and played parts of it for the class. She informed the group as well as entertained it. When Joe narrated his humorous experiences in going deep-sea fishing with his father, his purpose was partly to entertain, partly to inform. However, the primary purpose of all these speeches was to entertain.

IMPRESSING

In the elementary school children seldom give talks to impress. But Joe gave one at the end of the eighth grade. Because a sixth-grade teacher was retiring, the students in the school decided to give her a gift. At the same time, boys from the sixth, seventh, and eighth grades were chosen to pay tribute to her and to her work. Joe represented the eighth grade. In a genuine, sincere, and warm manner, he paid tribute to Miss Sayre. He told of some of the experiences in her classroom that had been particularly happy and about the characteristics that made children enjoy her. In fact, there were tears in the eyes of some members of the audience as he depicted what she had done for the children they all knew. He impressed his audience.

INFORMING

When Jane told how to make a dress, she was informing the class. When an eighth-grade group studied conservation, two of its members gave talks on soil erosion and on forest fires to inform the others about what is happening to the country's natural resources. Much of the speaking that is done in a classroom has for its purpose the giving of information.

PERSUADING

From the work on conservation, persuasive talks emerged. After the group talked about what was happening to the nation's forests, minerals, and water, they decided to do something to conserve these natural resources. They talked over the various plans and then invited their parents to the classroom to ask them to help in conservation. One boy thought New York State should provide assistance to tree farmers. The children persuaded their parents to take action about conserving some of our nation's resources.

PRINCIPLES OF FINDING THINGS TO TALK ABOUT

The purposes of speaking are closely related to finding topics for speeches. The purposes arise out of what happens in the classroom. Children themselves find something to talk about as they share their out-of-school experiences or as they take part in units of work in the classroom. When they prepare a program to which they invite their parents, their selection of topics will result from their own interests and experience, the nature of the occasion, and the requirements of their parents as listeners.

THE CHILD SELECTS THE SUBJECT HIMSELF

When a child moved from a small western New York town to New York City, the children in the third grade of which he had been a member sent him letters and cards. He replied by sending them a recording of the story of his adventures in his new home and town. As his father and he had gone on trips together, they had taken pictures of what they

FIG. 17. Learning about maple syrup. (*Neil Croom, University State Teachers College, New Paltz, N.Y.*)

saw. Consequently, the child also sent slides, numbered so that they could be shown with the talk more easily. He first told of his arrival in New York City and his stay with his family at a big hotel. Pictures taken from the hotel window accompanied this part of his talk. After he described his trip to the top of the Empire State building, he explained what Times Square was like in the daytime and at night. He gave an enthusiastic account of his trip to the opera. Again slides illustrated the activities. He reminded the children that in second grade they had read about the little red lighthouse and the great gray bridge. He pictured for them the great gray bridge and then explained how he and his father had climbed down to the little red lighthouse. Finally, he told about Christmas in his new home in a big apartment building and about Christmas decorations at Radio City. Slides also represented these experiences.

FIG. 18. Talking about maple syrup. (*Neil Croom, University State Teachers College, New Paltz, N.Y.*)

In another school, when the children in the eighth grade decided to learn more about conservation, they chose the topics they wanted to talk about. One child was interested in forest fires because he had seen one recently. Another wanted to discuss the conservation of water because he had been visiting in New York City during a water shortage.

Children in lower grades talk about such topics as pets, hobbies, games, excursions, people, and places. A second grader told his class-mates about his pet turtle. He explained how he got him, where he kept him at home, what he fed him, and why he liked him. This recital stimulated many of the other members of the class to talk about their pets. A third grader told about his father's job as a news dealer. He told where his father got the papers, how he delivered them to the news stands, and finally some of the trials of being a news dealer. Other children in the group contributed accounts of the work of their fathers. The child selects topics which he knows about and which interest him. Frequently, the topic is related to his school or family activities. Sometimes the teacher makes suggestions and guides a child's choice, but the final selection is his own.

THE CHILD SELECTS A SUBJECT AS AN OUTGROWTH OF AN OUT-OF-SCHOOL EXPERIENCE OR A CURRICULAR ACTIVITY

The subject the New York City child talked about was an outgrowth of his experiences outside of school. Out-of-school activities serve as topics to talk about in school. A child may have read a book he particularly liked, may have seen a television show he thought unusual or different, may have been to a play that excited his imagination, or may have observed an important news event. One youngster was present at the inauguration of Eisenhower. His vivid description aroused the interest of the children in inaugurations. Another child attended the unloading of the Barnum & Bailey Circus. He called his classmates' attention to the problems of unloading the animals, of moving them through the city streets, and of getting them ready for the big event.

At other times, talks grow out of curricular activities. For example, the members of the eighth grade, who were interested in conservation, spoke on:

Soil Erosion	Destruction of Timber
How the Earth Rotates	Fire Prevention in the Forest
The Soil and the Plow	Fish and Fishing
The TVA	Wild Animals
Sources of Water	Insects That Attack Trees
How to Make Water Behave	Diseases That Attack Trees
Enemies of Water	Planned Conservation of Water
People in the Forest	Planned Conservation of Land
Conservation of Wild Life	National Parks

These topics grew out of the children's study of conservation motivated by John's fishing and hunting. The children may want to investigate local history and report on it in class. Such an activity is described in a recent issue of *Childhood Education*.[1]

[1] C. Wittenburg, "Sharing Experiences in Local History," *Childhood Education*, Vol. 26 (November, 1949), p. 130.

As children plan to study together various areas, they find a variety of topics to report on: "Foods America Gives the World," "Women in Medicine," "Gravity," "Making of Aluminum," "Trains As Freight Carriers," "Working of the Telephone," "Development of the Modern Submarine," "Different Kinds of Trucks," "How to Fight a Fire," "How a Fire Alarm Works." What a child talks about depends on his experiences in and out of school, the kind of person he is, and his classmates.

FACTORS DETERMINING WHAT TO TALK ABOUT

THE CHILD HIMSELF

A child may have had a particular experience the group will enjoy hearing about. He may have a tradition in his family that is different, or his father may be engaged in an unusual occupation; for example, an eighth grader gave a talk on the operation of a rug-cleaning establishment. A thirteen-year-old girl told about weaving curtains on her own loom. Topics stem from the children's interests, hobbies, abilities, or experiences.

SPECIAL OCCASIONS

A second factor that influences the child's selection of a topic is the special occasion. During Book Week, the children of the seventh grade invited their parents to their classroom. They decided to advise their parents on what books to buy for their brothers and sisters. Members of the class drew on their favorite books and tried to sell them to their audience. Several of the students brought the books to show the audience how attractive they were. The occasion governed the selection of the topics.

LISTENERS

A third factor in the choice of topics is the listeners. Before the children in the seventh grade decided to tell their parents about children's books, they discovered that a large proportion of the parents give children's books as Christmas gifts. They thought that they could make their parents understand why they themselves had enjoyed and profited from certain books, although they realized they would have to treat some of the material in a new way because the school, town library, and bookstore had already sent out lists of recommended children's books. They questioned very seriously whether their parents would be willing to accept their opinions on this subject, but they felt that their evaluation of the books would be helpful to their parents. Their listeners' interest in children's books influenced their choice of topic.

THE TEACHER'S ROLE IN THE SELECTION OF A TOPIC

Because the teacher is aware of the influence of the child's interests, of special occasions, and of his classmates on the child's choice of topics, he uses this knowledge to stimulate speaking in the classroom. He does not assign 10 to 10:30 as the hour for oral topics and ask each child to prepare and deliver a short speech on "The Most Exciting Day of My Life." He does not even use the word "speech" or "talk." Rather, he takes advantage of opportunities that present themselves to encourage the sharing of information and ideas. An eight-year-old girl arrived early in the morning enthusiastic about the book *The Little House*, which she had taken home the night before. As her eyes sparkled and her voice showed her excitement, she told the teacher how the city crept up on the little house and how happy the little house was to be moved to the country, lived in, and loved. The teacher suggested that she tell her classmates about the book. A ten-year-old boy had been to the "Trip to the Moon" at the planetarium. As he said, "Boy, you really can feel yourself taking off to the moon," he communicated to the teacher the thrill of his adventure. The teacher asked him to share the experience with the group. His classmates wanted to know how to get there. After he conferred with his parents, he gave accurate, specific directions. A group was studying where the food in the big A & P comes from. Some children found out about frozen foods, fresh fruit, and vegetables; others, about meat, fish, dairy products, and bakery goods. After they had collected the information, they reported on it to their classmates. In these instances, the teacher influenced children in their choice of topics by taking advantage of the experiences of the children, the demands of the listeners, or the occasions when they were studying related areas.

COLLECTING MATERIAL

After a child has selected his topic, he collects material for his speech in several ways: (1) He reviews what he knows. (2) He observes and gains experience. (3) He makes inquiries of people who have special information. (4) He consults books and magazines.

THE CHILD REVIEWS WHAT HE KNOWS

When the eighth grade was studying conservation, one child decided to study the conservation of water. His reason for the choice was amusing. At first he announced, "I don't see any need for saving water." After thinking a little, he exclaimed, "I remember when I saved water." He announced that the previous year, when he had visited relatives in New York City, he had soaped himself, turned the shower off, and then, to rinse the soap off, turned the water back on; he had done this turning off and on to save water. He then recalled other ways his cousins had conserved water. Because he was intrigued with the idea of saving water on a larger scale, he decided to read more about it. From his visit to New York City, he knew a little about water conservation, for he recalled hearing about the rain maker and the proposed building of dams to supply New York City with more water. As the child finds something to talk about, he recalls what he already knows about the subject.

THE CHILD OBSERVES

After a child has reviewed what he knows about a subject, he begins to observe and to add to his own experiences. Speeches taken only from books are dull. When the students planned to study conservation of water, they decided to take some trips to help them understand phases of the subject. They visited the local watershed, discovered why so many evergreen trees are planted around a reservoir, found out how the level of water was recorded, and learned how the water was purified.

THE CHILD ASKS OTHERS

This group also visited an oil field to talk with its manager about oil conservation. Talking with experts is a second source of collecting material. In continuing the study of conservation, the eighth-grade group invited the forest ranger of the area to its classroom. When he came, he described for the children some of the methods used to protect the forest today. He explained how forest fires are prevented, detected, and fought. He told about the prevention of diseases in trees, the prevalence of insects that destroy trees, and the detection and elimination of these insects. The children learned more about conservation by talking with experts.

THE CHILD READS

Furthermore, the children read about conservation. Each child investigated the particular area he was covering. In some cases, parents

FIG. 19. The child uses the library. (*East School, Long Beach, N.Y.*)

helped with the project by finding materials and reading them with the children. The teacher brought to the classroom the following children's books, and each child read the sections that applied to his particular topic:

Bennet, H., and W. C. Pryor, *The Land We Defend*, New York, Longmans, 1942.
Brinser, A., *Our Use of the Land*, New York, Harper, 1939.
Caldwell, J., *Our Land and Our Living*, Syracuse, N.Y., Singer, 1947.
Gustafson, A. F., *Conservation in the United States*, Ithaca, N.Y., Comstock Publishing Company, 1944.
Parkins, A. E., *Our Natural Resources and Their Conservation*, New York, Wiley, 1939.

Reed, W. M., *America's Treasure*, New York, Harcourt Brace, 1930.
Shippen, K. B., *The Great Heritage*, New York, Viking, 1943.
Tippett, J. S., *Paths to Conservation*, Boston, Heath, 1937.

The children also read articles suggested by the teacher. He explained to them how to use the *Readers' Guide to Periodical Literature* and how to find the magazines they were looking for. Some of the children became very much interested in this project. They learned more about their topic through reading magazines and books.

The Child Records Material. Keeping a systematic record helps the child remember what he has read when he plans his speech. After doing some preliminary reading, the student makes a simple outline to serve as a guide to his reading. He may use the following headings in reading about sources of water supply:

I. Water is supplied by five sources
  A. Springs
  B. Dug wells
  C. Rock wells
  D. Sand and gravel wells
  E. Water drawn directly from rivers, ponds, and lakes

As the child reads about each of the topics, he records each item of information on a separate card and enough about the book or article to identify it. When he is quoting from a book, he encloses the sentences in quotation marks. He always indicates the page of the book or article from which he has taken his notes and puts the appropriate topic from his outline at the top of the card.

Illustration of a note card:

> Organizations for furthering conservation
> Tippett, J. S.
> (Pp. 223–224.)
> National Association of Audubon Societies. Purposes: "To prevent erosion, pollution of streams and waterways, wasteful lumbering, over-grazing, overhunting, useless destruction of natural wild-life habitats . . . " (p. 223).
> American Nature Association. Purpose: "To arouse interest of people in nature and to show how measures for conservation should and could be brought about . . . " (p. 224).

Illustration of a card describing a useful book:

Tippett, James Sterling   *Paths to Conservation*
                                 Boston, Heath, 1937.
Contains material on birds, trees, landscaping, state
flowers, meaning of conservation, wild life, and the
organizations which further conservation.
Conservation, pp. 207–236.
Bibliography on conservation, pp. 294–299.

For each speech, the child prepares a list of books and articles that
he has read. Information about books include the author, the title, the
place of publication, the publisher, and the date of publication. Information about magazine articles consists of the author of the article, the
title of the article, the name of the magazine, the volume number, the
month and the year, and the pages.

THE OLDER CHILD EVALUATES THE COLLECTED MATERIAL

The child in the upper grades evaluates the material he reads and the
authorities he interviews as far as he is able. He asks such questions as:

1. Who made the statement?
2. By what right did he make the statement?
3. Did he have sufficient opportunity to observe and to make use of the
observations?
4. Is he biased?
5. How long ago did he make the observation?
6. Have circumstances changed since he spoke?

ENCOURAGING THE CHILD TO FIND MATERIAL ABOUT A TOPIC

The teacher motivates the child to recall what he knows, to observe,
to make inquiries, and to read about his topic. By questioning, he
encourages him to remember what he already knows. For example, the
head of a student council wanted to remind the children to be careful of
the rights of those living near the school. He wanted to use examples of
cases where the rights had been violated. The teacher's question, "Can
you think of instances where property was damaged needlessly?"
helped him to remember what he already knew. The examples of children's stealing apples from a tree in a nearby yard and of boys' breaking
globes of street lights with snowballs became part of his speech.

The teacher also inspires children to observe and to make inquiries about aspects of their topics. A teacher told a ten-year-old girl about a frozen-food concern in her town. She went there, observed how cherries were sorted, washed, prepared for freezing, and finally packaged. As she talked with one of the foremen, she learned where the cherries were bought and where, when processed, they were sold. Her report was more interesting because of her observation and her inquiries. Teachers often provide experiences where children can learn from observation and inquiry. They visit the toy shop, the fire house, the city hall, the newspaper plant, the tomato fields, the canning factory, and the bus station. While they are visiting these places, they look carefully at the operations. They may talk to the owner of the toy shop, the fire chief, the mayor, or the editor. From talking with them, they learn more about the operations. Teachers in all grades encourage such activity.

Teachers also begin early to help children look up information in books and magazines. In the early grades, the form is simple. For instance, children in a first grade brought in as many different pictures of trucks as they could find. With the teacher's help, they deduced what the trucks were for and what goods they might carry. Investigation, in a simple form, had begun. When they study fire fighting, the teacher may bring in a number of books with pictures showing different types of fire engines. Again they are using books for a specific purpose—to find out more about fighting fires. Children become acquainted with the school library early in their careers, for they visit it to find a book that will be fun to read. Later, the teacher shows them how to use the card catalogue to find books which will prove helpful in their reports. Still later, he teaches them to use indexes. When they are ready to learn, he explains to them how to make a bibliography and how to take notes. In the middle grades, he asks them to give the author and the title; then he asks for the author, title, and date; and, finally, in the upper grades, he requires that they include all the usual bibliographic data. Each year, the child does a little more difficult reading and more recording of what he has read.

In the upper grades, the teacher begins to help him make judgments on the reliability of what he has read. He asks the child who the author is, who made the statement, when he made the statement, and whether he is reliable. By talking with the child, he helps him to judge the worth of what he has read.

The teacher encourages the child to make topical outlines. In the first grade, the teacher may ask, "How did we make our Jell-O last time?" As the children tell him, he places the steps on the blackboard:

1. Get the Jell-O and water ready.
2. Boil the water.
3. Measure two cups of hot water.
4. Mix the water with the Jell-O.
5. Let it cool.

Sometimes, when a child skips a step, the teacher asks, "Is that the very next step?" In a simple way, children are learning to organize. In the middle grades, he asks him to list the topics he is to cover.

ORGANIZATION OF MATERIAL

After the child has collected and evaluated his material, he then determines whether he has collected enough and of the right kind. He may find he needs to change his outline because of his material. In all likelihood, he possesses material he cannot use. In some cases, there are still gaps he needs to fill in. He will organize and adapt his material so that the listeners will understand it, follow it, and be interested in it.

LIMITING THE TOPIC

One boy was going to talk on the conservation of water. His preliminary outline included the topics of water supply, enemies of water supply, and means of conservation. As he read, he decided to talk only on the sources of supply of drinking water. His outline changed from one which consisted of three topics to one which listed five sources of water supply.

A girl who was to speak about conservation of our forests included the topics of forestry before 1900, imbalance of volume of wood caused by fire and excessive cutting, enemies of conservation, and requirements of tree farming. After doing some preliminary reading, she discovered that the outline was incomplete and that, furthermore, if she followed it, she would collect enough material for a dozen one-hour lectures. She limited her topic to the diseases that attack forests. Because the ranger showed the children a piece of elm afflicted with the Dutch elm disease, she became sufficiently interested to read about it and other diseases. Since an unusually bright six-year-old boy enjoyed animal stories, he wanted to tell his classmates that they were fun. He told the teacher he knew the stories of *Effelli, Peter Churchmouse, Baby Roo, Little Wild Horse, The Horse Who Lived Upstairs*, and *The Lazy Beaver*. The teacher pointed out that he would take a long time to tell the stories of all the animals but suggested he tell just enough about the two horse stories to make his classmates want to know more about them. He decided to tell just the main parts of *The Horse Who Lived Upstairs* and *Little Wild Horse*. Many children discover that they must limit their subjects because they choose areas too wide to cover adequately.

BEGINNING, MIDDLE, AND END

Even children in the first grade can be taught that a speech needs a beginning, a middle, and an end. One teacher uses the analogy of road signs. She says that the first sign announcing that the town is about to appear is the introduction, or the beginning, of the speech. She explains that it calls attention to the town. The body, or the middle, is the travel through the town. The conclusion, or end, is the sign that says, "Glad you visited us. You are now leaving Allegheny." She explains that, while you are in the town to look it over, you can avoid wasting time in aimlessly driving around by using a plan or map of the town to show you where you want to go. The trip will be more interesting, quicker, and easier. She points out that you can save the best spot until the end. She then points out that the plan or map for traveling through the town is analogous to planning a speech.

Jack was persuading his classmates to help prevent forest fires. He opened his speech in this way: "In Maine, in October, 1947, a forest fire destroyed 210,000 acres of forest. It wasted $32,000,000. It killed sixteen persons. The same kind of disaster could happen to you here in Sullivan County, over in the Shawangunk Mountains." He then went on to the body of his talk concerning ways to avoid fires in the forest. He ended with "Two-hundred-ten thousand acres of forest gone. Thirty-two million dollars worth of property thrown away. Sixteen dead. Don't let it happen in those hills we see from this window." He planned his introduction and conclusion after he had developed his main idea: When camping or picnicking in the forest, you eighth graders should be responsible for the prevention of fire.

Sometimes children are uncertain how to end a talk. One seven-year-old was telling how to plant a flower garden. Step by step, she told vividly and clearly what she had done. Finally, she stopped, hesitated, looked around, and said, "Well, I guess I'm through." When the teacher asked her what she could have said last to make her classmates remember her flower garden, she said, "I could have told them I'd help them if they wanted to plant one, or I could have invited them to come to see my garden."

PHRASING THE MAIN IDEA IN A COMPLETE SENTENCE

The teacher should encourage children to phrase the main idea of their speech or report in a single statement, such as the one mentioned in the preceding paragraph. The statement represents the idea that the speaker is using to entertain, inform, impress, or persuade his audience. The teacher should make sure that the child has a main idea. Having a clear understanding of the main idea prevents the introduction of unnecessary and unrelated details.

The teacher of the early and middle grades will not ask the child to state the main idea, but he will find out in an informal way whether the child has one. When the teacher suggested that the ten-year-old boy tell the group about his trip to the moon, he was sure that the child clearly knew his main idea—the planetarium's "Trip to the Moon" is an exciting adventure—even though he did not express it in words. Since a ten-year-old girl had been to Quebec during her Easter vacation, she wanted to tell her classmates about the trip. The teacher talked the trip over with her. One of the most interesting events was her talk with a ten-year-old boy from Quebec about his school. She stressed again and again how his school was more formal than hers. The teacher encouraged her to tell her classmates about this part of the trip. Although she never stated the main idea in words, it obviously was as follows: The schooling of one ten-year-old boy in Quebec indicates that the schooling in Quebec is more formal than that in this school. In each case the child knew what his main idea was.

DIVISIONS WITHIN THE SPEECH

For children in the elementary school, divisions are expressed in topical outline form, although occasionally children are mature enough to express them in sentence form. In either case, the divisions represent the major ideas related to the general statement. They should be clear and should not overlap. In the speech on the supply of water, the divisions are the five sources of water. In the topic of tree diseases, there could be two types of classification: (1) according to the types of insect that attack trees or (2) according to the types of tree which particular insects attack.

When the child asked his classmates to help prevent forest fires, he first showed why fires were a waste of natural resources and then went on to divisions concerning what could be done to prevent forest fires. In another speech, where a boy was proposing state aid for tree farming, he first explained what tree farming involved, then gave the reasons for its existence, and finally showed why state aid should be given to tree farmers. The first division was the definition of tree farming; the next division gave the reasons for its existence; and the final ones included the reasons for giving state aid to tree farmers. These divisions are typical of those made by children in the upper grades.

Kindergartners and first graders can list all the things they saw on a trip, or they can indicate the steps to take in following a recipe. Children in the third and fourth grade can reveal essential points they intend to cover. Fifth graders, in noting the main and sub points, are building a simple outline. Sixth graders make a more detailed one. Seventh and eighth graders may begin to work on sentence outlines if they are mature and if they have the necessary background. In all cases, the teacher is alert to see that the children include the necessary facts, omit extraneous details, and are orderly in their arrangement of material.

TYPES OF ORGANIZATION

Types of organization of speeches used in the elementary school are (1) time, (2) space, (3) causal relations, (4) classification, (5) making choices, (6) necessity, and (7) specific instance.

When the Events Occur. An example of organization based on time is the story of the boy who described his experiences in New York City. After he told about his arrival in September, he explained his activities in a time sequence. He gave a month-by-month account of what he had done in New York City from the month of September through the month of December.

Where the Events Occur. A child described a subway ride. He told first how he went downstairs, then down more stairs, through a turnstile where he put his money in a slot, down more stairs to a platform where he boarded the train. He explained each step of his trip in terms of where it happened.

Why the Event Occurs. A first-grade boy was explaining to his teacher why he wanted homework. He gave all his reasons as follows: (1) his brother had homework; (2) he would learn faster; and (3) he would like to have something to carry home in his book bag.

What Are the Types? The child's exposition of different types of water supply represents classification. He placed the sources of water in five categories: springs, dug wells, rock wells, sand and gravel wells, and water drawn from rivers, ponds, and lakes.

Why One Rather Than Another? The children were deciding whether to go to the zoo or to the post office. One seven-year-old, explaining why the post office was the better choice, gave all its advantages. A six-year-old girl, extolling the virtues of a trip to the zoo, made clear all the benefits to be gained from her proposal.

Must the Course of Action Be This One? Only one choice is feasible. A child made clear to his fellow second graders that they must learn to swim. If they are to have more fun in the water and if they are to be safe in it, their only course of action is to learn.

What Instance Illustrates This Point? A third grader demonstrated why boys should talk problems out rather than fight. He noted that one boy had a black eye and another a badly bruised leg because they fought instead of trying to talk over their differences. He explained that they could have settled their troubles through discussion.

CONSIDERING THE LISTENERS

The child should think in terms of his listeners as he organizes his speech. What statistics will appeal to them? Whom do they know as an authority in the field? What do they already know about the subject? In other words, the child considers the knowledge and interests of his listeners. Starting with what they know, he proceeds from the common ground. For example, when the children were trying to persuade their parents to do something about conservation, they started with grape production, which was familiar to their parents. The children explained how certain farms yielded more tons of grapes per acre than others and showed why this disparity existed. From this point, the children went on to what should be done about saving other natural resources, such as water, forests, and minerals.

Children may talk to one of three groups of listeners: (1) their classmates, (2) other children from a different grade, and (3) their parents. They may discuss the characteristics and interests of each group. One child made a rather astute observation as the members of his class were choosing books to be reviewed for their parents. He said, "My father will think a lot of this silly; you know most of our books appeal to mothers and not fathers. Our fathers are the ones who earn the money to buy the books." Because of this remark, the children discussed books that would appeal to their fathers. The comments were similar to these: "Dad doesn't think anything funny except Milton Berle." "Daddy always chases fires!" "My dad likes to take his car apart and put it back together again." After they had placed the likes, dislikes, and special interests of the fathers on the board, they listed those that occurred most frequently. They then analyzed the themes of the books to see how they fitted the interests of their audience.

In one case, a child wished to talk about a book of snakes. As he giggled, he said, "There isn't a thing up on that board that's like a snake." He pondered on how he could interest the parents in the book on snakes. A twelve-year-old girl said, "Snakes are like murder. Gory. They'll like them." But several members held this to be a silly reason. Finally, the child decided he would attack the problem by explaining to the parents how useful snakes are to our society. This approach was successful.

PUTTING THE SPEECH TOGETHER

After the child has selected his topic, collected material on it, and organized his ideas, he composes his speech. The teacher should help him be sure to use concrete and specific words, to see that his speech has unity, coherence, and a climax. His use of grammar and pronunciation should conform to the educated usage of the community.

USE OF CONCRETE AND SPECIFIC WORDS

Children should be taught to use concrete and specific terms. In a description of a trip, they tell interesting details and do not give an abbreviated time diary with generalized impressions. Skillful questioning by the students and the teacher helps the child to be concrete. When a child says that LaGuardia Airport is huge, the teacher asks him how huge. If he depicts a church as being very beautiful, the teacher questions him about the characteristics that make the church beautiful to him. One ten-year-old was telling about a Polish festival he had attended. He said the dresses were beautiful. The teacher asked him how he could give a vivid picture of the costumes. He responded by saying they were brightly colored, blue, green, and yellow. Finally, he was able to bring to class colored pictures of the Polish costumes. He and the class found words and phrases that described the gay colors and the picturesque quality of the costumes.

KEEPING THE SPEECH COMPLETE AND UNIFIED

Unity can also be taught through the use of pointed questions and suggestions. When a child was telling about tapping for maple syrup, he neglected to tell when it was done. One of the children asked, "When do farmers tap for maple syrup?" The child perceived that the time element was an important part of his speech that he had left out. Another ten-year-old was telling how to make lemonade. In the midst of his story, he proceeded to tell that lemons grow on trees in the South and that he knew the source because, when his aunt went south last summer, she sent him some. She went south because she had been sick with infantile paralysis. The teacher indicated that the members of the class were interested in learning how to make lemonade and that the speaker should save the story of his aunt's trip until another time. These children were learning the importance of completeness and unity.

KEEPING THE SPEECH COHERENT

Again through skillful questioning, the teacher points to coherence. One teacher said, "You suddenly jumped from going through the turnstile to being on the train. This jump is a big one. How could you make it easy for us?" Through the use of such a question, the teacher indicates the need for the relationship of the divisions to the general statement.

BUILDING THE HIGH POINT

In classroom dramatics, the play proceeds toward the high point. A high point also exists in a speech. A large part of building it depends on composition: the speech is so arranged that the strongest argument, the most exciting description, is near the end of the speech. The teacher helps the child to build the high point. He asks, What is the most important happening? Or he questions, What is the most exciting part of your account? He then suggests that he save this part for almost the end of the speech.

GRAMMAR

Teachers teach grammar in two ways, prescriptively and functionally. From a prescriptive point of view, grammar is a set of rules which guides the teacher in telling his students how to write and speak. He sets up separate periods in the daily schedule to teach the nominative case or the use of plurals. It is a formal approach which assumes that the rules of structure and usage do not change easily. This type of teaching grammar has its limitations in furthering communication. A child is likely to be bored with the acquisition of skills in grammar since he sees no reason for them.

From the standpoint of teaching speech, the functional approach is more effective. A child improves his grammar because he sees that he can communicate more clearly with others. He uses language for the purposes mentioned earlier: to entertain, inform, persuade, and impress. As he discovers that the successful carrying out of the purpose depends to some extent on grammatical usage, he is ready to learn. The teacher demonstrates that our language is a dynamic, changing tool and that both grammar and pronunciation change over the years. The functional approach tends toward a descriptive study: an analysis of the forms of grammar as used today in friendly intercourse by educated people. It is a description of usage in speaking based on the habits of cultivated men and women.

A teacher should have a knowledge of present-day research in language. If he is cognizant of it, he will not consider "It is me" or "Go slow" the expressions of the uneducated or uncultured. An interesting study[2] of attitudes toward grammatical usage was published in *Harper's* in 1949. It indicates wide variations in opinion on what teachers and the readers of *Harper's* consider correct grammar. Bodmer's[3] *The Loom of Language* shows how usage is changing and indicates that English is losing its inflections and that word order is increasingly important. Fries[4] has written *American English Grammar* from a descriptive point of view.

PRONUNCIATION

The trend in teaching pronunciation as well as grammar is descriptive rather than prescriptive. Kenyon and Knott's[5] *Pronouncing Dictionary of American English* is based on the pronunciations actually used by cultivated people of our generation. Every teacher should read their introduction. Pronunciation is constantly changing. A teacher may become narrow or intolerant, for he may consider the pronunciations

[2] N. Lewis, "How Correct Must English Be?" *Harper's Magazine*, Vol. 138 (March, 1949), pp. 68–74.

[3] F. Bodmer, *The Loom of Language*, New York, Norton, 1944.

[4] C. C. Fries, *American English Grammar*, Chicago, National Council of English Teachers, 1941.

[5] J. S. Kenyon and T. A. Knott, *Pronouncing Dictionary of American English*, Springfield, Mass., Merriam, 1944.

that he learned in high school or college as the only acceptable pro-nunciations. He may brand a pronunciation wrong with undue haste, not realizing that there exist variant pronunciations of many words. Emphasis on grammar or pronunciation should not be allowed to get in the way of communication.

The teacher can directly help each child to use grammar acceptably and pronounce each word in an approved way. A teacher may keep a file of cards on which he jots down the errors of grammar and of pro-nunciation which each child makes. He works with the child individually to correct his errors. Each year, the child speaks more acceptably. One fourth grader's card contained these items:

sang, sung	*n* for *ng*
did, done	*filum* for *film*
don't, doesn't	*kin* for *can*
good, well	omission final consonants, *ast* for *asked*
saw, seen	*cidy* for *city*
teach, learn	*jist* for *just*
went, gone	
naming yourself last	
agreement of subject and verb	
confusion in tenses	

The teacher explained the difference between *teach* and *learn* to the child. When she used the words correctly, he complimented her. He explained that the middle sound in *city* is *t* not *d*. When she said *city*, he praised her. In no instance did he interrupt her speaking. He called her attention to both errors and her correct usage when he spoke with her about speaking and writing.

The teacher does not attack all the errors at once. He works first with those which the child will be able to correct most easily and those which detract most seriously from his ability to communicate. As the teacher finds the child's usage on one item has improved, he moves on to the next. He does not hope to remove all errors during any one year.

GIVING THE TALK

After a student's preparation for his speech, he is ready to talk and his classmates are ready to listen. He must realize the meaning of what he is saying and say it with a lively sense of communication. His audi-ence should listen actively, accurately, and critically.

A CHILD'S REALIZATION OF THE MEANING OF THE WORDS AS HE SPEAKS THEM

The child must understand thoroughly what he is talking about. That the topic be self-selected and that it be interesting to the student are prerequisites to the thorough understanding of what he is talking about. When the topic has grown out of his own experiences or out of the classroom activities, he has a purpose in speaking to his classmates. He feels the necessity of re-creating his thought for the group. He is aware of the meaning of his ideas and of their emotional tones. By his voice, attitude, and posture he conveys the meaning to his audience.

A VIVID SENSE OF COMMUNICATION WITH HIS LISTENERS

First, the child's having a purpose in speaking helps establish a vivid sense of communication with his listeners. He wants his audience to learn from him, to enjoy his story or experience, to be persuaded by his speech. Secondly, a happy, friendly atmosphere in the classroom is conducive to real communication. The situation is in many ways conversational. Lastly, the child must make his classmates think and feel with him; they should be nodding, shaking their heads, or indicating by a gleam in the eye that they find him witty. He should be watching his audience for these signs and, on the basis of them, should be ready to adjust what he says and how he says it. In other words, a two-way active communication is obviously taking place.

LISTENING

Children should be taught to listen to each other attentively, accurately, and critically. If the speaker looks at his listeners, they are more likely to remain interested. Conversely, if the listeners keep their eyes on the speaker, he will be able to respond to them more wholeheartedly. The teacher can help promote two-way communication. He can explain to the children how the speaker and the listeners complement each other. He can set the scene in such a way that the children will think that the speaker and what he has to tell them are important. The listeners should not only be sure of the meaning and ideas that the speaker is attempting to convey, but they should also be judging the worth of what he is saying. They should examine the reasoning to make sure that the speaker's inferences are sound and that the support of the main idea is acceptable. They should be using what has been taught them to judge the speaker's contribution.

They should also take into account the child who is making the speech. Is he the kind of person who helps promote democratic living in the classroom? Is he a cooperative member of the group? Is he the kind of person who puts the interest of the group above his selfish interests? Is he the kind of person who collects material carefully before he speaks? When the teacher promotes two-way communication, careful thinking and preparation, and interest in what is being said, the students will listen accurately. If he insists that the children solve their own problems and that the solutions be based on accurate presentations of the problems and careful discussion of the solutions, children will be more likely to listen critically. Because he has encouraged good social living in his classroom, where the rights of all are respected and where all decisions are made carefully, the children are better able to judge each other's talks.

SUMMARY

A classroom environment should invite conversational speaking. The teacher should promote a free, friendly atmosphere, should take advantage of opportunities for the children to gain experience stemming from their interests, and should be aware of the level of the group and of the individuals within the group. In essential respects, giving a talk is like good conversation. The purposes of classroom speaking are (1) entertaining, (2) impressing, (3) informing, and (4) persuading. In finding topics to talk about two principles are paramount: (1) that the subject be self-selected and (2) that it grow out of either curricular work or an out-of-school experience. The four factors involved in the selection of a topic are (1) the purpose, (2) the speaker, (3) the occasion, and (4) the listeners.

In collecting material, the child reviews what he knows, observes, inquires of authorities, and reads on the subject. He evaluates the material and organizes it. In planning his speech, he includes an introduction, body, and conclusion; he organizes his material in relation to the main idea. Divisions according to time, space, classification, specific instances, evaluation, and necessity may be used. He adapts his material in the speech to his audience and composes it so that it is unified, complete, coherent, grammatical, and climactic. He re-creates his thought at the time of his delivery and maintains with his listeners a vivid sense of communication. The listeners listen to the speaker accurately and critically.

EXERCISES

1. List talks that might be given during a school period of a week to entertain, impress, inform, or persuade.

2. List topics for speaking suggested by a unit of work similar to the one on conservation noted in this chapter.

3. Make a bibliography of children's books in a certain area such as "Alaska," "Trains," or "The Postal Service" which would prove useful in a unit for a specific grade and would provide material for making talks.

4. Take down as nearly as you can a speech given by a child in a classroom. Indicate how the child followed some of the principles mentioned in this chapter.

5. Indicate specifically how special occasions may influence the children's choice of topics.

6. Show specifically how a child's interests may influence his choice of topic.

7. Show how talks might emerge from experiences of children out of class.

8. Indicate how you would help a child organize his material in the grade you intend to teach. Assume he is to talk about a specific topic.

BIBLIOGRAPHY

SOURCES FOR FURTHER READING

Baldrige, M., "Three Decades of Language Study," *Childhood Education*, Vol. 26 (November, 1949), pp. 117–121. Discusses the studies of language that are significant in teaching children.

Berry, A., "Listening Activities in the Elementary School," *Elementary English Review*, Vol. 23 (February, 1946), pp. 69–79. Explains how to improve listening.

Blackman, M., "That Their Voices May Not Quake," *Childhood Education*, Vol. 26 (November, 1949), pp. 114–116. Contains ways to encourage children to share their experiences.

Bryant, D., and K. R. Wallace, *Oral Communication*, New York, Appleton-Century-Crofts, 1948. Discusses how to prepare, organize, and deliver the different types of speeches.

Ernst, M. S., *Words*, New York, Knopf, 1950. Discusses how words grow and change. Designed for the upper grades.

Gale, R. J., "Steps to the Good Oral Report," *Elementary English*, Vol. 23 (May, 1946), pp. 214–218. Discusses outlining and suggests how topics can be developed.

Gilman, W. E., B. Aly, and L. Reid, *The Fundamentals of Public Speaking*, New York, Macmillan, 1951. Treats clearly and comprehensively the theory and practice of public speaking.

"Language Arts in the Elementary School," *Bulletin of the Department of Elementary School Principals* (special issue), Vol. 20 (July, 1941), pp. 259–316. Gives suggestions for things to talk about and principles to follow in speaking.

Lewis, C., "Tell It from Your Mouth," *Childhood Education*, Vol. 26 (November, 1949), pp. 110–113.   Tells how to bring out spontaneity in children in their sensations and perceptions.

Lindahl, H. M., "Vitalizing the Language Program," *The Elementary English Review*, Vol. 21 (December, 1944), pp. 286–291.   Includes outline of work illustrating how both oral and written language may be made alive through functional, integrated language activities organized around meaningful, interested learning experiences.

Lundin, E., "Learning to Make Short Talks," in *Language Arts in the Elementary Schools*, Twentieth Yearbook of the Department of Elementary School Principals, Washington, National Education Association, 1941, pp. 296–302.   Tells how to help children make effective talks.

McMillin, M., "How to Make an Outline," *Instructor*, Vol. 54 (February, 1945), pp. 14–16.   Illustrates class procedures in learning to construct both paragraph and topical outlines.

Markovin, B., "Growth through Speaking and Listening," *Elementary English*, Vol. 26 (March, 1949), pp. 129–131, 141.   Shows the value of active participation in well-planned activities in developing the foundation for effective language through speaking and listening.

Murphy, G., "We Also Learn by Listening," *Elementary English*, Vol. 26 (March, 1949), pp. 27–28.   Considers purposeful, accurate, critical, and responsive listening.

Perrin, P., "Teaching Realistic Grammar," *Elementary English*, Vol. 22 (February, 1945), pp. 41–45.   Discusses the teaching of grammar in the elementary school from a descriptive point of view. Lists some so-called grammatical errors that need more realistic treatment.

Pooley, R., "Contributions of Research to the Teaching of English," *English Journal*, Vol. 27 (April, 1948), pp. 170–175.   Indicates the influence of research on teaching of usage.

Risden, G., "What Is the Evidence?" *Childhood Education*, Vol. 27 (September, 1950), p. 24.   Gives examples of stimulation of thought in six-year-olds.

Seegars, J. C., and R. H. Seashore, "How Large Are Children's Vocabularies?" *Elementary English*, Vol. 26 (April, 1949), pp. 181–194.   Cites studies which question such widely held beliefs as that the initial vocabulary of school children is small, that the rate of growth is small, and that it is necessary to control carefully the nature and the number of new terms.

Wilt, M., "What Is the Listening Ratio in Your Classroom," *Elementary English*, Vol. 26 (May, 1949), pp. 259–264.

Winans, J. A., *Speech-making*, New York, Appleton-Century-Crofts, 1938, pp. 11–40.   Discusses the principles of delivery.

8 Discussion

Discussion is an integral part of classroom living. All day long children talk about questions of common interest. They plan their work. They prepare to go on a trip; they talk about it afterwards. They decide on a story to tell with puppets; they make arrangements for putting on the show before the school. They are finding answers to their own inquiries. This habit of discussion is an important fact in most elementary school classrooms. The spirit of inquiry, brought about by a willingness to talk things over freely, accounts in many cases for the successful management of a classroom.

DISCUSSION BY AN EIGHTH-GRADE GROUP

The story of a discussion of a problem by an eighth-grade group with about twenty-five members is typical of the discussions held in many classrooms. This eighth grade was in a type of private school, and its members were soon to leave to go to a public high school. This grade staged and produced the story of the Erie Canal, on which they worked long and hard. Some of the students did the dancing; others, the choral speaking; others, the singing; and still others, the acting. Several student teachers in music worked with the children and played some of the parts which needed mature characterizations. Together the music student teachers and the eighth graders planned and carried out the business organization, the printing of tickets, composition of the programs, and the designing and the construction of costumes and scenery. The eighth graders were proud of their accomplishment when the performance was over. As they counted their profits, they discovered that they had over $100. They had not anticipated a profit.

The question of what should be done with the money arose. Lanny, a particularly glib and persuasive child, immediately came to his feet and described what a wonderful dance they could give. He pictured an orchestra very like the one the college students of the town hired; he described punch and fancy cakes. Nan fell in immediately with the idea and proceeded to paint a still more glowing picture. She suggested that they invite boys and girls outside the class. Her final enthusiastic comment was that no eighth-grade class in the school had ever given a grown-up dance with a live orchestra.

At this point, the teacher called the attention of the students to the problem: the spending of $100. She indicated that they had offered just one solution: spending the money for a dance with a live orchestra. She asked them to investigate the problem more thoroughly and suggested they set up criteria by which to judge the proposals. A committee worked on this assignment and proposed that they should spend the money so that it would be satisfactory to all members, would bring prestige to the class, and would be a practicable expenditure. The members of the class agreed to these criteria.

Jane, one of the leaders of the group, posed another question, "Do we have a right to make a decision on the spending of the money by ourselves when our music student teachers helped us to earn it?"

For a while they considered whether they should invite the music student teachers to participate in the discussion. Jackie indicated that student teaching was required. Jane replied that they had, nevertheless, given much more of their time than was required in their student teaching. Harold claimed, a bit belligerently, "They like us; they don't care what we do with the money."

Jane responded with "Maybe they don't, but at least we should consult them."

The group went off on a tangent as to who had done more work, the student teachers or the eighth graders.

At this point, the teacher again summarized briefly, indicating that they had introduced another problem: Should the music student teachers who had helped with the work take part in deciding how to spend the money?

Helen said that they couldn't have put on the show without them; and, in addition, a matter of ethics was involved: the music student teachers had a right to take part in the decision. The group decided to invite the music student teachers to the classroom to participate in the solution of the problem. When the music student teachers came, the eighth graders told them that they followed certain rules in discussion. For example, they stated that they did not interrupt, that they did not monopolize but listened attentively, and that they were willing to consider points of view different from their own. They explained the criteria by which they were judging the proposals.

Again the floor was open for discussion. Lanny again depicted the glories of a big eighth-grade dance. Enthusiasm for a dance ran high. Helen, however, suggested that $100 was a lot of money to spend on a dance and that she felt they should give a gift to the school with it. She pointed out that other classes had given smaller gifts. Their gift would be an impressive one. In addition, she called their attention to the fact that they should be considering all solutions to the problem and not debating whether they should have a dance. The teacher asked Lanny and Helen to be patient and not to try to convert the members of the class to their views. She reminded them they were thinking the problem through cooperatively.

Some felt the gift was the wiser solution; some felt the dance was. Most of the children were thinking carefully and accurately. When their classmates discovered their reasoning was faulty, they pointed it out to them. Harold said that he didn't believe in giving gifts to a school; pretty soon the school would expect the members of the class to earn the teacher's salary. Mary pointed out that the first part of his argument was sound, that the school authorities and not the children should provide materials for a classroom. But she indicated that the second part, expecting the members of the class to earn the teacher's salary, was a little absurd. She remarked that, because she knew there were certain pieces of equipment the boys and girls in the classroom could profit from, she would be glad to see the money used for this purpose.

Mark said that he felt he owed a great deal to the school in that it had given him opportunities he wouldn't have had in another school. After he named some of them, he suggested that they use the money to buy equipment for the school. Johnny pointed out that Mark was appealing to the emotions of the group because they were leaving. He asked that this type of appeal be left out of the discussion. Again, the teacher summarized the advantages and disadvantages of both gift and dance. Shortly, it became obvious that the group was veering toward the purchase of a gift for the classroom. After considerable discussion, they finally arrived at a consensus: to spend the money for a gift—there was basis for action.

The next problem to be solved was: What gift should the eighth grade give the school? Someone suggested that a committee of the eighth graders and the music student teachers select it. Several members objected strenuously to this mode of operation. They declared that, because they had all shared in the making of the money, they wanted a share in its spending. One of the music student teachers suggested a playback machine combined with a radio and some records. Faye said that a playback machine was already available and they could borrow records from the music library. Jill pointed out that the borrowing of records presented a problem in that it involved a trip to another building. They discussed the advantage of having the use of the machine during the noon hour. They disagreed about costs, for which they did not have accurate information. This fact the teacher pointed out to them.

Another student suggested a wire recorder. The children examined this solution. Some of the children explained they already had the use of a tape recorder when they wished. Others felt they would like to have a machine more readily available so that they could record important speeches and musical events. Others noted that they often wouldn't be in school to record events when they were taking place. Someone suggested that they could record their discussions and analyze them afterwards. Others declared that, because they had already heard themselves, they knew what was wrong with their discussions.

Again the teacher summarized: this time she noted the advantages inherent in buying a playback and radio and those in buying a wire recorder. She suggested that they needed more accurate information as to the cost of the various machines and their effectiveness. A committee was appointed to go to the stores selling the equipment, to visit the audio-visual authority in the school, and to consult *Consumer's Guide* concerning values of the various pieces of equipment. Lanny went back to the advisability of giving a dance; at this, Jane called him on lacking courtesy and on obstructing group action. Because she did it tactfully, Lanny responded quickly to the suggestion.

With the information obtained by the committee, the children at a later date discussed the possible gift: a radio and playback or a wire recorder. They decided on the radio and playback.

DISCUSSION BY A THIRD-GRADE GROUP

To illustrate that discussion is an integral part of a classroom, the story of third graders who trimmed their Christmas tree with mittens follows:

The project started when Johnny brought to school a small poster gaily decorated with a mitten tree. After he had read to the class the poem that told about the tree's being in the garden of Snow Suit Town on the shore of the Stocking Cap Sea, he explained that the tree held as many mittens as it could. Discussion, for the purpose of pooling information, then took place. The children were interested in the tree, who sponsored it, and what happened to the mittens. They learned that the American Friends Service Committee had initiated the idea and that the mittens were sent to children in Austria, France, Germany, Finland, Japan, Korea, and Italy. They found out that during the war a great many sheep had been killed and that factories where wool is made into yarn had been destroyed. These children in foreign lands, therefore, needed warm mittens.

Later in the morning, Sandra told the story *Paddy's Christmas*. The children discussed the concept of "being happy from the inside out" and related this idea to the Christmas spirit. The notion of the mitten tree reasserted itself. The children agreed that knowing the mittens were going to keep the hands of children in other lands warm would make them happy from the inside out. After the children discussed the rather abstract idea and its meaning, they translated it into specific action, for they felt a mitten tree would make them feel happy from the inside out.

Since they had chosen to undertake the project, several problems for discussion immediately presented themselves: (1) How could they enlist the help of their parents? (2) How could they earn money to buy the yarn or mittens? As they talked over the first problem, they decided that they would write a letter to their parents to tell them about the project. They first discussed what the letter should include. These items they wrote on the blackboard. Then they dictated the letter to their teacher, examined its content, revised, and reworded it until it satisfied all of them.

The following day the children attacked the second problem, how to raise money for the mittens. They decided on these solutions: a popcorn sale, a cookie and cake sale, selling old newspapers, and putting on a puppet show for the first two grades. They discussed other means, but they decided that these were the most satisfactory ones in the light of the amount of time they had, their own capabilities, and the help they could expect to get from those outside their classroom. Each of these activities involved discussion on how to initiate them and how to carry them through. For example, the children talked about how to get cookies for their cookie sale. They agreed to make some themselves and to ask their mothers for others. However, they felt that adding an additional chore to their mothers' burdens was unfair if they did not relieve them in some way. They settled on taking care of a younger brother or sister, doing dishes, dusting, or in some other way lightening their mothers' work. Their projects were successful, for they made $9.30 from the popcorn, $14.40 from the cookies, $2.00 from the sale of old newspapers, and $1.00 from their puppet show.

FIG. 20. The mitten tree. (*Neil Croom, University State Teachers College, New Paltz, N.Y.*)

The last discussion was concerned with the purchasing of their tree and mittens. They talked over the kind of tree they wanted, how much they would spend for it, and where they would go to shop for it. The requirements for the tree were set up: (1) It must be tall and straight. (2) Its shape must be pretty. (3) It must have thick branches. They arrived at these three after considering many other criteria. They decided three were enough, for they did not have enough money to be too particular. After a careful consideration of the problem of buying mittens, they decided to ask two of the mothers to do it for them because they realized that they did not have available the necessary time or transportation. The projects progressed smoothly because the teacher and the children used discussion (1) to pool their information and (2) to solve the problems involved.

DEFINITION

Group discussion is cooperative conversation by members of a group who are sharing information and opinions on a topic or who are finding solutions to a problem under the guidance of one of their members. This definition emphasizes that discussion serves two purposes: (1) to pool information and (2) to hunt for and find the answer to a problem. Children may study various aspects of a topic and present these aspects to the group through discussion. The third graders learned about the mitten tree through questioning the one boy who knew. Children may have run into a problem: the eighth graders' problem was how to spend the $100 that they had earned. When children search for the answer, they define and analyze the problem, discover its available solutions, and determine which solution they consider best and how they could put it to work. For example, the third graders considered a number of ways to earn money to buy mittens. Both in pooling information and in hunting for a solution to a problem, children are thinking together. They may not agree; but when they discuss a problem, they consider the solutions in terms of the good of the group. The eighth graders did not agree on their solution at first; but, as they analyzed the problem and thought it through, they arrived at a decision. "Cooperative conversation" means that the members are participating actively in terms of listening, thinking about the problem or the topic, and contributing their thought to the group. Both the eighth graders and the third graders were working hard to solve their problems. "Under the guidance of one of their members" implies that one of the students or the teacher is helping the discussion to move forward. In both examples mentioned, the teacher was the leader.

TYPES OF DISCUSSION

In the chapter on Giving Talks, the problem of conservation provided topics for speaking. When the children and the teacher investigated conservation, they discovered that they needed more information.

Therefore, they planned their reading and reporting. The giving of reports took the form of discussion, used to impart information. After they had acquired the information, they felt that, through their talking with experts and through their reading, they should decide which solutions to particular problems were better than others. They wished to acquaint members of their audience with various points of view. Again the form was discussion; in this case, both sides of the question were presented, and the purpose was an analysis to help in policy determination. In one case, the purpose was to impart information and, in the other, to present the various solutions of the problem. The discussions took various forms: a round table, panel discussion, dialogue, symposium, and lecture-forum.

ROUND TABLE

Members of the class and the teacher planned together the work on conservation. They decided on the necessary trips, the people to be invited to the classroom, and the activities of the class that would carry out the planned work. They arrived at decisions through discussion. Members of the class worked together to analyze and solve the problem and to evaluate the solutions. In round-table discussions, a fairly large number of members talk together under the direction of a leader. In both examples given, the discussions were round-table ones with all members of the class participating. This type is used most frequently in the classroom.

PANEL DISCUSSION

Six members of the class studied tree farming; they discovered what it involved and how it operated. They discussed their findings as a group. They made no set speeches when they presented the requirements to their listeners. The listeners were permitted to question the group to help them understand what tree farming involved. In panel discussion, four to eight members talk together before an audience to give various aspects of the problem or topic under the direction of a leader. The talks are followed by a question-and-answer period.

DIALOGUE

John, who probably knew more than the rest of the class about conservation, questioned the forest ranger. The members of the class participated at the end of the hour. Dialogue is the questioning of an expert by a skillful person. The listeners may later ask questions of the leader or the expert.

SYMPOSIUM

The children held a symposium on the prevention of forest fires. Five children prepared speeches on the work of the forest ranger, education of the public, prevention through legislation, work of the junior forest ranger, and necessary care by individuals who enter the forests. The chairman introduced each speaker, announced his topic, and later conducted a question-and-answer period. In a symposium, individuals introduced by the discussion leader give speeches; the chairman later conducts a question-and-answer period.

FORUM

The forum is the conducting of a meeting using the types of discussion as indicated earlier. The first part usually consists of the presentation of the problem and its solutions through panel, dialogue, symposium, or lecture form. The second part consists of questioning by the listeners.

In no case will the teacher teach the form of discussion as such. However, as he sees opportunities where a particular type of discussion will prove useful in the management of pooling information or solving a problem, he tells the group. For example, the eighth-grade teacher recognized that the symposium would be a good form for the discussion of the prevention of forest fires.

VALUES OF DISCUSSION IN POOLING INFORMATION
TEACHES THE INDIVIDUAL RESPONSIBILITY FOR ACQUIRING INFORMATION

When a child knows he is responsible for collecting information for the entire class, he does it more carefully and thoroughly. He realizes that the group is dependent on him for information about a certain topic or area. He will, therefore, search for it in as many sources as possible and, with the help of his teacher, will do his investigation systematically.

ALLOWS THE CHILD TO FOLLOW HIS OWN INTERESTS

When a child is particularly interested in an area, he is given an opportunity to go into it more thoroughly. He receives information in other areas from other members of the class. For example, one child studying conservation had a particular interest in tree farming because he had visited his uncle's tree farm. Therefore, he read widely in the area of tree farming, profited from his reading, and imparted worthwhile information to his classmates.

EXPEDITES SHARING OF INFORMATION ALREADY AVAILABLE

Sometimes children already have at hand information they can share through discussion. The boy who knew more about the mitten tree exemplifies this situation. The third-grade children also shared their information and feelings about the Christmas spirit. In one sixth-grade class, twelve different children had visited Niagara Falls. The collective information of all twelve was information useful to the group and easily and readily obtained.

VALUES OF DISCUSSION OF PROBLEMS

Group discussion of problems has two primary values: (1) it promotes careful, exact thinking on the part of the group, and (2) it furthers better human relationships among members of the group.

PROMOTES CAREFUL, EXACT THINKING

Children collect all possible evidence before they make judgments. They learn the importance of facts as a basis for evaluating a solution. Children not only gather the necessary information from available and reliable sources but they judge its worth. Facts are not useful unless they serve a purpose. Equally important, then, are the ideas about the question formulated from the facts. The group examines the ideas carefully, thinks critically about them. From this examination, they decide the best answer to the question and decide on a policy. Ideally, the children have been thinking carefully and accurately and have been aware of the processes of thinking of their classmates.

In the discussion by the eighth graders, Harold stated that, if the group started buying equipment for the school, soon it would be expected to pay the teacher's salary. One of the eighth graders rebuked Harold for his statement by pointing out that, whereas the first part of the statement was true, the deduction was not. Another child's attention was called to the fact that he was making undue use of emotion in appealing to the group in terms of what the school had done for its members. In other words, the children were learning to think more carefully and to reason more accurately.

DEVELOPS BETTER HUMAN RELATIONSHIPS IN THE GROUP

The participant in a group discussion learns about other people, how they act, and how they react. A group discussion is an excellent place to observe how people get along with others. Some teachers have used discussion as a means of studying interpersonal relations. This writing deals with the more formal approach: the use of discussion as a means of getting people who believe differently to talk together and to arrive at understanding. It places a premium on group deliberation. Each member has a chance to state his opinion. No one dominates. By developing habits of cooperative, reflective thinking, it makes participants aware of obstacles to group thinking like prejudice and dogmatic statements. Some boys and girls change their minds as they consider the problem more carefully or as they find out new facts. When they arrive at a decision, all assent to it. Students learn to accept the results of democratic action.

In the eighth-grade classroom, all its members were seeing democracy work. Lanny, the glib, talkative child, learned that some students held opinions different from his and that the group attached significance to what others said. He began to understand that he must carefully examine opinions expressed by others. As one child debated rather than discussed the issues, an alert child called his debating to his attention. He responded quickly to her suggestion. Although many of the boys and girls had originally wanted to have a dance, they decided to buy equipment after they had considered the problem. Finally, as they arrived at a decision, all assented to it. Admittedly, Lanny was disappointed, for his enthusiasm for the dance had run high, but he accepted the decision gracefully. They were learning to live with their group in a democratic society.

LIMITATIONS OF DISCUSSION OF PROBLEMS

DISCUSSION IS SLOW

Action cannot always await the result of group discussion. Admittedly, times exist when a teacher must make a decision quickly and when the decision is his responsibility. Occasionally, in the deliberation of a problem, both the teacher and the brighter students will be impatient with the group. Group discussion needs time to find the necessary facts, to discover and understand different viewpoints, and to resolve possible conflict. The value of group deliberation claimed for discussion is also one of its weaknesses. General participation means the inclusion of students with mediocre minds and limited ability to express themselves. At times, the slow minds help to make group discussion confused and dull. The alternative to group discussion is for the teacher to make all decisions. This more dictatorial method moves rapidly and efficiently, but today's children are to live in a democracy and not in an authoritarian state. The discussion of the eighth-grade problem was slow; its narration is telescoped here. Actually, it consumed several hours. At one point, it ceased until the group found out more about prices of various pieces of equipment. Nevertheless, each child was happy that he had had a chance to participate in making the decision.

DISCUSSION APPEARS TO LACK ORDER

Discussion to some seems to lack order. Reflective thinking is not always orderly, sure, and definite. It follows no prescribed pattern; for example, it cannot be fitted into a syllogism. Individual reflective processes do not progress clearly toward an objective. They move by fits and starts, retract themselves, sometimes move down one-way streets. Therefore, reflective thinking of the group moves in a similar way. Group discussion does not pretend to be a finished performance of thought. Admittedly, many speaking situations do not call for discussion; for example, the political rally discussed in the chapter on assemblies had as its purpose moving the students to action. Discussion does not belong in such a program. The thinking involved in discussion is problem solving.

TOPICS FOR DISCUSSION

Not all topics provide valuable experiences. Certain requirements for discussion exist: (1) The discussion topic should be within the range of experiences of members of the group. (2) It should be concerned with a problem that is important to the group. It may be a problem of the classroom, community, or nation that needs solving. (3) It should be controversial, except where group discussion is used as a technique to impart information to others. (4) It should serve, as far as possible, as a basis for planning the activities of the classroom.

INFLUENCE OF EXPERIENCE OF THE GROUP

The topic should be within the range of the group's experience. The problem of the eighth graders as to what to do with $100 which grew out of a school experience was a good one for group discussion. The problem of how to earn money for the mittens emerged from the desire of the third graders for a mitten tree. Both questions were well within the range of the experience of the individuals of the groups. Another eighth grade had been studying motion pictures. Because they had seen several foreign films, one of the class suggested a discussion on the topic of whether foreign films were better than American films. After exploring the topic a little, the boys and girls decided that their experiences with foreign films were so narrow that they could not discuss the problem intelligently. This suggestion for discussion, even though it grew out of curricular work, was a poor one because the children were too limited in their experience.

IMPORTANCE TO THE GROUP

The topic should be based on a problem that is important to the group discussing it. The discussion of spending the $100 carried meaning to the members of the eighth grade, for they had made the money and wanted to be sure they had a voice in its spending. The boys and girls of a third grade discussed what kind of Christmas party to have, whom to invite, the type of entertainment to offer, and what refreshments to serve. This topic was significant to the members of the group discussing it. A fourth grade discussed the rerouting of traffic through their town. The existing routing interfered with the play activities of some of the children; a proposed routing threatened the play of others. Because many of the children were directly involved, the problem was important to the group.

CONTROVERSIAL NATURE OF THE TOPIC

Thirdly, the topic should be controversial unless its purpose is to impart information. The spending of $100 by the eighth graders had several possibilities. The problem of how to earn money to buy mittens had a number of solutions. The discussion question should be one capable of being answered in several ways.

On the other hand, members of a class use discussion to impart information. For example, a second-grade group was studying trains. After the children had read several books on trains and had visited the railroad station and the roundhouse, they discussed what they had read and seen. The responsibilities of the conductor and the different kinds of trains were typical items of information brought out through group discussion. Members of the group investigate different phases of the problem, discover the needed material, and report to the group by means of discussion.

BASIS FOR PLANNING CLASSROOM ACTIVITIES

Lastly, children plan their work through discussion. When they plan a trip, they discuss when to go, how to go, how to be safe and courteous while on the trip, how to get permission to visit certain places, and what to ask when they get there. They make use of group discussion to plan such classroom activities as the kind of assembly program to produce. The third graders mentioned earlier planned putting on their puppet show, running their cake sale, and purchasing of their Christmas tree. Where children use group discussion for such a purpose, it teaches democracy well.

DISCUSSING A PROBLEM

In group discussion of a problem, there are five steps:

1. Locating and defining the problem. Is there a real problem? Is it important? How can we state or define it?
2. Analyzing the problem. Is it new or old? How did it develop? How big is it? What are its causes and effects? Why must we do something about it? On what basis can we judge the solutions?
3. Examining suggested solutions. What are the solutions? Who suggested them? Do they have axes to grind? Has any one tried any of the suggested solutions? What would be their effects? What are the advantages and disadvantages of each solution?
4. Selecting the best solution. What seems best for us?
5. Putting the solution to work. What can we do to put it to work? How can we best put it to work?

Children in all grades proceed through the five steps. In the early grades the teacher does not talk in terms of analyzing the problem. Rather, he asks questions. The following questions asked of the third-grade group when it attacked the problem of finding ways to earn money are typical:

1. How can we earn money to pay for mittens for the mitten tree? This question states the problem.
2. What have we done before to earn money? How much do we need? How quickly must we earn it? These questions analyze the problem.
3. What are the ways in which we can earn money? Who would do the work in each of the ways? These questions locate possible solutions.
4. Which are the best ways for us to earn money? This question leads to a tentative conclusion.
5. How can we start and carry through the projects to earn money? This question suggests ways of putting the solution to work.

The eighth-grade group followed the five steps enumerated above.

STATING THE PROBLEM

The situation of the eighth graders became one of discussion only after the teacher stepped in with the suggestion that the children investigate the problem to see whether there weren't other possible solutions. Up to that point, the speaking situation was a persuasive one in which Lanny and Nan were advocating a particular line of action. Had the teacher not entered the picture here, the discussion might have been around the following topic: What kind of party shall the eighth-grade group have? After the teacher intercepted the ball, the definition of the problem in this instance seemed obvious: What should the eighth-grade group do with the unexpected profit of $100? But the word "should" in the question needed defining. If the children had talked about its meaning in this instance, the discussion might have been more fruitful.

ANALYZING THE PROBLEM

The group had $100 in its treasury which it had earned and which it wanted to spend. The criteria by which the members of the class were to judge the problem were revealing. Two were obvious: that they spend the money to bring satisfaction to the group and in such a way as to be most practicable in the school. The third, that they spend it to bring prestige to the class, posed a problem. None of the students questioned this statement. Should the leader have provoked discussion on this point? or was she giving evidence of objective leadership in accepting it?

EXAMINING POSSIBLE SOLUTIONS

There were two solutions: (1) to spend the money for a dance and (2) to spend it for a gift to the school. The discussion of the two solutions showed a combination of maturity of thought and childlike notions. The children's desire to emulate their elders in giving a dance and their idea that the gift would be a kind of memorial to them are indexes of characteristics of the group. The students showed maturity in detecting false reasoning in their examination of the solutions. Harold was not allowed to get by with the overstatement "Pretty soon they will expect us to pay the teachers' salaries." As another child emotionalized the argument by saying that they should give the school a gift because of what it had done for them, a boy pointed out he was appealing to their affection for the school. When another lad said that most eighth-grade classes have a recording machine in their rooms, he was asked to support his statement. Since he knew of only two, his generalization was a bit hasty. One of the girls noted this hasty generalization. They examined the two possible solutions carefully.

SELECTING THE BEST SOLUTION

Their reasons for their choice of giving a gift again showed adolescent attitudes. They felt that they would be remembered kindly, that the gift would serve as a "memorial" to their class, that it would give their class prestige in the school community, and, finally, that it would avoid parental criticism of their trying to be too grown-up. Some of the children wanted to have the dance just for the reason that it was a "grown-up activity."

PUTTING THE SOLUTION TO WORK

A committee was formed to investigate which piece of equipment was the better buy. The committee was to consult with the audio-visual expert in the school and the printed sources containing recommendations of buying audio equipment. It was then to present a report to the group for action.

BEHAVIOR OF THE GROUP IN THE DISCUSSION OF A PROBLEM

During a child's elementary school years, when he learns to converse actively, he observes the codes of courtesy. Behavior that is effective in conversation is equally effective in group discussion. The good participant in either takes an active part without monopolizing, listens carefully, speaks only when he knows what he is talking about, and considers all points of view. Furthermore, he sticks to the subject and feels responsible for carrying forward either the conversation or discussion.

TAKING AN ACTIVE PART WITHOUT MONOPOLIZING

The child takes part but he does not monopolize. If he learns in the lower grades to take his turn, to give other members a chance to play with a certain object, and to share, he will be more likely to be a good participant in discussion. When he realizes early in his school career that he has a definite part but cannot do all the talking, he is learning a lesson in good human relationships which will serve him throughout his life.

LISTENING CRITICALLY

Members of a discussion group listen to each other attentively. Critical listening is a part of analytical thinking and careful, prepared speaking. The child will be an active listener. He is analyzing what the speaker says as he talks, examining the speech for defective reasoning, and accepting new ideas and new information. Even though most participants are silent most of the time, they respond actively to what is said. Somewhat linked to active listening is the child's waiting patiently to question someone's analysis. The good conversationalist does not interrupt but waits quietly until the speaker finishes. The effective member of a group discussion also bides his time. He keeps his thoughts until the chairman recognizes him. He shows respect for the opinions of others.

SPEAKING BASED ON KNOWLEDGE AND BACKGROUND OF THE PROBLEM

Before the children attack a problem, they gather the necessary information. They attend lectures, make reports on readings, visit institutions, and inquire of the authorities in their areas who are available. They not only collect the material but also assimilate and organize it. As far as they are able, they evaluate it. They examine it to see whether it is clear, whether it is consistent, whether the sources are reliable. Older children ask such questions about the authority as the following: Is he biased? Did he have all the facts? Is he qualified in terms of character and intellect to serve as an authority? They make sure that they have read both sides of a controversial question so that they can see the whole problem clearly.

The discussion participant does not speak until he has completed this preparation. Furthermore, he thinks before he speaks. He does not talk merely to gain the floor. On the other hand, he does not think so long that the group is on the next step while he is still preparing to speak on the last. Many children respond too quickly and without sufficient information; others wait too long and prepare what they have to say too thoroughly.

CONSIDERATION OF ALL POINTS OF VIEW

The child does not close his mind to a point of view different from his own. As he considers the points of view of others and analyzes their positions carefully, he will keep his mind open and is willing to change it. He does not make statements like "Everybody knows that." When he finds the group opposed to his opinion or his course of action, he acquiesces gracefully and does what he can to help them in the solution they have chosen. Many of these attitudes he has learned in living with others in the classroom in the lower grades. In other words, he adjusts to the group. The best adjustment comes from a genuine respect for himself and for the others in the group.

KEEPING DISCUSSION RELEVANT

He does not make irrelevant comments or distract the discussion from the main issues. When he discovers the discussion veering from the main issues, he reminds the group of the principles or problems they are talking about. Even though a comment shows him as brilliant, witty, or very wise, he refrains from making it unless it furthers the solution of the problem.

SHARING GROUP RESPONSIBILITY

Lastly, he assumes his share of group responsibility. He does not sit back and let the others make the decisions. He listens actively, thinks critically, and adds his bit to the group deliberation when it is needed. He feels a need to be part of the thinking of the group.

HELPING THE CHILD BE AN EFFECTIVE MEMBER OF THE GROUP

The teacher helps the child be an effective member of a discussion group. In his talk with the child who has a tendency to monopolize, he helps him to see that he is not being quite fair to the other members of the group. By skillful questioning, he helps the child to listen critically. He commends the child who shows he has listened well. He encourages the child to find out all he can about the problem by bringing material to class, by suggesting other sources, and by motivating the group to take trips and to speak with those who know about the topic. By his own attitude and by a reminder, "Let's hear all sides of the question," he furthers consideration of all points of view. "Let's stick to the point," "Let's stay with the issue," or "That idea doesn't belong" are phrases the children have learned from the teacher and ones that they use when needed. In all his work, he motivates each individual to be a responsible member of a group by comments of encouragement and by assignment.

FUNCTIONS OF THE LEADER

The leader as well as the participant has responsibilities in group discussion. He must keep the discussion moving forward, must keep it to the problem to be solved, and must develop in the participants attitudes of critical thinking. In order to solve the problem, he should make sure he fulfills the functions of a leader. He serves as a constructive guide who is helping each person do his own thinking and contribute to the group. There are several aspects to the problem of leadership in group discussion: promoting critical thinking, encouraging participation of all students, stating the problem, motivating the acquisition of necessary information, careful handling of conflict, and keeping order.

PROMOTION OF CRITICAL THINKING

The leader must keep the students thinking carefully. As their reasoning becomes careless, he skillfully questions to point out fallacies. For example, if a child generalizes on too few instances, the leader will ask him on what basis he is making his generalizations. When he uses language that is colored, slanted, or not exact, the leader will ask for the exact meaning. Or he will suggest giving an example. When the child makes an overstatement, the leader will say, "Lets examine that statement carefully a minute." If the child makes an unsubstantiated claim on the basis of statistics, the leader will say, "Where did you find your statistics?" He keeps the discussion to the issues, repeats them when necessary. Summarizing the discussion at intervals also helps indicate how far the discussion has gone and what form it has taken.

ENCOURAGING PARTICIPATON OF ALL STUDENTS

Part of the desire of all students to participate comes from an atmosphere conducive to discussion and to the clarification of issues. The atmosphere will be an inquiring, friendly one in which the group is striving to study all aspects of a problem and to reach a decision. The leader prevents domination by the more aggressive members and encourages the shy ones to participate. He may resort to calling on the quiet ones, asking for their contributions tactfully by questions such as "Do you agree with John, Mary?"

STATEMENT OF THE PROBLEM

The leader states the problem accurately and fairly. He defines it clearly and carefully. He may believe in a particular solution; nevertheless, he will abide by the consequences of the conclusion reached by the group. He does not superimpose his solution. He does not give weight to the solution he favors by calling on particular individuals or by coloring his summations.

FINDING FACTS

The leader should help to bring out all facts. If the group has set the stage for discussion by its assignment of readings and by the preparation of an outline for the discussion, inquiry is based on facts, and the solution on evidence.

HELPING THE DISCUSSION TO MOVE FORWARD

When the teacher is the leader, he helps the children to follow the traditional steps of discussion: (1) statement and definition of the problem, (2) analysis of the problem, (3) possible solutions, (4) tentative conclusions, and (5) suggestions for working out the chosen solution. Frequently, he achieves this organization through skillful questioning and summaries. When the child acts as a leader, the teacher and he frequently talk over questions he may ask before the discussion takes place.

TACTFUL HANDLING OF CONFLICT

The leader handles conflict tactfully. He will encourage students to make statements representative of different points of view, and he establishes an objective attitude toward them. Whenever reasoning is faulty, he does not react emotionally but questions clearly. The spirit is one of working together to find the best solution.

KEEPING ORDER

In conclusion, the leader keeps order. He requires that members of the group address the chair in formal discussion; in informal discussion, he asks that they wait their turn. He sees to it that one member does not always have the floor and that each has an equal chance. He promotes calm, friendly discussion, not heated argument.

Mary was chairman of the hobby committee. The group decided that they had many different and interesting hobbies which they would like to show others. Before Mary presided at the first meeting of the class, the teacher talked over with her the problems that would present them· selves. They included the following:

1. When would they have the show?
2. Whom would they invite?
3. How would they invite their guests?
4. Should they have a program?
5. Would they serve refreshments?
6. How many exhibits should they have?
7. Would they have rules for the kinds of exhibits?
8. How would they set up their exhibits?

The teacher and she also talked about how she would encourage all her classmates to participate, how she would keep order, and how she would handle her classmates during the discussion.

TALKING OVER DISCUSSION

Children should talk over their classroom discussion of problems, for when the discussion is merely a "bull session," its utility is decreased. To make sure that discussions serve a purpose, that the leader has been effective, and that the children have participated successfully and constructively, they make a list of questions to be asked members of the group. Different age groups ask different questions. The following are questions asked by an eighth-grade group:

1. Did each boy and girl understand the problem?
2. Did each boy and girl contribute either information or a comment which helped solve the problem?
3. Did each member react constructively to criticism?
4. Did he listen attentively and critically?
5. Did he keep clearly in mind the purpose of the discussion?
6. Did he cooperate with other members and with the leader?
7. Did he wait for recognition by the chair?
8. Did he reason carefully and analyze his classmate's reasoning?
9. Did he state his opinion honestly but impersonally?
10. Did he state facts accurately?
11. Did he speak clearly, distinctly, and audibly?
12. Did he communicate with his audience?

Concerning the leader, they asked as follows:

1. Did he help the group feel comfortable?
2. Did he state the problem accurately?
3. Did he encourage all members to participate?
4. Did he offer accurate summaries along the way?
5. Did he handle conflict tactfully?
6. Did he help to keep the discussion progressing?
7. Did he offer a good summary and conclusion?

About the group, they asked as follows:

1. Did it understand all facets of the problem?
2. Did it collect the necessary information?
3. Did it cooperate with the leader?
4. Was its group spirit one of united inquiry?
5. Did it arrive at a satisfactory conclusion or solution of the problem?

Younger children talk over their discussion more simply. The following are questions asked by members of a fifth grade:

1. Did we speak without raising our hands?
2. Did we interrupt?
3. Did we stick to the point?
4. Did we think before we spoke?
5. Did we learn as much as we could about our problem before we started talking about it?
6. Did we listen to others carefully?
7. Did we cooperate with each other and the leader?
8. Did we speak loudly and clearly?

A careful evaluation of discussion from time to time points up accurate thinking through of problems.

DEBATE

Throughout the chapter, the advantages of discussion have been emphasized. It is democratic and cooperative. It is reflective, a process where thought takes form. It applies system to solving a problem. It respects the opinion of each individual. But what if the members of the eighth grade had not agreed on giving equipment to the school? If Lanny and some of his classmates had stuck firmly to their initial position of having a dance, an impasse would have occurred. The members of the group could not have discussed the issues forever; a decision had to be made. The problem was not a theoretical one where the children could have agreed that differences existed and that each member had a right to his own opinion. Instead, the problem was a practical one that needed a decision. Had an impasse occurred, the teacher would have had two alternatives: (1) to settle the problem herself or (2) to suggest debate. Debate is preferable to dictatorship since it is the way of democracy.

Debate is the presentation of argument between two groups who represent positions in opposition to each other. In the instance of the eighth graders, one side would have presented arguments for having a dance; the other, for not having the dance. After each side had presented its case, the decision would have been made by voting. Debate usually occurs under parliamentary procedure. The motion is made and then debated. Sometimes the group modifies its stand and compromises. The majority rules. The United States Congress, the state legislatures, faculty meetings, and student council meetings represent places where debate occurs and where decisions are made through voting.

The teacher prefers cooperative discussion, but he realizes that times exist when members of the group will not agree. In such cases he encourages them to present the arguments for each side as effectively as they can and then to vote. The minority abides by the decision of the majority.

SUMMARY

Group discussion is cooperative conversation by members of a group who are sharing information and opinions on a topic or who are finding solutions to a problem under the guidance of one of their members. The types of group discussion are: round table, panel discussion, dialogue, symposium, lecture-forum, and forum.

The topics for group discussion should grow out of in-school or out-of-school experiences of the members of the group, should be important to the group, and should, as far as possible, serve as a basis for the planning of activities of the class. Topics are of two kinds: (1) those that impart information and (2) those that solve problems. Each has its place in education.

The values of group discussion in imparting information are as follows: (1) It teaches the individual respect for information. (2) It allows a child to follow his own interests. (3) It expedites the sharing of information already available. The values of group discussion of a problem are the following: (1) It promotes careful, exact thinking on the part of the group. (2) It furthers better human relationships among members of the group.

Discussion of a problem involves defining and locating the problem, analyzing it, examining suggestions for its solutions carefully, selecting the best solution, and finding out how to put the solution to work. Members of the group will prepare for discussion by gathering all the available information and by testing the information for its clarity and accuracy. The teacher, through skillful questioning, encourages the children to follow the steps of discussion mentioned above.

Participants observe the codes of courtesy for conversation. They take part but do not monopolize; they listen attentively and critically. They do not interrupt and speak only when they have sufficient knowledge and background to support their statements. They are objective and consider points of view different from their own. They keep within the realm of the discussion problem and assume their share of group responsibility.

The leader keeps the students thinking carefully and aids in the participation of all members. He states the problem clearly and accurately and summarizes when necessary. He handles conflict tactfully and does what he can to see that the problem is discussed from all angles. The children talk about the discussion to determine whether the members have participated constructively, whether the leader has been effective, and whether the group has benefited from the discussion.

The teacher prefers cooperative discussion, but when children cannot make up their collective mind, debate is the preferable way of solving the problem. It is the presentation of argument between two groups who represent positions in opposition to each other. It usually occurs under parliamentary procedure. The motion is made, debated, and voted on. Sometimes it is amended or changed before the final vote is taken. The majority rules.

EXERCISES

1. List questions that might be discussed in the grade you plan to teach.

2. Hold a round-table discussion on the following topic: Are elementary school children given enough opportunity to solve the problems of their own classrooms?

3. Analyze the discussion at the beginning of the chapter from the viewpoint of the leader's role in the discussion.

4. Indicate ways in which the leader might have changed the course of this discussion.

5. Read the chapter on reasoning in one of the texts on discussion and show how the discussion of reasoning by adults is applicable to children's discussion.

6. Show how discussion could be used during a typical school day's program in the grade you plan to teach. Be specific.

7. Show how discussion could be used to plan the work of the grade you intend to teach. Be specific.

BIBLIOGRAPHY

SOURCES FOR FURTHER READING

Baird, A. A., *Argumentation, Discussion and Debate*, New York, McGraw-Hill, 1950. Gives the theory and principles of discussion. Indicates the differences between discussion and debate.

Baker, H. V., *Children's Contributions in Elementary School General Discussion*, Child Development Monographs, No. 29, New York, Teachers College, Columbia University, 1942. Reveals the contributions of children to general class discussions in grades 2, 4, and 6 in three schools of different socioeconomic levels in New York City.

Beery, A., "Experience—the Source of Communication," *Childhood Education*, Vol. 27 (February, 1951), pp. 278–281. Shows how common experiences foster discussion and illustrates how discussion grows out of in-school experiences.

Bowden, F. B., "Conversation and Discussion in the Elementary School," *Elementary English Review*, Vol. 24 (May, 1947), pp. 293–302. Discusses stimulation of, and topics for, conversation and discussion.

Bryson, L., "The Limits of Discussion," *Journal of Adult Education*, Vol. 9 (June, 1937), pp. 260–264.

Dewey, J., *How We Think*, Boston, Heath, 1933, Chaps. 1, 2, 5, 6. Discusses the process and product of thought and the steps in reflective thinking.

Ewbank, H. L., and J. J. Auer, "Decision Making: Discussion and Debate," *Bulletin of Secondary School Principals*, Vol. 32 (January, 1948), pp. 34–39. Gives principles of discussion; reveals the difference between discussion and debate.

———, *Handbook for Discussion Leaders*, New York, Harper, 1947. Contains the principles and methods of group discussion.

Hatfield, W., *An Experience Curriculum in English*, Report of the National Council of Teachers of English, New York, Appleton-Century-Crofts, 1935, pp. 144–147, 170–173. Notes objectives for discussion. Lists techniques to be acquired.

McBurney, J. H., and K. G. Hance, *The Principles and Methods oj Discussion*, New York, Harper, 1939. Contains the phases of understanding, preparing, and participating in discussion.

McMillan, M., "Panel Discussions in the Upper Grades," *The Grade Teacher*, Vol. 65 (January, 1948), p. 57. Covers the preparation and techniques of panel discussion.

Murphy, G., "We Also Learn by Listening," *Elementary English*, Vol. 26 (March, 1949), pp. 127–128. Treats purposeful, accurate, critical, and responsive listening.

Roths, L. E., "Improving Classroom Discussion," *Education Research Bulletin*, Vol. 24 (January, 1945), pp. 6–13. Outlines the requirements of the problem to be discussed by children. Includes questions to ask concerning the techniques and values of discussion.

Thomas, O., "Discussion: Let's Have More of It," *School Executive*, Vol. 69 (August, 1950), pp. 51–53. Shows the necessity of discussion directed by teachers who understand the problem in the classroom to promote leadership and a better citizenry.

Thouless, R., *Straight and Crooked Thinking*, New York, Simon and Schuster, 1932. Indicates the obstacles to reflective thinking.

Utterback, W. E., *Group Thinking and Conference Leadership*, New York, Rinehart, 1950. Includes methods of group discussion.

Wagner, R. H., and C. C. Arnold, *Handbook of Group Discussion*, Boston, Houghton Mifflin, 1950.

9 Conducting a Meeting

As boys and girls work and play together, they frequently organize into a club. They write and adopt a constitution; they elect officers; they propose action. Their action may have to do with arrangements for playing football or going on a picnic. They use parliamentary procedure to bring order, system, and justice to the settlement of these problems.

VALUES OF PARLIAMENTARY PROCEDURE

Parliamentary procedure is logical; it applies common sense to getting business transacted easily and quickly. When a child learns the rules of parliamentary procedure as he needs them, he sees why they make sense. They are logical, for their purpose is to expedite business. For example, all argument must relate to the motion on the floor. If a member introduces extraneous matter, he is ruled out of order. Because the members attack one subject at a time, they must organize their thinking around one topic. The orderliness of the procedure aids them in getting their problems solved more efficiently.

In addition, parliamentary procedure provides for the full and fair democratic expression of the opinions of every member of the assemblage. Advocates of both sides of an issue have a chance to make their choices of action known and to give their reasons for their judgments. The assemblage debates the question as long as it desires. Parliamentary procedure protects the rights of each individual to participate in the meeting. Through discussion of the motion and the use of subsidiary and incidental motions, the minority makes its voice felt. But the majority rules and votes for what it decides is best. This procedure is the essence of democracy.

USE OF PARLIAMENTARY PROCEDURE
IN THE ELEMENTARY SCHOOL

Just how much parliamentary procedure can be taught in the elementary school? If children use its form consistently in their meetings from the third grade on, they may be using all the motions listed on page 211 by the time they are in the eighth grade. The learning will have been a gradual process based on the needs of the group in its meetings. Probably no group below the third grade uses parliamentary procedure.

A third-grade group can organize into a club and the children usually enjoy it. Often they ask for it, for their parents are members of the Rotary, Kiwanis, Lions, and Garden Clubs. When they are prepared for it, they choose a president carefully. They select a member who is fair, takes his responsibility seriously, and shows the qualities of leadership. Parliamentary procedure governs the election. Third graders can write simple constitutions. They can introduce business in the form of motion. The children arise, address their president as "Mr. President," and wait to be recognized. They use the words "I move that . . . " to get their business on the floor. Many times they like the formality of parliamentary procedure.

In each successive grade, the boys and girls learn more of the forms. Many eighth-grade members would shame their parents as parliamentarians. It is important that parliamentary procedure be taught in terms of its usefulness in all grades. For example, a child may say during a meeting, "I'd like to change that motion. Why can't we go on the picnic Thursday rather than Tuesday?" The teacher explains that parliamentary procedure takes care of the discussion of this change by "amending the motion." He tells the children how to do it. The motion is meaningful to the child, for he has learned it through the actual transaction of the business of the class.

THE FOURTH-GRADE GROUP ORGANIZES A BIRD CLUB

The fourth-grade group became interested both in identifying birds and in recognizing their calls. They got up at 5:30 to go on bird hunts. They ordered records to listen to the calls the different birds made. They kept a bulletin board on which they posted the names and pictures of birds that the members of the group saw. For a while for those children birds were their principal interest.

One day, Jeffrey suggested that the members of the class form a bird club. They were delighted with the suggestion and they talked first about the name of their club. They decided to call themselves the Whatsit Bird Club because they so frequently asked, when they saw or heard a bird, "What is it?" Next they talked about who should belong to their club. They agreed to include all the members of their own class and considered asking some of the fifth graders who were interested in birds. But they decided against inviting any outsiders. The next question they asked was "What shall we do as a club?" They chose to take care of the bird bulletin board, to make birdhouses, to go on bird walks, and, generally, to learn more about birds. They decided to meet once a week. Finally, they elected officers: a president, a vice-president, a secretary, and a bulletin-board carer. They did not plan on using money for any activity; therefore, they dispensed with a treasurer.

When the children elected officers, they already knew the phrase "I nominate Jerry." They also selected "counters" to count the votes. Each time the counters announced who had received the most votes. They did not know about closing nominations. This bit of procedure the teacher taught them.

The teacher also suggested that they write down the name of their club and the decisions they had made about it. He said that this material was called a constitution. He further advised that a committee selected by the president undertake this task. The children already knew how committees functioned, for they did much of their work through committees. The committee wrote this constitution, and the teacher suggested that they head each different item *Article* and number them in order:

THE WHATSIT BIRD CLUB

Article 1

Members of our fourth grade belong to the Whatsit Bird Club.

Article 2

We will learn the names and calls of more birds, make birdhouses, go on bird walks, and keep a bulletin board on birds.

Article 3

Our officers are a president, a vice-president, a secretary, and a bulletin-board carer.

Article 4

Our club will meet at two o'clock Friday afternoons in our classroom.

The committee learned some of the fundamentals of writing a constitution: inclusion of the club's name, its purpose, listing of its officers, and naming the meeting time and place.

Before the second meeting, the teacher and the president talked over procedure. Jeffrey and he agreed he would follow this order:

1. We will begin our meeting.
2. The secretary will tell us what happened at our last meeting.
3. The constitution committee will tell us about the constitution.
4. What do we want to do as a club?

Jeffrey called the meeting to order. He then asked Katy, the secretary, to read her report. The report follows:

MINUTES OF THE WHATSIT BIRD CLUB

April 22, 1953

We decided to have a club. We are going to call it the Whatsit Bird Club. Jeffrey was elected president. Helen was elected vice-president. I, Katy, was elected secretary. Cary was elected bulletin-board carer. Jeffrey asked Helen, Mark, and Kathie to write a constitution. We are going to meet Friday at two o'clock.

Katy

Jeffrey asked the group whether it would like to change the minutes. No one volunteered. He then called on the constitution committee to give its report. Members of the group liked it as it stood, but the teacher suggested that they vote on it. Then they talked about what they wanted to do. Different members wanted to make a birdhouse, take a bird walk, go on a trip to the Museum of Natural History. The teacher advised that they talk about one item at a time and asked Gloria to express her wish like this: "I move to go to the Museum of Natural History." They discussed going there and finally voted to go. As they talked about the arrangements for the trip, Jeffrey decided he needed a committee. He appointed one and asked it to report at the next meeting.

Some of the children had never had any contact with parliamentary procedure; others already knew almost all they used during the two meetings. Both groups learned the following parliamentary devices through actual participation: electing officers, writing a simple constitution, appointing a committee, following the orders of the day, reading the minutes, giving a committee report and acting upon it, introducing new business, and voting on motions.

As the meetings progressed, they learned other forms. They learned to move that the meeting adjourn. They found out that they must finish one piece of business before beginning another. One day, one child moved to send for bird cards, another to invite a professor who knew about birds to class. The teacher told them how to finish one item before starting another. He advised the president to say, "We're talking about sending for bird cards now. Save your motion about inviting the professor until later." They also discovered that what they had to say should pertain to the motion on the floor. At another meeting one child talked on and on about a movie she had seen that had no particular bearing on the motion. Cary said, "We're wasting time." The teacher explained the principle of all discussion's being pertinent to the motion on the floor; he suggested that Jeffrey, the president, say, "Please stick to the motion on the floor."

In a sixth grade, strangely enough, the children learned to use one of the most difficult of motions, the previous question. One day, two boys became very argumentative about the price to charge for their school newspaper. Finally, the president said, "Look, you've talked long enough. Let's act." At this point the teacher told them there was a motion which took care of such situations. He recommended that they word it this way: "I move we stop talking about the motion." He explained that if two-thirds of the children wanted to stop talking about the motion, they voted on it immediately. This group found it a particularly useful motion, for the group contained three or four argumentative die-hards.

Children learn parliamentary procedure as they are ready for it and as they need it. In most grades, the teacher supplies the necessary information, but in the seventh and eighth grades children may make use of a manual on parliamentary procedure written for children.

A fairly comprehensive list of principles of organization and of motions is included here for the teacher. In many classes, the teacher will use very little of it. Frequently, he will use the ideas but in less formal language. At other times he will simplify the procedure to make it easier for children to follow and to understand. For example, in the conducting of business, the chairman is not likely to say, "Keep your remarks pertinent," but rather, "Stick to your point." He is more likely to say, "Please don't be rude" than, "Kindly keep your remarks impersonal." Instead of "amending a motion," he will probably use the phrase "changing a motion." When he refers to how the motion is to be changed, he will use such phrases as: taking out the words, putting in the words, or changing the motion to . . . As long as the child understands the ideas and principles, the wording is immaterial.

Probably very few eighth graders will use all the motions noted here. But in some cases where children have used parliamentary procedure from the third grade on, they will surprise their teacher with their knowledge of parliamentary procedure. The writer recalls hearing an eighth-grade parliamentarian conducting a meeting smoothly and easily. His correct usage of "Please keep your remarks impersonal," of "There's already a main motion on the floor," and of "Laying on the table takes precedence over referring to a committee" showed he had more knowledge of parliamentary procedure than most adults have.

PARLIAMENTARY PROCEDURE FOR THE TEACHER

ORGANIZATION OF A CLUB

Any person may call a group together and preside until a presiding officer is elected. He explains the purpose of the meeting and conducts the election of a temporary chairman and secretary. The newly elected chairman now takes over. A member introduces a resolution to form a club. After it has been passed, the chairman chooses or the group elects a committee to draft the constitution and its by-laws.

Adoption of a Constitution. A constitution usually consists of eight parts: (1) the preamble, which explains and describes the purpose of the organization; (2) the name of the club; (3) those entitled to membership; (4) a list of the officers and their duties; (5) when and how frequently the meetings are to be held; (6) the method of amending the constitution; (7) what percentage of the total membership constitutes a quorum; and (8) the by-laws, which include more details concerning the organization, such as the payment of dues and the method of electing officers. After the committee has drawn up the constitution, its chairman presents it in full to the organization. He then reads it section by section. If the assemblage desires, any part of it may be amended. It is then read a third time as it has been amended. The last step is the final vote on its acceptance.

CONSTITUTION AND BY-LAWS OF THE SEVENTH GRADERS OF THE
MARY MILLER SCHOOL

Preamble

The object of this club shall be to help the teacher plan the work of the sixth grade, to aid her in carrying out its activities, and to arrange for certain social events of the class.

Article 1. Name.

1. The name of this club shall be "The Seventh Graders of the Mary Miller School."

Article 2. Membership.

1. There shall be two kinds of members: regular and honorary.

2. The regular members shall be those who are regularly enrolled in the seventh grade of the Mary Miller School.

3. The honorary members shall be the teacher, the principal, and any seventh-grade students who may move away from the Mary Miller School during the year.

Article 3. Officers.

1. The officers of this club shall be a president, vice-president, secretary, and treasurer.

2. The duties of these officers shall be those which are usually performed by these officers.

Article 4. Meetings.

1. There shall be two kinds of meetings: regular and special.

2. The regular meetings of this club shall be held Friday at ten o'clock in the seventh-grade classroom throughout the school year.

3. The special meetings of this club shall be called by the president.

Article 5. Amendments.

This constitution may be amended as follows: The amendment must be presented in writing at a meeting two weeks before the meeting it is to be voted upon, and it must be passed by a two-thirds majority of the members of the class.

Article 6. Quorum.

A quorum of this club shall be 90 per cent of the class.

BY-LAWS OF THE SEVENTH GRADERS OF THE MARY MILLER SCHOOL

Article 1. Parliamentary authority.

The rules of order to be followed are those explained in O. Garfield Jones's *Junior Manual for Group Leadership.*

Article 2. Dues.

The dues of the Seventh Graders of the Mary Miller School shall be 10 cents per semester.

Article 3. Officers.

1. Officers shall be nominated from the floor and elected by secret ballot.

2. Elections shall be held twice annually at the second meetings of the first and second semesters.

Article 4. Amendments.

The by-laws may be amended by a two-thirds vote of the members present at a regular meeting. The amendment in writing must be submitted at the meeting the week before it is to be voted on.

Election of Officers. After the group has adopted the constitution and by-laws, it is ready to elect officers. The temporary chairman calls for nominations from the floor or asks for the report of the nominating committee. In some organizations, the constitution decrees that a nominating committee make the nominations. If a nominating committee has made the nominations, the chair asks whether there are any additional nominations. When there is no nominating committee, members arise, address the chair, and nominate their candidates. Nominations do not require a second. After the nominations have been made, the presiding officer closes them, or a member moves to close them. This motion needs a second and a two-thirds vote. The election may be accomplished by a show of hands or by ballot. Immediately after his election, the president becomes the presiding officer. The organization then elects the vice-president, secretary, and treasurer.

DUTIES OF OFFICERS

President. The president presides at all meetings and maintains order. He sees that the meetings follow a prescribed routine, allows the introduction of business, and gives all the members who wish to do so an opportunity to discuss the motions. To expedite business, he makes sure it is expressed in the form of a motion. If a member suggests an action, the chairman asks that he put his suggestion in the form of a motion. The chairman never uses the pronoun "I" but rather "the chair." For example, he says, "The chair rules that Jane is out of order." His duties as a presiding officer will be explained in greater detail later.

Vice-president. The vice-president takes the place of the president when the president is absent and performs his duties.

Treasurer. The treasurer is the bookkeeper of the organization; he keeps a record of all expenditures and all income. For his own protection, he gives receipts for all the money he takes in and asks for receipts for all the money he gives out.

Secretary. The secretary's main duty is to keep minutes, a record of all that has transpired during a meeting. The minutes include (1) the kind of meeting, regular or special, (2) the name of the organization, (3) the date and hour when the meeting was called, (4) the name of the presiding officer, (5) a record of those present, (6) action taken on the minutes of the previous meeting, (7) a record of the main motions that were not withdrawn, who introduced them, and what happened to them, (8) points of order and a record of all other motions not defeated or withdrawn, (9) the time of adjournment, and (10) the signature of the secretary. The secretary also takes care of the correspondence of the club as directed by it and its president.

MINUTES OF THE MEETING OF THE SEVENTH GRADERS OF THE
MARY MILLER SCHOOL

A regular meeting of the Seventh Graders of the Mary Miller School was held Friday, January 12, 1952, at ten o'clock in the seventh-grade classroom. Those absent were Kay and Judy. The President, John, presided. The minutes of the previous meeting of January 5, 1952, were read and approved.

Jane, chairman of the committee appointed to select the picnic date, submitted the report of the committee. She announced that the committee had selected May 10, 1952, as the best date in view of all the circumstances. Jane moved that the report be adopted. The motion was seconded and carried.

As there was no unfinished business, the president called for new business.

Harry moved that the class present its puppet show, *Snow White and the Seven Dwarfs*, at the first available date to the entire school. The motion was seconded and carried.

Helen moved that a committee of four be chosen by the chairman to make arrangements for the presentation of the show and that its chairman report progress at the next meeting. The motion was seconded and carried. The chair appointed Faye, Jim, Joe, and Mary as members of the committee.

Jim moved that the meeting be adjourned. The motion was seconded and carried.

Respectfully submitted,
Mary K. Brown
Mary K. Brown
Secretary, Seventh Graders

ORDER OF A MEETING

The following is a typical order of business: (1) call to order, (2) roll call by the secretary, (3) reading, correcting, and approving the minutes of the previous meeting, (4) announcements by officers of the club, (5) reports of standing committees and reports of special committees, (6) finishing old business, (7) introducing new business, and (8) adjournment.

The president usually calls the meeting to order by rapping on the desk with a gavel or by saying, "The meeting will please come to order." He then asks the secretary to call the roll and to read the minutes of the previous meeting. After the secretary has read the minutes, the president asks, "Are there any corrections or additions?" If there are none, he says, "The minutes stand approved as read." When the minutes are corrected, he says, "The minutes are approved as corrected."

The president then calls for announcements and then for reports of committees. The chairmen of the committees present the reports and usually move their acceptance. When a report is lengthy, the chairman first presents it as a whole and then section by section. The group amends any part of it that it wishes. The chairman then rereads it, and the group approves the whole report as amended. The secretary files the approved and unapproved reports. If business is left over from a previous meeting, the chairman proceeds to it; for example, a main motion may still be on the floor. The president repeats the motion for the benefit of the members of the group and opens discussion on it.

After the old business has been concluded, the chairman asks for the introduction of new business. A member arises, saying, "Mr. Chairman." The chairman allows him the floor by stating his name. The member then introduces the business by the phrase, "I move that . . . " Another member, who does not need to be recognized, seconds the motion by saying either "I second the motion" or "Second." When the motion is not seconded immediately, the chairman asks, "Is there a second?" When there is none, the chairman announces that the motion has been lost for want of a second. After the second, discussion starts immediately. If it does not arise spontaneously, the chairman says either "The question before the house is . . . " or "It has been moved and seconded that . . . "; and then he asks, "Is there any discussion?" After the discussion has ended, the chairman calls for a vote. Where he has any feeling that the group does not know the motion on the floor, he repeats it. For example, "It has been moved and seconded that . . . All those in favor say 'aye.' All those opposed, 'no' "; After the vote, he indicates whether the motion has been carried or lost.

The chairman calls for a vote in any one of four ways: (1) by a show of hands, (2) by asking members to stand, (3) by proclamation, *i.e.*, "All those in favor say 'aye'; all those opposed, 'no,' " (4) by secret ballot, in which case he appoints tellers who pass out the ballots, collect them, and count them. A member may ask for a recount of the votes if he doubts the decision of the chair. To do this, he calls, "Division."

DUTIES OF THE CHAIRMAN

The chairman, as stated earlier, is responsible for the order of the group. He does not allow a member to speak unless he addresses the chair. There is no prescribed order for recognition, but the chair usually recognizes the maker of the motion first, then those who have not spoken, and finally those on opposite sides of the question. When a member speaks without addressing the chairman, he admonishes him with "Kindly address the chair." Two of his other responsibilities are that members do not introduce extraneous discussion and that they keep their remarks impersonal. In the eventuality of extraneous discussion or personal remarks, he says, "Kindly keep your remarks pertinent" or "Kindly keep your remarks impersonal." The chairman also makes sure that there is only one main motion on the floor at a time. If a member introduces a second main motion, he says, "There is already a main motion on the floor." This statement temporarily disposes of the second main motion.

To act as an impartial judge is the duty of the chairman; therefore, he cannot take part as a member of the group. For example, when the voting is done by acclamation, by standing, or by a show of hands, he does not vote, except in the case of a tie. But he may vote in secret ballot provided that he places his ballot in the box before the counting takes place. He does not present a motion or enter discussion while he is in the chair. When he wishes to do either, he asks the vice-president or another officer to take charge of the meeting. He does not force the group to vote. When there is no more discussion, he asks, "Are you ready for the question?" If the response is "Question," he puts the motion to vote.

TYPES OF MOTIONS

In parliamentary procedure motions fall into five categories: (1) main motions, (2) privileged motions, (3) subsidiary motions, (4) incidental motions, and (5) renewal motions. Motions in the second and third groups have an established precedence. Those in the fourth group take precedence only over the motions to which they apply. Privileged motions concern the meeting as a whole; subsidiary motions concern the main motion. Some of these motions require a second, while others do not; some are amendable, others not. Some may be debated; others may not be. In certain instances, the person who already has the floor may be interrupted. Some of these motions require a majority vote;

others need a two-thirds vote. This information and the order of precedence are summarized in table on page 211.

The Main Motion. The main motion introduces into the assemblage business upon which the assemblage must act. It concerns such items as plans for a picnic, for the presentation of a program, for a meeting to be held with another group, or for procedures to be followed in an athletic contest.

Privileged Motions. Privileged motions have precedence over incidental motions, subsidiary motions, and the main motion. Their purpose is to protect the rights and comfort of the members of the group. They involve problems such as the heating or lighting of the room, calling for the orders of the day, taking a recess, and adjourning. They are so important that they require the direct and immediate attention of the group.

Incidental Motions. Incidental motions take precedence only over the motions out of which they arise. They are voted on before the subsidiary motions are discussed or voted on. This procedure is logical in that the group takes care of the most urgent motions first. Incidental motions arise from some circumstance in the meeting. For example, a member may feel that the chair has made a decision contrary to parliamentary law and may wish to ask for an appeal from his decision. Another member may wish to request information from the maker of the motion. These items are obviously of more immediate concern than those of the subsidiary motions.

Subsidiary Motions. The subsidiary motion modifies the main motion. Its purposes are (1) to change the debate on the main motion, as by amending it; (2) to dispose of the question for that particular meeting, as by postponing the motion indefinitely, by laying it on the table, or by referring it to a committee; (3) to postpone action until a certain time; (4) to stop debate by requesting an immediate vote; or (5) to fix a time limit on individual speeches by limiting or extending debate. All subsidiary motions take precedence over the main motion; that is, they must be disposed of before discussion or voting on the main motion takes place.

Renewal Motions.[1] Some motions bring up business for further consideration. They have the rank of main motions and are introduced only when no motion is on the floor. This procedure is logical, for they are like new business. These motions have to do with reconsidering action

[1] See W. Gilman, B. Aly, and L. Reid, *The Fundamentals of Speaking*, New York Macmillan, 1951, p. 564.

PARLIAMENTARY MOTIONS AND THEIR ORDER OF PRECEDENCE

Rank, name, and type of motion	Is a second required?	Is the motion amendable?	Is it debatable?	What vote is needed for passage?	May it be introduced while another has the floor?
PRIVILEGED MOTIONS					
1. Fix time of next meeting	Yes	Yes	No	Majority	No
2. Adjourn..............	Yes	No	No	Majority	No
3. Take a recess.........	Yes	Yes	No	Majority	No
4. Questions of privilege..	No	No	No	None	Yes
5. Call for orders of the day	No	No	No	None	Yes
INCIDENTAL MOTIONS*					
Withdraw a motion....	No	No	No	Majority	No
Object to consideration of the question......	No	No	No	⅔	Yes
Point of order.........	No	No	No	None	Yes
Appeal from a decision of the chair.........	Yes	No	Yes	Majority	Yes
Suspend rules.........	Yes	No	No	⅔	No
Request information...	No	No	No	None	No
Parliamentary inquiry..	No	No	No	None	Yes
Motion related to voting	Yes	Yes	No	Majority	No
Closing nominations...	Yes	Yes	No	⅔	No
Division of the assembly	No	No	No	None	Yes
SUBSIDIARY MOTIONS					
6. Lay on the table.......	Yes	No	No	Majority	No
7. Call for the previous question...........	Yes	No	No	⅔	No
8. Limit or extend debate	Yes	Yes	No	⅔	No
9. Postpone to a certain time...............	Yes	Yes	Yes	Majority	No
10. Refer to a committee...	Yes	Yes	Yes	Majority	No
11. Amend..............	Yes	Yes	Yes	Majority	No
12. Postpone indefinitely...	Yes	No	Yes	Majority	No
RENEWAL MOTIONS					
Reconsider...........	Yes	No	Yes	Majority	Yes
Rescind..............	Yes	Yes	Yes	⅔ or Majority†	No
Take from the table....	Yes	No	No	Majority	No
MAIN MOTION..............	Yes	Yes	Yes	Majority	No

* These motions have no rank but grow out of other motions.
† See explanation of rescind, p. 216.

already taken or rescinding it. The motion to take from the table is included in this group.

The motions listed in the table will be explained and the form in which they are stated indicated. The motions are listed in order of precedence. Each motion has precedence over all those which follow it. In the case of incidental motions, no single one has precedence over another, but any one of these has precedence over the subsidiary motions. For example, if a main motion is on the floor, if it is amended, if it is laid on the table, and, then, if a motion is made to recess, the order in which they are disposed of is (1) to recess, (2) to lay on the table, (3) to amend, and (4) to take action on the main motion.

PRIVILEGED MOTIONS

1. *Fix the Time of the Next Meeting.* **Form**: "I move that, when we adjourn, we adjourn until Friday at three o'clock." When there is no other motion on the floor, this motion is treated the same way as a main motion. If there is another, this motion takes precedence over all, is not debatable, and can be amended only by changing the time. It requires a second and a majority vote.

2. *Adjourn.* **Form**: "I move that we adjourn." This motion takes precedence over all other motions except that of fixing the time of the next meeting. It requires a second, is not debatable or amendable, and requires a majority vote.

3. *Take a Recess.* **Form**: "I move to take a recess." The group may wish to recess to eat lunch, to rest, or to await the report of a committee. The motion requires a second, is not debatable, is amendable, and requires a majority vote.

4. *Question of Privilege.* **Form**: "I rise to a question of privilege." The chairman answers, "State your question of privilege." The member then states it, "I request that I be allowed to open the window." The motion is concerned with the comfort and rights of the group. It does not require a vote unless there is an objection. It obviously needs no second, is not amendable or debatable.

5. *Orders of the Day.* **Form**: "I call for the orders of the day." This phrase calls to the attention of the presiding officer that there is particular business scheduled for the meeting. The chairman responds to the motion by asking the secretary what the orders of the day are. It obviously does not require a second or a vote and is not amendable or debatable.

INCIDENTAL MOTIONS

Withdraw a Motion. Form: "I beg leave to withdraw my motion." The chairman responds with "Jane has asked leave to withdraw her motion. Unless someone objects, permission is granted." This action, however, must occur before the motion is stated by the chair; otherwise, the motion must go to vote. Furthermore, if someone objects, the motion is put to the vote. The motion requires no second; it is not amendable or debatable. It is carried by a majority vote.

Objection to Consideration of a Question. Form: "I object to the consideration of this question." The motion must be made before the assemblage has begun debate. The chairman immediately asks, "Shall the question be considered?" Usually objections are made when someone feels that the matter is not within the province of the group to consider. It does not require a second, requires a two-thirds vote, and is not debatable or amendable.

Point of Order. Form: "I rise to a point of order." The chairman then asks the member to state his point. The chair then rules by saying either, "Your point is well taken" or "Your point is not well taken." No vote is called for unless someone disagrees with the chair's ruling. It obviously requires no second and is not debatable or amendable.

Appeal from Decision of the Chair. Form: "I appeal from the decision of the chair." The chair then responds with "Shall the decision of the chair stand? All in favor say 'aye,' opposed, 'no.'" A majority vote or tie vote upholds the decision. Usually, a member does not appeal a decision unless there has been a parliamentary error which seriously confuses or interferes with the business of the meeting. The motion requires a second, is amendable and debatable, and needs a majority vote.

Suspend the Rules. Form: "I move that the rule . . . be suspended." This motion applies to standing rules, such as those relating to the order of business. It requires the consent of all the members of the assembly or a two-thirds vote. It is not amendable or debatable and needs a second.

Point of Information. Form: "I rise to a point of information." The chairman responds by saying, "Please state the point." The member asks either the chairman or the member who offered the motion. The purpose is to request more information concerning the motion on the floor. It obviously needs no second or vote and is not amendable or debatable.

Parliamentary Inquiry. Form: "I rise to a parliamentary inquiry." The chairman replies with "State your inquiry." The member does so. The chairman then gives the necessary information. Clearly no second is necessary; the motion is not debatable or amendable, and no vote is taken.

Motions Related to Voting. Form: "I move the vote be taken by ayes and noes." Or the member may indicate that the vote is to be taken by show of hands, by ballot, by rising, or by roll call. The chairman usually says, "If there is no objection, the vote will be taken by ballot" (or whatever method was suggested). These motions are amendable but not debatable; they require a second and a majority vote.

Closing Nominations. Form: "I move the nominations be closed." It is not debatable, is amendable as to time, needs a second, and requires a two-thirds vote.

Division of the Assembly. Form: "Division." A member calls this word out because he thinks that the chairman has made a mistake in his announcement of a vote. No second is necessary. The chairman then calls for a show of hands or a rising vote so that the vote may be counted more carefully.

SUBSIDIARY MOTIONS

6. *Lay on the Table.* Form: "I move the question be laid on the table." This motion postpones action. The member who introduces it may feel that other business is more important. It requires a second, a majority vote, and is not amendable or debatable.

7. *Call for Previous Question.* Form: "I move the previous question." The chairman responds with "The previous question has been called for," or he may use the phrase "A motion has been made to close debate." The purpose of the motion is to stop further debate and force an immediate vote in order to save the time of the assembly. Because debate is cut short, the motion requires a two-thirds vote. It also requires a second and is not debatable or amendable. When the motion is carried, the chairman proceeds to call for a vote on the question on which debate has been stopped.

8. *Limit or Extend Debate.* Form: "I move that debate be limited to three minutes for each member" or "I move that debate end at eleven o'clock." The aim is to set a limit on the time spent in debate for members of the group or for the group as a whole or to extend the time already set for debate. The motion requires a second and a two-thirds vote; it is not debatable. It may be amended as to time set.

9. *Postpone to a Certain Time.* Form: "I move the matter be postponed until . . . " (a specific date). When this date arrives, the ques-

tion is then part of the orders of the day. A motion is usually postponed until more information may be acquired, until a larger group is present, or until persons who are vitally concerned about the matter under discussion are in attendance at the meeting. The motion is debatable and amendable; it requires a second and a majority vote.

10. *Commit, Refer, or Recommit.* Form: "I move the matter be referred to a committee of three to be appointed by the president to report at the next meeting." If the committee is to have power to act, this item should be included. The motion always includes three items: the number on the committee, how they are to be selected, and when they are to report. When the chair appoints the members of the committee, he first mentions the name of the person who is to be the chairman of the committee. The purpose of this motion is that the matter under discussion may be studied by a smaller group, who will bring recommendations to the larger group. The motion is debatable and amendable. It requires a second and a majority vote.

11. *Amend.* An amendment to a motion may be made in five ways: (1) by striking out certain words, (2) by striking out certain words and inserting other words, (3) by inserting words, (4) by adding certain words, and (5) by substituting a new motion. The member introduces the amendment in this way: "I move to amend the motion by striking out the words . . . and inserting the words . . . " The chairman puts the amendment to vote first. He says, "We shall now vote upon the amendment which is . . . " The assembly votes on the amendment. When the assembly passes the amendment, the chairman calls for a discussion of, and a vote on, the original motion as amended. The amendment must be pertinent to the main motion. A member may move an amendment to the amendment but no more. The motion is debatable and requires a majority vote.

12. *Postpone Indefinitely.* Form: "I move the matter be postponed indefinitely." The effect of this motion is usually to kill the matter under discussion, although it is sometimes used to test the strength of a motion. It requires a second and a majority vote. It is debatable and not amendable.

RENEWAL MOTIONS

Reconsider. Form: "I move the question . . . be reconsidered." Since the motion can only be made by a member who voted with the majority, the chairman asks whether the member making the motion voted with the majority. When the motion to reconsider is carried, the chairman takes a new vote on the question. This motion must be made at the same meeting where the question was considered or at the following meeting. It requires a second. It is debatable where the motion to which it applies is debatable; otherwise, it is not. It is not amendable and requires a majority vote.

Rescind. Form: "I move to rescind the action . . . " If previous notice is given, a vote can be rescinded by a majority; otherwise, it is necessary to have a two-thirds vote of those present or a majority of all members of the club. It requires a second, is debatable and amendable.

Take from the Table. Form: "I move the question . . . be taken from the table." The purpose of this motion is to bring up for consideration a matter previously laid on the table. It requires a second, is not debatable or amendable, and requires a majority vote.

SUMMARY

Parliamentary procedure provides for full, fair, and free discussion by members of the group, allows the majority to rule but respects the rights of the minority, and aids in expediting the business of a group. Children should be taught the elements of parliamentary procedure gradually and as they feel the need for it in conducting the business of their club or class.

Organization of a club involves a preliminary meeting, at which a temporary chairman and a secretary are elected and provisions made for the drawing up and the adoption of a constitution. After the constitution has been accepted, officers are elected. Usually, a president, vice-president, secretary, and treasurer serve a permanent organization. The president serves as chairman of all meetings, preserves order, and gives all members an equal opportunity to participate. The vice-president takes charge when the president is unable to attend. The secretary keeps a record of the meeting and takes care of correspondence. The treasurer handles the finances of the organization.

A meeting follows this order: call to order, roll call, reading, correcting, and approving the minutes, announcements by officers, reports of standing and special committees, finishing old business, introduction of new business, and adjournment. There are five types of motions: main motions, incidental motions, subsidiary motions, privileged motions, and renewal motions.

EXERCISES

1. Indicate how parliamentary procedure can be introduced into the elementary school in a particular grade.
2. Attend a meeting of adults. Determine how well its participants follow parliamentary procedure.
3. Attend a meeting of children. Indicate how much use they make of parliamentary procedure.
4. Point out specifically how a particular motion can be introduced when the need arises.
5. Show how the language in several of the motions can be made less formal.
6. Show how one procedure in the organization of a club might be simplified.

BIBLIOGRAPHY

FURTHER SOURCES OF READING FOR THE TEACHER

Gilman, W., B. Aly, and L. Reid. *The Fundamentals of Speaking*, New York, Macmillan, 1951, Chap. 27. Explains parliamentary law in simple clear terms. Annotated bibliography.

Leigh, R. D., *Modern Rules of Parliamentary Procedure*, New York, Norton, 1937. Rules of parliamentary procedure indexed for easy use.

Robert, H. M., *Rules of Order*, rev., New York, Scott, Foresman, 1951. Contains the complete rules of parliamentary procedure adapted to the use of organizations. The official authority on all matters not contained in the constitutions or by-laws of organizations.

Stevenson, F., "A Course in Parliamentary Procedure As an Approach to Leadership Training for Adults," *School and Society*, Vol. 69 (Apr. 30, 1949), pp. 315–316. Lists the values of parliamentary procedure.

Sturgis, A. F., *Learning Parliamentary Procedure*, New York, McGraw-Hill, 1953. Tells how to make use of parliamentary procedure. Discusses organization of a club and kinds of motions. Shows how the organizations function in their meetings and when they use parliamentary procedure.

———, *Standard Code of Parliamentary Procedure*, New York, McGraw-Hill, 1950.

BOOKS ON PARLIAMENTARY PROCEDURE FOR CHILDREN

Bailard, V., *So You Were Elected*, New York, Whittlesey, 1946, Part 1. Contains a discussion of parliamentary procedure. Includes the order of meeting, duties of the officers, reports of the treasurer and secretary, adoption of a constitution. Adapted to boys and girls of the upper grades.

Craig, A. E., *The Junior Speech Arts*, New York, Macmillan, 1949, pp. 390–412. Includes a simplified, clear description of the principles of parliamentary procedure. Shows how to introduce business, how various motions are introduced, the use of parliamentary terms, the organization of a club or society, and a sample meeting. Upper grades.

Jones, O. G., *Senior Manual for Group Leadership*, rev. ed., New York, Appleton-Century-Crofts, 1949. Contains a fairly complete treatment of parliamentary procedure with motions indexed for easy usage. Could be used in the seventh or eighth grades.

————, *Junior Manual for Group Leadership*, New York, Appleton-Century-Crofts, 1934. Contains rules of parliamentary procedure. Arranged so that it can be easily used. Can be used in intermediate and upper grades.

Henry, W. H. F., and L. Seeley, *How to Organize and Conduct a Meeting*, New York, Noble, 1926. Includes the organization of a meeting, order of a meeting, duties of officers, discussion of a question, and types of motions. Written for the upper grades.

Weaver, A. T., and G. L. Borchers, *Speech*, New York, Harcourt Brace, 1946, pp. 420–431. Includes a discussion of parliamentary procedure that can be used profitably by seventh and eighth graders. Written in a simple, clear style.

10 Assemblies

School X has a program of assemblies that the children enjoy, that are learning experiences for them, that are a constructive influence on their school spirit and on the attitudes of their parents toward the school. A committee of children and a teacher plan a few of the programs as auditorium performances, but most of them are outgrowths of the work of particular groups. The school houses two sections of grades 1 through 8. Grades 1 through 3 and 4 through 8 have their own sets of programs. On occasions such as Christmas, the whole school comes together for an assembly. Because these programs are effective educational experiences for the children and members of the community, the programs for one year for grades 4 through 8 are listed and described briefly.

A PROGRAM OF ASSEMBLIES

September: *Cinderella*. A marionette show. Produced by outsiders and attended by the entire student body.

"1952." A dramatization of a theme for each month of the year. Produced by all grades for the entire school.

October: "Education Today." A dramatization of scenes from various classrooms. Produced by members of grades 4 to 8.

"Political Rally." A rally to encourage the children to vote in the mock election. Produced by the fifth grade.

November: "What Is Sound?" Demonstration of experiments concerning sound. Produced by the sixth grade.

December: *The Boy on the Meadow*. A musicodramatic production. Produced by the eighth grade for all the school.

January: "Food Prices." Debate, The Federal government must institute a more rigorous form of controlling food prices. Debate by the eighth grade.

"March of Dimes." A plea for money for the March of Dimes. Produced by the seventh grade.

February: "The Solar System." Explanation and demonstration. Produced by the seventh grade.

"Swing Your Pardner." A demonstration of square dancing. Produced by the sixth grade.

March: "Know Your Literature." Celebration of Book Week. Produced by children from grades 4, 6, 7, and 8.

April: *Pinafore.* An operetta. Produced by the fifth grade.

John Darling. A dramatization of a folk tale. Produced by the fifth grade.

May: *Hansel and Gretel.* A puppet show produced by the fourth grade.

"Living Art." Tableaux representing famous pictures, accompanied by music or speaking. Produced by grades 4 to 8.

June: *John Peter Zenger.* A dramatization of Zenger's life. Produced by the eighth grade.

A MARIONETTE SHOW PRODUCED BY A PROFESSIONAL GROUP

This artistic performance of *Cinderella* motivated the children in the various grades to make puppets or marionettes and to put on their own shows. All the children in the school came to this production.

"1952" PRODUCED BY ALL THE GRADES FOR THE ENTIRE SCHOOL

The children in the various grades told a story about each month of the year through pantomime or dance and song or choral speaking. At the right of the stage stood a calendar, approximately 3 feet by 6 feet, with "pages" for each month. The upper part of the page contained a scene representing the month; the lower part, the letters JAN. or FEB. Two children dressed in page's costume opened the show by tearing off the title, "1952," from the calendar. As each scene was about to begin, they reappeared, tore off the preceding page, and left the one indicating the title of the scene that was to follow. The members of the assembly committee assigned each of the groups of children a month. They asked them to prepare a scene with pantomime or dance and to interpret it through speaking or singing. They indicated the approximate time that each group might use. They also asked each group to design and paint its page of the calendar. To keep the pages of the calendar uniform they gave out the paper on which the scenes were to be painted. The children in each group decided what they wanted to do to interpret the month and how they wanted to show it on the calendar.

The second-grade group played January. A chorus from the class seated in the audience sang "Jingle Bells" while on the stage other members, dressed in snow suits, snowballed each other, pulled a sled around, and walked on snowshoes. Some of the eighth-grade girls had constructed a large snowman from chicken wire and papier mâché. While the chorus sang a song about the snowman, two children put on the snowman's stovepipe hat and stuck a pipe in his mouth. For December, the sixth grade portrayed Christmas by speaking the Biblical story of the birth of Christ in chorus and by showing the nativity scene in the form of a tableau. The whole assembly participated in the story by singing the appropriate Christmas carols as they occurred in the story. Children in the other grades depicted the other months: February, Washington's Birthday; March, winds; April, spring rain; May, Maypole dance; June, wedding bells; July, swimming; August, vacation time; September, beginning of school; October, harvest time; November, Thanksgiving.

"EDUCATION TODAY" PRODUCED BY GRADES 4 TO 8

The assembly committee asked the seventh and eighth grades to plan an assembly for Education Week. A committee of the students from both grades and their teachers planned the program and assigned parts of it to each of the five grades. Traditionally, the school children invited their parents and friends to this assembly. This year, they put on scenes that were typical of various classrooms: performing science experiments, making puppets, reading, dramatizing scenes from books, cooking, and planning a trip. A narrator tied the scenes together by reading from her diary. She started with the highlights of her education in the fourth grade and proceeded to the time she was ready for high school. As she completed reading what had happened in a grade, members of that grade played the scene. The diary in itself was a piece of excellent creative writing. Her reading of it was an effective introduction to the various scenes, for she put the audience in the right mood and told them what to expect.

"POLITICAL RALLY" PRODUCED BY THE FIFTH GRADE

The children divided the auditorium session equally as to time to give one-half to the Republicans and one-half to the Democrats. Their purpose was not to change the opinions of the members of their audience but to get them to vote. The eighth graders had already held registration and were to take charge of after-school voting of all the children in grades 4 to 8 for the presidential candidates. Members of the fifth grade led the group in singing political songs and in giving cheers. They delivered rousing speeches. They gave away buttons, pamphlets, and even pencils. The experience was an exciting one for the members of the audience.

"WHAT IS SOUND?" PRODUCED BY THE SIXTH GRADE

This assembly consisted of a demonstration of a series of experiments about sound. The members of the group demonstrated elements of sound: vibration, resonance, and the media of vibration. They showed the difference between noise and tone. They indicated qualities of sound: volume, pitch, and duration. As a conclusion, different individuals played the same tune on a recorder, a piano, a violin, and finally on glasses of water. They had marked the glasses beforehand to indicate how much water they needed to obtain certain pitches. After one boy had made a big show of pouring the water in carefully, another casually played the tune. The master of ceremonies then asked the audience questions as to why the tones varied. The children had planned that, if no member of the audience knew the answer, one of the children on the stage would respond to the question.

A MUSICODRAMATIC PRESENTATION PRODUCED BY THE EIGHTH GRADE

The Boy on the Meadow is a German folk story of a stepmother's kind treatment of her own two youngsters and of her cruel treatment of her stepchild at Christmas time. When the stepchild goes out into the meadow, he finds a poor, ragged boy wandering; he gives him his own new shoes and then sees a vision. After he returns home, he tells the story to his stepmother, who pooh-poohs the idea and punishes him. At nightfall, as the youngsters go to bed, they put their shoes outside for St. Nicholas to fill. The stepmother fills her own children's shoes but puts nothing in the stepchild's old, worn-out shoes. In the morning, the stepchild's shoes are filled to overflowing with gold coins. The stepmother realizes the error of her ways and thereafter treats all the children alike. At the point where the children go to bed, the traditional Christmas story was played with pantomime and song, ending with the Nativity scene. It was an unusual and impressive Christmas program.

DEBATE ON FOOD PRICES

"The Federal government must institute a more rigorous form of controlling food prices" was the subject of a debate produced by the two sections of the eighth grade. The audience served as judges for the two debating teams.

"MARCH OF DIMES" SPONSORED BY THE SEVENTH GRADE

Interested children from several grades conducted an assembly to raise money for the March of Dimes. Three of the children who had had polio formed a panel to discuss what the foundation had done for them. Four boys had earned money for the fund the previous summer by selling lemonade. A dozen children had put on a neighborhood show to raise money. Each of the two groups explained what it had done and suggested that other children might be interested in similar projects. A group of boys and girls also dramatized a scene in which parents were talking about the financial help the foundation had given them and what it had meant to them. The purpose of the assembly was to persuade the students to give money to the foundation.

"SWING YOUR PARDNER" PRODUCED BY THE SIXTH GRADE

Square dancing became the popular pastime of the members of the sixth grade. Because they wanted to share their enjoyment of swinging their partners, they put on an exhibition of square dancing. All the children in the school came to the program.

"THE SOLAR SYSTEM" PRODUCED BY THE SEVENTH GRADE

The seventh-grade group had been studying the solar system. They had become very interested in the stars and their positions in the sky. After they had learned about them, they asked to share their knowledge with the other students. Therefore, they placed on the stage a network of strings to which they attached the various stars. They then explained the solar system to the members of the audience.

"KNOW YOUR LITERATURE" PRODUCED BY MEMBERS OF GRADES 4, 5, 7, AND 8

The children in these four grades produced brief scenes from four children's books: Ruth Sawyer's *Roller Skates*, Esther Forbes's *Johnny Tremaine*, Alice Davis's *Timothy Turtle*, and Don and Betty Emblem's *The Palomino Boy*. As each scene was introduced, the title of the book and its author were shown on a "cover." The children had designed and painted the covers in their art work.

AN OPERETTA PRODUCED BY THE FIFTH GRADE

Since the boys and girls in one of the fifth grades were studying operettas, they had listened to and learned some of the rollicking, gay songs of *Pinafore*. Because they were interested in its story and music, and because they particularly enjoyed them, they decided to share their enthusiasm with the other children. They dramatized *Pinafore*, using just the main plot. A narrator in the form of a grandfather told his two grandchildren about the performance. To help the audience understand the story, the narrator told it, and then children on the stage repeated it in their dialogue and in their songs. The children wrote the script and memorized the lines. The script follows:[1]

H.M.S. PINAFORE

SCENE I: OUTSIDE CURTAIN.

GRANDFATHER. (*Remains in chair at the side of the stage throughout the play.*) Those young ones. You just cannot depend on them any more. When I was a boy and someone was taking me visiting or to a party, I was always ready on time. I used to get there an hour early. I cannot remember when I have been late for anything. It's two o'clock now, and the matinee performance of *Pinafore* begins at two o'clock. No sir, I've never been late for anything in all my life . . . well . . . anyhow, not recently.

NAN. (*Coming in the door with Bill.*) Hello, grandfather, Here we are.

BILL. Hi! We're here. Let's go.

GRANDFATHER. Not so fast. Not so fast. I'm not as young as I used to be. And where have you been? We haven't much time. Why, I remember once when I came late to my aunt's birthday party . . . no . . . that can't be right. I was never late anywhere. What was I saying? Oh, yes. Why, I remember the last time I saw *Pinafore*. It was in New York. Yes, New York. The best performance I ever saw. That stage was the biggest I had ever seen. Right in the middle of it was the deck of the ship H.M.S. "Pinafore." She was lying in Portsmouth Bay, England, and on her decks was a crew of English sailors a-scrubbing and a-polishing. There were a lot of little bumboats around the ship, and when the curtain opened, the sailors were all singing "We Sail the Ocean Blue."

(*Curtain opens, chorus sings "We Sail the Ocean Blue"*)

GRANDFATHER. My, how they could sing. But soon they had to stop, for a bumboat woman selling all kinds of trinkets came on board to sell her wares to the sailors. This was Buttercup, their favorite. Now do not ask me why she was called Buttercup because even she did not know.

(*Buttercup sings "I'm Called Little Buttercup." The sailors crowd around to buy wares. Ralph Rackstraw, however, hangs back looking sad.*)

BUTTERCUP. Who's the lad who buys no wares of me? Why is he so sad? Has he no sweetheart?

[1] Script written by the fourth grade of the Campus School, State Teachers College, Fredonia, N. Y., under the direction of Miss J. Anderson.

DEADEYE. He has a sweetheart all right—the Captain's daughter. (*Laughs*)
He, a common sailor wants to marry Josephine, the Captain's daughter.
Poor soul. Poor soul. Poor Ralph Rackstraw.

BUTTERCUP. Ralph Rackstraw? That name . . . (*Quietly*) Little did I
think I'd ever . . . (*Confusion amidst sailors as the Captain boards the ship.*)

A SAILOR. Here comes the captain.

CAPTAIN. Good morning. I hope you are all well.

SAILORS. Very well, sir.

CAPTAIN. Well, there's work to be done. Off to your jobs, men. Off to your
jobs. Ah, Buttercup.

BUTTERCUP. Sir, you are sad.

CAPTAIN. That I am. That I am. I have my troubles. My daughter is sought
in marriage by Sir Joseph, our Admiralty's First Lord. But she will have none
of him.

BUTTERCUP. Poor Captain. Poor Captain.

Curtain

GRANDFATHER. Now, that's a sorry lot, isn't it? Why won't Josephine
marry Sir Joseph? You don't know Sir Joseph! He is prim, portly, and proud.
But he is always followed by his sisters, and his cousins, and his aunts. Who
would want to marry him and his sisters, and his cousins, and his aunts?

SCENE II: THE SAME

SIR JOSEPH. (*Sings "The Ruler of the Queen's Navy" and "I Am the Monarch of the Sea."*) That's the man I am today. But I wasn't always the ruler
of the Queen's Navy. I had to work my way to the top.

COUSINS *et al.* How? How come?

SIR JOSEPH. (*Sings "When I Was a Lad."*)

Curtain

GRANDFATHER. See, that's Sir Joseph. Poor Ralph. But he was a brave lad
and finally he told Josephine he loved her. She would have nothing to do
with him, because she was a Captain's daughter and he was a man of low
birth. But Ralph knew what to do. He drew out his pistol and threatened to
shoot himself. What could Josephine do? She said she would marry him and
they planned to elope. That was the end of the first act.

NAN. It sounds like a good play. Shall we go now, Grandfather?

GRANDFATHER. Well, the second act is the best. I remember it especially.
It's the night Josephine and Ralph plan to elope. The Captain is talking to
Buttercup.

Curtain

SCENE III. THE SAME

CAPTAIN. Misfortunes crowd upon me. All my friends have turned against
me.

BUTTERCUP. Don't be too sure, good Captain. There is a change in store
for you, a great change.

CAPTAIN. A change?

BUTTERCUP. Yes, things are seldom what they seem.

CAPTAIN. What do you mean?

BUTTERCUP. Wait and see. Wait and see.

Curtain

GRANDFATHER. Right there I began to wonder. What did Buttercup mean? I didn't think about it very long because Deadeye came up to the Captain and told him about the elopement. The Captain caught the guilty parties in the act.

Curtain

SCENE IV: THE SAME

CAPTAIN. Hold it all of you. Josephine, where are you going?

JOSEPHINE. With Ralph Rackstraw.

CAPTAIN. He's scarce fit company for you.

RALPH. Captain, hold it. I've dared to look at your daughter because I am an Englishman.

(*Chorus sings "I Am an Englishman."*)

(*Sir Joseph appears with his cousins, et al.*)

SIR JOSEPH. What's the meaning of this disturbance? Who is eloping? Why, Josephine . . . and a common sailor. Seize this man. Bind him with chains. Take him to the dungeon.

BUTTERCUP. Stop! I have something to say. (*Buttercup sings "The Farming Song."*)

SIR JOSEPH. Do I understand? You were foster mother to both Captain Corcoran and Ralph Rackstraw and that they were exchanged as babies? Can this be possible? Then Ralph Rackstraw is the Captain and the Captain is Ralph Rackstraw.

BUTTERCUP. Yes.

SIR JOSEPH. Let the men appear before me. Captain, come here. So you were Ralph and Ralph was you.

CAPTAIN. So it seems.

SIR JOSEPH. After this, I cannot marry your daughter. She is the daughter of a lowly sailor. Here, you take Josephine and treat her kindly.

CREW. Hurrah for Captain Ralph! Hurrah for Corcoran! Hurrah for the "Pinafore"!

(*Finale, all songs repeated.*)

Curtain

GRANDFATHER. So you see. Ralph was the Captain, and the Captain was Ralph. Buttercup made a terrible mistake. Yes, Nan?

NAN. Grandfather, it's two o'clock.

GRANDFATHER. Merciful heavens! So it is. We've got to hurry. I've never been late to anything in my life.

A FOLK TALE PRODUCED BY THE SIXTH GRADE

The folklore of early America was the source of material for another assembly. The sixth-grade group found that the first story, "John Darling," in McCloskey's *Yankee Doodle's Cousins* proved ideal for dramatization. It is the one mentioned in the chapter on creative dramatics which has to do with a fishing contest sponsored by Sal, the best cook on the Erie Canal, in order to choose a husband. Her favorite catches few fish, but she saves the day by hanging her red head over the side and thereby enticing the fish into the boat.

A PUPPET SHOW PRODUCED BY THE FOURTH GRADE

The fourth graders made the puppets, constructed the stage, and produced the puppet play *Hansel and Gretel*. They used the public-address system so that the audience could hear the puppeteers easily.

"LIVING ART" PRODUCED BY GRADES 4 TO 8

The industrial arts department constructed a large gold frame and behind it draped velvet on screens. Costumed children posed as the characters in different famous pictures while members of a particular class interpreted the picture in song or in speaking. For example, while one child posed as the Madonna, the eighth-grade group sang "Ava Maria." One fourth-grade girl depicted Jan Vermeer's "The Cook." The children obtained bowls and baskets very like the ones in the picture. The girl was costumed simply with a sweater, blue velvet, and a headdress made from white cloth. In this instance, one of the girls wrote and read a poem telling of all the good food the cook was fixing. A fifth-grade girl posed as the lady in "Portrait of a Lady" by Roger van der Weyden. An old brown velvet suit brought from home, a wide red belt, and some cheesecloth dyed tan sufficed for costuming. The children, as a group, wrote a poem about the thoughts of the lady and the music teacher helped them to set it to music. All the members of the group sang it. The seventh-grade group studied Botticelli's "The Nativity," Fra Angelico's "Journey of the Magi," and Fra Filippo Lippi's "Virgin Adoring the Child"; from this group, they selected "The Nativity" for which they spoke as a group Eugene Field's "Song," which tells the story of the birth of Christ. After each portrayal, a copy of the picture that the groups were portraying was shown on the screen.

BIOGRAPHY PRODUCED BY THE EIGHTH GRADE

The members of the eighth grade dramatized part of the life of John Peter Zenger.

PLANNING ASSEMBLIES

A committee of children, one from each of the ten grades, planned the year's assembly program with the guidance of a seventh-grade teacher. They decided beforehand that some of the assemblies should include members of several grades as participants and the whole school as an audience. They felt that this type of participation developed a unified school spirit. "Living Art," "1952," and "Education Today" represent types of assemblies in which a number of groups participated. All the school children came to *The Boy on the Meadow, Cinderella,* "1952," and "Swing Your Pardner." In cases where members of various groups were participating, the committee worked out the format of the program carefully so that the production would have unity.

Most of the programs grew out of classroom experiences. For example, as one group studied the folklore of the early American days, it decided to dramatize *John Darling.* Another learned about the solar system and wanted to share their knowledge. Still another group found pleasure in the story and songs of *Pinafore;* it felt other children in the school would be pleased with *Pinafore.* As the sixth-grade group experimented with sound, they asked to show their demonstrations to the other children. When a group found an experience it wanted to share, its members presented it to the assembly committee. Almost always the committee approved its presentation. On some occasions, where too many programs were available, the committee suggested that the students put on their program for a smaller audience, such as another grade or two or three other grades.

REQUIREMENTS FOR ASSEMBLY PROGRAMS

THE MATERIAL FOR THE ASSEMBLY IS THE WORK OF THE CHILDREN

The committee set up certain principles to follow in planning programs. The first principle was that the children plan and carry out the work for the assembly with the guidance of the teacher. The committee asked that the ideas for the programs originate with the children. Some of the scripts were very childlike—perhaps appallingly so to some adults. The following is an excerpt from the prologue of *John Darling:*

> Now John had a girl and her name was Sal.
> She cooked for him on the Erie Canal.
> When he asked for her hand, she said she didn't know
> For she had beaux from Albany to Buffalo.
> She had some hair that was red as fire,
> And at night it shone like a ball of fire.
> She was six feet tall and an awful dope,
> And sometimes John gave up all hope.

This poem expressed the children's viewpoint of what Sal was like.

THE PRODUCTION OF THE ASSEMBLY IS THE RESPONSIBILITY OF THE CHILDREN

Along the same lines is the second principle: the children accept and carry the responsibility for the performance. The committee asked that, when it was feasible, the teacher sit with the audience. On the whole, the children handled emergencies well. For example, a seventh-grade student who was to bring a large map to the stage was absent. After the performance had begun, the children discovered that they had no map. They closed the curtains, and one little girl led community singing while one of the boys brought the map to the stage. Usually, the group assigned particular responsibilities to individual students; for instance, one student was chairman of the properties committee and another, chairman of the scenery committee. Each group made sure that someone was taking care of the different tasks.

THE ASSEMBLY SHOWS THE PARENTS THE SCHOOL'S EDUCATIONAL PHILOSOPHY

The third principle was that the assemblies show parents and the members of the community what the school is doing and indicate to them in a concrete way the educational philosophy of the classes. One group of parents may think that the school is all reading, writing, and arithmetic, while another group may consider that too much time is spent on "frills." After the assembly on sound, a parent remarked in complete amazement, "Why, those children know more about sound than I do." After the dramatization of *John Darling*, a mother said, "This kind of thing is so much better for youngsters than the private elocution lessons I used to take."

THE ASSEMBLY FURTHERS GOOD SPEECH IN CHILDREN

The fourth principle was that the assemblies further good speech in children. In explaining the science experiments, the children did not memorize their explanations, they talked extemporaneously about their subjects. When they imparted information, they gave it in an easy, conversational style with meaning and did not orate in an unintelligible fashion. Where the program was dramatic, the youngsters interpreted the lines and characters intelligently. Each child knew what the charac-- ter was saying, why he spoke as he did, and why he reacted to another character the way he did. They created character rather than exhibited themselves. Their programs gave evidence of good speech education.

THROUGHOUT THE YEAR, THERE EXISTS A VARIETY OF PURPOSES IN THE PROGRAMS

Earlier, in Giving Talks, the four kinds of speeches were explained: impressive, entertaining, informative, and persuasive. Assembly programs have the same purposes. Occasions for impressive assemblies are few but are frequent for the other types. In this school year one program was mainly impressive, *The Boy on the Meadow*. Several had entertainment as their primary purpose, such as the puppet show, *Hansel and Gretel*, and the square dancing. Quite a few were informative, such as the discussion of sound and the explanation of the solar system. Several were persuasive, as "The March of Dimes" and the debate on price controls. The year's program should include assemblies which achieve different purposes well. The purpose of a program put on in another school was to inform the students of the healthful values of certain vegetables and to persuade the members of the audience to eat these vegetables. One child dressed as spinach in faded green crepe paper and another costumed as a carrot in a garish orange extolled the virtues of their respective vegetables. Spinach looked sickly, lifeless, and dull and spoke in a most unconvincing manner. Carrot hailed her virtues with such bombastic oratory that the timid were glad to escape her as she jumped off the stage. Lettuce looked, sounded, and acted wilted. The program neither informed nor persuaded well. The purpose of each program should be clear, and throughout the year the programs should achieve different purposes.

To summarize, it is important that the assembly represent the kind of effective speech education that is being carried on in the school. It is essential that it originate and be developed as the responsibility of the children with the guidance of the teacher, that it represent the educational philosophy of the school accurately, that it include programs with different purposes, and that to a large degree it grow out of the curricular work of the school.

MATERIALS FOR ASSEMBLIES

The chapters throughout this book suggest materials, since assemblies should grow out of curricular work. Creative dramatizations, production of plays, discussion on topics of mutual interest, talks about topics such as conservation, oral reading, choral speaking, and puppetry are suitable activities for assemblies. Other assemblies might include patriotic programs, open discussion of school problems, school sings, student talent programs, programs for special days and weeks such as Pan American Day, Columbus Day, Constitutional Day, Be Kind to Animals Week, and programs growing out of other school experiences in art or music.

Children's literature motivates programs. Rosemary and Stephen Vincent Benét's *A Book of Americans* makes an interesting basis for an assembly. Biographies, such as Esther Averill's *Daniel Boone*, Marion Brown's *Young Nathan* (the story of Nathan Hale), and Robert Lawson's *Ben and Me*, inspire auditorium programs. Books like *The First Thanksgiving*, by Lena Barksdale, Tasha Tudor's *A Tale for Easter*, and Sadie Weilerstein's *What the Moon Brought* (story of Jewish festivals) inspire dramatizations of the various festivals. *One God, the Ways We Worship Him* explains the fundamentals of the Jewish, Catholic, and Protestant religions. In one school, it served as a source for an assembly program. *The American Annual of Christmas Literature and Art*, published every year by the Augsburg Publishing House, Minneapolis, Minn., contains material that is unusual. For example, the 1950 issue includes the story of the use of candles at Christmas, Christmas in the city a long time ago, traditions of the holiday season in England, Sweden, France, Poland, and Norway, and a number of the less-known Christmas carols. It contains many ideas for assembly programs. Books about countries also motivate auditorium activities. Frances Frost's *Legends of the United Nations* contains stories from many lands. Children's literature is the source of many assembly programs.

DISCUSSING THE ASSEMBLY

After the children have put a program on, they evaluate their performance. They talk over the areas in which they did well and those where they can improve their program. They ask such questions as:

1. Did the program accomplish the intended purpose?
2. How could we have organized it so that it would have gone off more smoothly?

3. Could the audience hear and understand us?
4. What in the content could we have improved for our particular audience?
5. Did the audience listen to our program actively?
6. Did the audience understand our content?
7. Did the audience respond to our performance?
8. If we were to repeat the performance, what would we change?

FIG. 21. Discussing the assembly. (*University State Teachers College, Fredonia, N.Y.*)

SUMMARY

Assemblies grow out of the speech activities that are included in the curricular work of the school. Those planning assemblies should keep in mind the following five requirements: (1) The children plan and carry out the work with the guidance of the teacher. (2) The children accept and carry the responsibility for the performance. (3) The assembly shows the parents what the school is doing and its educational philosophy. (4) The assembly program furthers good speech in children. (5) The year's program includes assemblies with different purposes. Assembly programs may be based on special days or weeks, units of work in the school program, and children's literature. After children have put on an assembly, they evaluate it in terms of its purpose, its presentation, and its effect on the audience.

EXERCISES

1. Discuss the place of the assembly in the educational program of the school.

2. Plan an assembly to celebrate a special event or a holiday that would involve several grades.

3. Describe an assembly that might grow out of a unit of work in the classroom.

4. Indicate specifically how the assembly can help in the community's understanding of the school.

5. Show how a specific piece of children's literature can serve as a basis for an assembly.

6. Attend an assembly given by children. Show its purpose. Analyze the assembly to see whether it follows the requirements for assemblies mentioned in this chapter.

7. Give examples of classwork of the grade you intend to teach that can be shared with other children in an assembly.

BIBLIOGRAPHY

Crawley, M. H., "It's Good to Live Here," *National Education Association Journal*, Vol. 39 (October, 1950), pp. 504–505. Describes a series of assemblies built around the topic, "Zeal for American Democracy."

Espenlaub, D., "Christmas in One World," *Childhood Education*, Vol. 24 (December, 1947), pp. 188–189. Shows the portrayal of Christmas in various countries, for example, Mexico.

Ferry, E. D., "Our Own Plays: An Experience in Creative Writing," *Elementary English*, Vol. 28 (March, 1951), p. 135. Explains how a third-grade group puts on an original play in assembly.

Lolita, Sister Mary, "Haydn Lives Again," *Educators' Music Magazine*, Vol. 27 (January, 1948), pp. 18–20. Tells about an assembly based on Haydn.

Montgomery, C., "Good Will toward All Men," *Childhood Education*, Vol. 24 (December, 1947), pp. 184–186. Gives an account of a Christmas program using a fifteenth-century carol to represent "the olde idea" and using the customs of lands such as Finland, Spain, and Africa to represent "the new idea."

Opal, J. M., "Book Week in an Elementary School," *Elementary English*, Vol. 26 (October, 1949), pp. 308–322. Discusses Book Week and the use of an assembly to culminate the week.

Simonson, E., "The School Assembly Program," *Elementary English Review*, Vol. 22 (November, 1945), pp. 258–260. Tells the "story of America." Includes the leading events in the history of our country. Produced by the fourth, fifth, and sixth grades.

Todd, J. M., "Manila Tagboard and Tempera Paint," *American Childhood*, Vol. 36 (April, 1951), pp. 2–3. Explains the use of an assembly to show children's paintings.

Turner, K. W., "Auditorium English," *Grade Teacher*, Vol. 65 (April, 1948), p. 64. Tells about assemblies representative of people of many lands, such as Indians, Italians, and Northern Europeans.

Whittenburg, C., "Sharing Experiences in Local History," *Childhood Education*, Vol. 25 (November, 1949), pp. 130–132. Contains the account of an assembly produced by eight-year-olds for parents and schoolmates. Tells of the planning, carrying out, and evaluating of an assembly, "Local History Is Fun." Includes description of material in the assembly.

Wirt, M. H., "The Play, the Auditorium, the Assembly," in *The Role of Speech in the Elementary School*, Washington, National Education Association, Department of Elementary School Principals, 1946–1947, pp. 79–84. Gives the philosophy of building a play for presentation in an assembly.

Zachar, I. J., "An Assembly Committee at Work," *English Journal*, Vol. 34 (November, 1945), pp. 476–480. Relates the organization of the assembly through a teacher-student committee.

II The Role of the Classroom Teacher in Correcting Speech Difficulties

School X is a school where the administrators, parents, teachers, and specialists cooperate to further the growth of each child. Part of the growth of the child concerns the development of his ability to communicate with others. When a child does not communicate well, the staff of the school and the parents work together to improve this ability. Mr. Howard, a speech correctionist, and other members of this faculty work together to solve the problems of oral communication. Because a speech difficulty hinders oral communication, a committee of teachers asked Mr. Howard to prepare a report for the staff, "The Classroom Teacher's Responsibility for the Child with a Speech Difficulty." The group asked him to cover (1) the definition of a speech difficulty; (2) the difficulties which the teacher is most likely to find in his classroom; and (3) the teacher's part in the program of speech correction. Mr. Howard wrote the following report:

DEFINITION OF A SPEECH DIFFICULTY

All teachers listen to what children are saying. Beyond this point, however, they listen in different ways, partly because of their varying interests and background. For example, Miss Bright notes voice quality; Mr. Brown, word usage; and Miss Jacobson, particular sound variations. Miss Jacobson makes a careful analysis of the sound variations of her children. All teachers, however, indicate when a child's way of speaking interferes with what he is saying. When his speech attracts attention to itself, even though his environment is fairly comfortable, he has a speech difficulty. This difficulty in, or barrier to, communication is detected by teachers in their listening. For example, one youngster may substitute one sound for another, as *mudder* for *mother* or *lethon* for *lesson*. Another may repeat sounds and syllables and hesitate frequently enough to distract the listener. Still another may sound as if he has a very bad cold. Statistics indicate that from 3 to 12 per cent of the school population have speech difficulties that interfere with communication. The Midcentury White House Conference reports that 5 per cent of children between the ages of five and twenty-one are seriously handicapped by speech disorders.[1] The correctionist and the teacher work together to help the child with the speech difficulty.

TYPES OF SPEECH DIFFICULTIES

ARTICULATORY DIFFICULTIES

Most frequently, teachers meet articulatory difficulties, which account for about 3 per cent of the speech difficulties in the elementary school.[2] This number is more than all the other speech difficulties combined. Articulatory defects include the following:

1. Substitution of one sound for another; for example, a child says *wed* for *red*, *wiwy* for *lily*, or *fum* for *thumb*.
2. Omission of sounds; for example, a child says *dum* for *drum*.
3. Distortion of sounds; for example, the *s* sound may have some of the characteristics of the *sh* sound.

The causes of these difficulties are varied: organic difficulty of the articulatory organs, dull hearing, psychological difficulty, persistence of childish habits, and faulty learning.

HARD-OF-HEARING SPEECH

As has been indicated above, the hard-of-hearing youngster often has an articulatory difficulty. This difficulty is sometimes accompanied by one in voice. In some instances, a hearing loss may not be significant enough to cause any speech difficulty. Nevertheless, even in these cases, a barrier to communication often exists. Although the child can speak properly, he may not be hearing all that goes on around him. In other words, two-way communication may not be taking place. In the United States there are 3,000,000 children with impaired hearing. A survey of 23,347 children in the Detroit schools indicated that 4.5 children out of

[1] American Speech and Hearing Association Committee on the Midcentury White House Conference, "Speech Disorders and Speech Correction," *The Journal of Speech and Hearing Disorders*, Vol. 17 (June, 1952), p. 130.
[2] *Ibid.*

100 had impaired hearing.[3] The Midcentury White House Conference reports 0.5 per cent children with impaired hearing with speech defects.[4]

Certain symptoms indicate that a child may have a loss of hearing. Certain vowel and consonant sounds are distorted or omitted, depending upon the type of hearing loss. The sounds affected are contingent on what pitches the child does not hear accurately and on his ability to observe how sounds are made. His voice may become softer or louder than usual, again dependent on the type of hearing loss. If a child has a perception loss (due to injury or damage to the nerve of hearing), his voice tends to become louder. On the other hand, if he has a conduction loss (due to physical impairment of the ear), his voice tends to become softer. The child with a significant loss of hearing ignores verbal directions or confuses them. He does not respond when someone talks to him. Frequently he asks the teacher or other children to repeat explanations. He watches the speaker unusually closely and sometimes turns his head to one side to listen to the speaker more carefully. A hard-of-hearing child's performance based on reading usually surpasses his performance based on oral explanations. Sometimes he complains of dizziness, head noises, or earaches. Because these signs indicate that the child may be hard of hearing, the teacher should report them to the correctionist and to the school health authorities. Frequently the classroom teacher is the first to suspect that a child is hard of hearing.

Next most frequently, vocal defects and stuttering occur. Approximately 1 per cent of the school population stutter, and about the same percentage have fairly serious problems of voice. The Midcentury White House Conference reports that 0.7 per cent of children stutter and that 0.2 per cent have serious voice difficulties.[5]

DIFFICULTIES OF VOICE

Difficulties of voice fall into three categories: volume, pitch, and quality. First, children may speak too loudly or too softly. Second, they may speak on the same pitch, at too high a pitch, or at too low a pitch (in general, every person has an average or fundamental pitch level at which he produces voice with the greatest ease and effectiveness). Third, their voices may be disagreeable or unpleasant; for example, they may

[3] L. Keller, "Hearing Survey in Detroit Schools," *Journal of Exceptional Children,* Vol. II (March, 1945), pp. 168–183.

[4] American Speech and Hearing Association Committee on the Midcentury White House Conference, *loc. cit.*

[5] *Ibid.*

be nasal, denasal, breathy, hoarse, or strident. With a nasal voice, a child sounds as if he is talking through his nose. With a denasal one, he sounds as if he has a cold. The causes of difficulties of volume, pitch, and quality of voice fall into these classifications: (1) physical, (2) emotional, and (3) functional. The first category accounts for a large number of difficulties. Mary Brown's voice was thin and light. She frequently complained of feeling tired. In her case, a medical examination revealed a severe case of anemia. The second category, emotional causes, is often noted by laymen. A typical comment is "She's a nagger; her voice fits her." Voice is not always an index to personality, but at times the vocal defect is one of many symptoms of maladjustment. Lastly, the cause may be functional. Because one child imitated a movie actress with a low pitch, her voice became hoarse and unpleasant.

STUTTERING

A stutterer's speech interferes with the reception of his ideas by his listeners. No one stutterer's speech is exactly like a second's. Symptoms of one stutterer were blocking on some sounds, repetition or prolongation of sounds, repetition of syllables or words, and spasms of the speaking mechanism. On occasion, he spoke fluently. Many stutterers manifest such symptoms. Others present a different group. For example, some stutterers speak slowly in a hesitating fashion. Their speech is monotonous. They try to speak on inhalation. Almost always some situations exist in which a stutterer does not stutter; for example, he may be able to act in a play or speak over the telephone. Sometimes he stutters worse than other times.

The causes of stuttering are not known. Many theories exist, but research has substantiated no particular one. Van Riper's[6] *Speech Correction: Principles and Methods*, Reid's[7] article in the *Journal of Speech Disorders*, Ainsworth's[8] in the same journal, and Hahn's[9] *Stuttering: Significant Theories and Therapies* contain summaries of present-day theories.

The following theories of the causation of stuttering are prevalent:

[6] C. Van Riper, *Speech Correction: Principles and Methods*, New York, Prentice-Hall, 1947, pp. 267–274.

[7] L. Reid, "Some Facts about Stuttering," *Journal of Speech Disorders*, Vol. 11 (1946), pp. 3–12.

[8] S. Ainsworth, "Integrating Theories of Stuttering," *Journal of Speech Disorders*, Vol. 10 (1945), pp. 205–219.

[9] E. H. Hahn, *Stuttering: Significant Theories and Therapies*, Stanford, Calif., Stanford University Press, 1943.

(1) There exists in the stuttering child a weakness of the neuromuscular system causing it to break down. (2) Adults and/or other children in the stutterer's environment have handled his normal hesitations and repetitions unwisely: (3) Emotional conflicts, which show themselves in the symptoms of stuttering, exist in the child.

Breakdown of the Neuromuscular System. The belief is quite widely held that the neuromuscular system of the stuttering child is not so adequate for speaking as that of the nonstuttering child. The weakness of the central coordinating system shows up in the child's speech under strain. For example, if he has a severe illness, accident, or other shock which acts as a precipitating cause, the stuttering appears.

Undue Attention to Children's Natural Hesitations. Parents, adults, or other children have disapproved of, or called attention in an unpleasant way to, the child's normal repetitions and hesitations. Consequently, he stutters. No young child has fluent, easy speech. Small boys and girls repeat sounds, stop talking completely, and break the rhythm of their speech. The speech patterns of adults set high standards of performance for children; many children receive pressure to reach toward these standards. A parent may say, "Stop that stuttering," or he may scowl, frown, or in some way obviously show his irritation at the child's slow, hesitating statements.

Emotional Conflict. One stuttering child, an orphan, always asked for approval by declaring that no one loved him in order to hear it denied. He was afraid of dogs, of the dark, of the merry-go-round. Frequently, he had severe nightmares. Another stuttering child did not get along with other youngsters. He always chose children younger than himself to play with and then bullied them. When securely hidden, he would throw stones at adults and other children. Instances such as these show, in particular, stuttering youngsters' inabilities to adjust to their environments. In such cases, some authorities regard the stuttering as a symptom of a basic personality problem or the inability of an individual to adjust to his social environment.

All three causes seem to apply to some stuttering children. For example, Janey's grandmother stuttered. Janey, a five-year-old, seemed to have difficulty in learning to eat neatly. She did not run well. Quite obviously, she had some difficulty coordinating. Her mother was an overly anxious, worried person who was always busy. Janey's speech irritated her, and she let Janey know it through her manner and her scolding. The standards she set for Janey in cleanliness and obedience were very high. Lastly, Janey had many fears: of staying alone, of the dark, of closed-in places. Instead of becoming part of a group, she often sat by herself. Multiple factors seem to be involved in Janey's stuttering.

CLEFT-PALATE SPEECH

Two speech difficulties caused by physical abnormalities or conditions are those associated with cleft palate and with cerebral palsy. The figures for the incidence of cleft palate are fairly low. In Wisconsin, during 1942 to 1945, 1 child out of 798 was born with a cleft palate.[10] The Midcentury White House Conference reports that 0.1 per cent of children have cleft-palate speech.[11]

Cleft palate or lip is the abnormal survival of embryonic fissures. Sometimes only a cleft of the lip occurs; evidently, development then becomes normal, and the palates are joined. Sometimes there is no cleft of the lip, but clefts of the teeth ridge (the ridge behind the upper teeth) and the hard and/or soft palates occur. In these cases, the early stages of development were normal, but the later stages were arrested. The cause of cleft palate is not known.

In the speech of the child with a cleft palate, all sounds pass directly into the nose; consequently, his speech has a very nasal quality. All the vowel sounds are nasalized, and most of the consonants have nasal characteristics. In the sounds p, b, t, d, k, and g, he is unable to build up the air to explode; therefore, they are defective. Often b, d, and g take on the characteristics of the sounds m, n, and ng. The sounds f, v, s, z, sh and zh, and the two th's are also defective, since the child with a cleft palate cannot control the air stream coming through the mouth. Because s and z require the direction of the air stream down a narrow channel, they are likely to be the most seriously affected of the fricative sounds. Frequent inhalation and considerable use of a kind of catch before vowels are also distinctive traits. Certain mannerisms frequently go along with cleft palate. The child twitches his nose as if he were sniffing. The winglike structures of the nose constrict to compensate for the failure of the nasal port to close.

CEREBRAL-PALSY SPEECH

Cerebral palsy is a disturbance of the motor function due to damage to the brain during or shortly after the birth of the infant. Approxi-

[10] G. M. Phair, "Wisconsin Cleft Palate Program," *Journal of Speech Disorders,* Vol. 12 (December, 1947), p. 411.

[11] American Speech and Hearing Association Committee on the Midcentury White House Conference, *loc. cit.*

mately 7 out of 100,000 children born each year have cerebral palsy. Because of the appearance of the cerebral-palsied child, laymen sometimes label him feeble-minded. He is likely to look sleepy and sometimes stupid, for he cannot control the muscles of his face to register emotion. The majority of cerebral-palsied children are intelligent and can grow to take their places in society. Fifty per cent are average; 5 to 10 per cent are bright; 10 per cent are idiots or low morons; and the rest are substandard.[12] The Midcentury White House Conference reports that 0.2 per cent of children between the ages of five and twenty-one have cerebral-palsied speech.[13]

Although the speech of the cerebral-palsied youngster is normal when the muscles of the articulating organs are not affected, in most cases it is slow, jerky, and labored. The rhythm is faulty, with many unnatural pauses. The quality of the voice may be weak, falsetto, or tremulous. The consonants are likely to be inaccurate, particularly in such cases as *t*, *d*, *n*, and *l*, in which the tongue is lifted to the teeth ridge. The speech of one cerebral-palsied child is different from that of a second. The different types of cerebral palsy and the muscles that are affected influence the speech.

THE CLASSROOM TEACHER'S RESPONSIBILITY FOR SPEECH DIFFICULTIES

Members of a school staff are effective in working with children when they work as a team. In the case of speech difficulties, the school doctor checks the physical health of the child. The psychologist helps the teacher and the correctionist understand both the child and his parents. The principal calls on resources of the community, such as the medical specialists and the social worker. The correctionist works directly with the speech of the child and coordinates some of the special services. But the classroom teacher knows the child best since he is with him all day.

In general, what does the classroom teacher do for a child with a speech difficulty? He is interested in his development, in the furtherance of effective communication in the classroom, and in the establishment of good human relationships within the group. What is good educa-

[12] M. E. Pusitz, "Speech Correction in the Cerebral Palsied," *Journal of Speech Disorders*, Vol. 4 (September, 1939), pp. 205–218.
[13] American Speech and Hearing Association Committee on the Midcentury White House Conference, *loc. cit.*

tion for the child with normal speech is good education for the child with a speech difficulty.

UNDERSTANDING THE CHILD

First, the teacher works hard at understanding the child. He goes over his cumulative reports carefully to learn what he can about the child. When the speech difficulty is closely related to the personality of the child, the reports are particularly helpful. He supplies his teammates with information which can help them understand the child. He reports the child's behavior in the classroom and on the playground and how he gets along with other children. He gives details of his special abilities and interests. He describes the home situation. With this information as a background, all the teammates help the child to adjust to his environment.

ACCEPTING THE CHILD

Part of this adjustment lies in accepting the child as he is, helping the other children accept him as he is, and encouraging the child to live with his difficulty successfully. The teacher plays a most important role in furthering acceptance of the difficulty. He may feel sympathy toward the stutterer; the students may feel derision; the stutterer himself may be quite self-conscious about his speech. When the teacher controls his feeling and accepts the stutterer with his speech difficulty, he and his classmates are more likely to adopt the same attitude. One teacher encourages a wholesome attitude on the part of the children by pointing out that all of them have difficulty with some phase of learning; reading, arithmetic, or spelling, and that children differ from each other in ways of speaking, appearing, and behaving. With guidance, children accept a handicapped child readily. The author saw a badly crippled child play a part in a play with his classmates. They approved him as a performing member, made the necessary provision for his infirmity, such as pushing his crutch toward him, and expected him to do his share in the play. Both he and his classmates accepted his handicap. The author also saw a hard-of-hearing youngster participating in creative dramatics in which he was the lion. He crouched like a lion, roared like one, and quite completely gave the illusion of being a lion. True, when he roared, "I am the lion," he did not articulate clearly. But he did have more ability to portray character than most of the other children. One of his classmates said, "Sydney has more oomph than the rest of us." The other youngsters accepted him with his poor articulation and recognized that he was an effective cooperative participant in their play. In both instances, unusually fine teachers skillfully laid the foundation for the handicapped child's acceptance by the entire group.

FURTHERING EFFECTIVE COMMUNICATION

The second important factor is that the classroom atmosphere invite communication. When the children plan their work together, when they enjoy playing together, they must talk and they must listen. Furthermore, as they go on purposeful trips, as they make puppets, as they act in a play, they have something worthwhile to discuss. A classroom with an aquarium, an interesting bulletin board, and a corner for reading good books invites talk. The material in earlier chapters on speech activities tells about ways in which teachers have fostered effective communication. Again, because the teacher is the one who is with the child as he communicates to a group, he does more to interest him in speaking than does any other single individual.

BUILDING GOOD HUMAN RELATIONSHIPS

The third factor is that a good relationship among the children and between the children and the teacher encourages speaking. When there exists a warm, friendly feeling in the classroom, when the youngsters enjoy each other and their teacher, speaking is made easier. By encouraging the children to participate in decisions, by helping them feel that they solve their problems through discussion, and by assuring them that they have a necessary and vital part in the school program, the teacher promotes a feeling of belonging and of responsibility to the group.

HELPING THE CHILD SPEAK WELL

Lastly, under the guidance of the correctionist, the teacher works directly with the speech of the child. For example, after the correctionist had taught one ten-year-old child to say the sound l correctly, the teacher reinforced the learning of this sound in the classroom by helping the child say it as he had been taught and by commending him when he incorporated the sound in his conversation. He helps in other ways:

in the ear training of students, in the recognition of their errors, and in the establishment of habits of acceptable voice and diction.

The teacher is the captain of the team whose purpose is to correct a child's speech. The teacher knows the child best, is familiar with the home situation, and is able to study closely the child's response to the program. As the classroom teacher and his teammates, the correctionist, the psychologist, and the physician, play the game more skillfully, the season becomes more successful and more children learn to control their speech difficulties.

THE SPEECH CORRECTIONIST AND THE CLASSROOM TEACHER ATTACK SPEECH DIFFICULTIES

The kindergarten teacher, Miss Martin, visited Mr. Howard the next week because the speech of several of her children gave her concern. She felt that a large percentage of her kindergarten youngsters had difficulty with articulation. For example, she pointed out that one child said *sed* for *sled* and *bwown* for *brown*. Mr. Howard told her he felt that many of these substitutions were the normal articulatory patterns for children in the kindergarten but that he would check them for her. He indicated that maturity alone remedies many young children's speech difficulties.

MATURITY IN RELATION TO ARTICULATORY DEFECTS

Mr. Howard cited the following table compiled by Davis[14] which shows the ages at which most children are able to articulate certain sounds (*s*'s and *z*'s are listed twice because distortions in these sounds occur when children lose their front teeth):

3.5 years—*p, b, m, w, h.*
4.5 years—*t, d, n, g, k, ng, y.*
5.5 years—*f, v, s, z.*
6.5 years—*sh, zh, l, th* as in *thin, th* as in *then.*
8.0 years—*s, z, r, wh.*

Because of the preponderance of five-year-olds within Miss Martin's group, many of her children were still acquiring sounds. Mr. Howard

[14] I. P. Davis, "The Speech Aspects of Reading Readiness," in *Newer Practices in Reading in the Elementary Schools,* Seventeenth Yearbook of the Department of Elementary School Principals, Washington, National Education Association, 1938, p. 283.

told her that *l* and *r* in blends in words such as *drown* and *fly* were often difficult for children. He reminded her that she was very patient with her children's inability to handle their zippers easily and that in most cases both the ability to fasten the zipper and the ability to articulate certain sounds would come with increasing maturity.

Studies show considerable variability in the ages at which children master certain skills. This same principle is true in the acquisition of sounds. Some children speak clearly at four years of age; others are eight before they make all their sounds accurately. Girls generally develop languagewise faster than boys. Irene Poole[15] points out that not until girls are six and a half years of age do 50 per cent attain mastery of all consonant sounds. The boys take approximately a year longer before they acquire the same mastery. In a study of articulatory errors of children, Roe and Milisen[16] conclude that growth and maturation eliminate many sound errors in the first four grades. They also indicate that maturation does not effect noticeable improvement in the speech sounds of higher grades.

NATURAL HESITATION IN YOUNG CHILDREN'S SPEECH

Louise was another child with whom Miss Martin needed help. She described Louise as a vivacious five-year-old who sometimes hesitated and sometimes repeated sounds. Miss Martin felt that this was a normal phenomenon, as others in her group hesitated and repeated to about the same degree. But Louise's parents were concerned, for Louise's great-aunt stuttered badly. Louise's parents tended to set very high standards for her in many ways, such as cleanliness, tidiness, correct grammar, and good manners. After seeing Louise, the correctionist agreed with Miss Martin's diagnosis. He suggested that they both talk with Louise's mother to encourage her to listen for *what* the child said rather than *how* she said it. He also recommended Wendell Johnson's[17] "An Open Letter to the Mother of a Stuttering Child" to the parents, for it contains sound advice for parents whose children stutter or for parents who think their children stutter.

---

[15] I. Poole, "Genetic Development of Consonant Sounds in Speech," *Elementary English Review*, Vol. 11 (June, 1934), p. 161.

[16] V. Roe and R. Milisen, "The Effect of Maturation upon Defective Articulation in Elementary Grades," *Journal of Speech Disorders*, Vol. 7 (March, 1942), p. 44.

[17] W. Johnson, *Speech Handicapped School Children*, New York, Harper, 1948, Appendix XIII, pp. 443–451.

SEVERE ARTICULATORY DISORDER

Miss Harvey, first-grade teacher, was the next caller. She came to Mr. Howard saying, "Janey doesn't talk so that I can understand her. The other children translate for me." The correctionist agreed that Janey was difficult to understand and that her speech pattern was a complex one. She could say *p*, *b*, *t*, *d*, *s*, *z*, *m*, *n*, and *ng*, although at times she substituted *b* for *p* and *d* for *t*. She used *t* and *d* for *k* and *g*, *t* and *d* for the two *th*'s, *p* and *b* for *f* and *v*, *w* for *l* and *r*, *s* and *z* for *sh* and *zh*, and *s* and *z* for *ch* and *j*. She frequently omitted many consonants; for example, she said, "Aye ad a new dah ome" for "I have a new doll home," "Ayuh oh?" for "Where are you going?" and "It oke" for "It's broken."

The correctionist explained that Janey's pattern of substitutions was unusual and that no cause was apparent. Her hearing was normal and she tested average in intelligence by a nonlanguage test. She did not begin to speak until she was four years old. He further noted that she was afraid, timid, and depended on a sister who was overprotective and oversolicitous of her. He explained that Janey's mother was cooperative and intelligent but severely handicapped by being confined to a wheel chair. He showed how the school psychologist and the kindergarten teacher of last year had helped Janey in her adjustment and described the progress she had made in kindergarten.

Setting up Situations Conducive to Communication. In talking over the situation with Mr. Howard, Miss Martin decided to set up situations which would encourage Janey to talk. Mr. Howard asked her if she would report them to him. The following situations were typical of the ones she reported. When another child brought his dog to school, Miss Martin suggested that Janey talk with it so that it wouldn't be lonesome. Janey did and loved the talk. The teacher took advantage of other opportunities where Janey could communicate successfully. She told Janey how the plant manager's face had lighted up when Janey had thanked him for taking the group through his plant. After the group had picked grapes, Janey helped "read" the recipe for making grape jelly. Members of the class took a train trip. All of them, including Janey, planned it beforehand and talked about it afterward. Miss Martin did an unusually fine job of encouraging Janey to communicate. Through such activities Janey felt that she *could* talk.

Listening to Sounds and Distinguishing between Them. At this stage, Mr. Howard started ear training with Janey. To Janey *f* sounded like *p*, to her *pibe* for *five* did not sound unusual. She was unaware that she had made a substitution. She did not have the ability to discriminate, for she did not recognize the sound or identify it in any particular way. The speech correctionist was training her to hear the sound. Children learn words and, often, sentences as a whole; they do not separate the word into the various sounds. The correctionist was teaching Janey to isolate the sound, to identify it, and finally to compare the sound she substituted with the sound others used.

With Mr. Howard's help, the classroom teacher helped Janey to listen to sounds. Miss Martin read *ShhhBang, A Whispering Book*,[18] *The Noisy Book*,[19] *A Kitten's Tale*,[20] *Cock-a-doodle-doo*,[21] and *Rain Drop Splash*[22] because they contained sounds children enjoy repeating. The children went on a listening walk. When they came back, they told what they had heard: the squeak the wheels made when the car went around a corner, the click as gas was poured into the gas tank of a car, the burr of an airplane, the chug-chug of the slow freight train, the rustle of the leaves, and the songs of the birds. Another type of listening activity was one in which the children decided whether sounds were alike or different. The teacher made sure that they knew the concepts of the words "alike" and "different." She then struck two glasses of water with different amounts of water in them. She hit a block of wood and a block of iron. She rang two bells with similar sounds, then two with different sounds. Finally, she said nonsense syllables like "ray way," "ray, ray," "fay, kay." To make sure the children were listening rather than watching they put their heads on their desks. Janey enjoyed the game and developed in her ability to discriminate between sounds.

Developing Responsibility in the Child. The psychologist also played a part. He continued conferences begun last year with Janey, and he and Miss Martin talked about ways to help Janey. Janey's sister usually waited for Janey at three o'clock to escort her to the bus. Miss Martin suggested to the sister that Janey be allowed to go to the bus alone. Last year, Janey would not go to the speech room unless Mr. Howard came after her. She held tightly to his hand while she went with him. Then the kindergarten teacher suggested that another child would like to go along to see what happened. Finally, Janey was encouraged to make the trip alone. This year, Miss Martin asked her to do an errand on her way to the room. In many such ways, the classroom teacher helped Janey become a more independent and responsible child.

[18] M. W. Brown, *ShhhBang, A Whispering Book*, New York, Harper, 1949.
[19] M. W. Brown, *The Noisy Book*, Chicago, Scott, Foresman, 1939.
[20] A. Chalmers, *A Kitten's Tale*, New York, Viking, 1946.
[21] B. Hader and E. Hader, *Cock-a-doodle-doo*, New York, Macmillan, 1939.
[22] A. R. Tresselt, *Rain Drop Splash*, New York, Lothrop, 1946.

Reinforcing the Teaching of the Correctionist. After Mr. Howard had taught Janey to say *f* and *v*, Miss Martin encouraged Janey to say them correctly in the classroom. She complimented Janey when she said "five." One day Miss Martin brought a picture of a fox in the woods. The picture contained many objects the names of which contained *f*'s or *v*'s. She and Janey talked about the picture. In an easy, casual way she motivated Janey to use *f* and *v* where they belonged.

Throughout the year, Miss Martin helped Janey in four ways: (1) by helping her adjust to speaking situations, (2) by helping her listen to sounds and distinguish between them, (3) by helping the family treat Janey as a more mature child and realize the need for her being responsible for herself, and (4) by reinforcing what the correctionist had taught her.

STUTTERING

The third grade, with Miss Jones as a teacher, contained two children with serious problems. The first of these was Johnny, who stuttered.

Miss Jones became aware of Johnny's difficulty with speech almost immediately. He repeated many sounds: "I c-c-c-can't go now." "Wh-wh-where d-d-d-did you p-p-put the scissors?" Now and then he opened his mouth but no sound came forth. His speech did not flow smoothly because he broke his sentences in many unnatural places. Frequently he used the word "well" to start a sentence. He tended to speak faster than the other members of the group. His lips often quivered as he spoke. His difficulty with his speech was apparent to any observer in the classroom.

Johnny did not always stutter. As he took part in a play, he spoke smoothly. When he participated in choral speaking with his group, he spoke easily. On many days, he repeated or blocked infrequently. After a long vacation, his stuttering was more severe. He sang with the group well. As he played the role of a Swedish papa, he did not stutter at all. At times, he manifested many symptoms of stuttering, at other times, he manifested few or none.

During the first two weeks of school, Miss Jones found that Johnny was a good student. He helped plan the visit to a canning factory and to a fishing boat. While on the boat and at the factory, he asked intelligent questions of those in charge. As he returned to the classroom, he liked to talk about the experiences and made worthwhile contributions to the group discussion. He seemed to have little fear of speaking even though he took a long time and had great difficulty in getting out what he wanted to say. He read well and liked to read. He did his number work accurately and rapidly; he grasped its concepts quickly. In art, he did not like to paint; he preferred to draw with a pencil or crayon. He was always dissatisfied with his paintings, for he felt they were "sloppy." On the whole, he was interested in his school work and did well in it.

On the playground, he played quite well with other children. He seemed to stutter less on the playground than he did in his classroom. He liked to throw the basketball even though he did it poorly. If he failed to get the ball in the ring consistently, he became very angry. As a teammate in games, he usually was cooperative. On the whole, he was willing to wait his turn and to let the other boys and girls "star," but there were times when he insisted on being captain and when he monopolized the basketball. Once in a while he would bully younger children.

As Miss Jones noted the stutter, she went to the central office for his file to learn about his background, his previous work in school, and his adjustment to his group. She found out that he came from a home of average economic status. The father was a skilled factory worker. Johnny was the youngest child, with a brother, fifteen years old, in eighth grade and a sister in an out-of-town college. A paternal grandmother also lived in the home. Miss Jones discovered that Johnny was a bright boy with an I.Q. of 124 according to a Stanford-Binet test administered by the school psychologist the previous year. She found out that he had done well in reading, arithmetic, social studies, and spelling, and that on achievement tests he was approximately two years ahead of the norms in almost all subjects. Consistently, however, his previous teachers reported his tendency to want to excel in almost all his school work and to want to draw, write, and paint perfectly. He evidently adjusted to his group better each year, for she found evidence of increasing participation in group activities and a growing ability to share. His health report was excellent.

Mr. Howard told Miss Jones more of Johnny's background. The grandmother was a kind of matriarch who ruled the family with a gloved hand. The mother was an overly anxious, worried individual, earlier confused about Johnny's stuttering. She had believed many of the tales circulated about stuttering; for example, she had made arrangements for chiropractic treatments. She reported that he had begun to stutter when he was four years old after one of their neighbors had frightened him severely. From her own story, she was at times too strict and at other times too lax with him. She did not maintain regularity in meals, sleeping, or disciplinary action with Johnny. Mr. Howard had learned that she was very severe in handling Johnny.

Mr. Howard called in the school psychologist, who reported that Johnny's brother and Johnny resented each other. The brother was unsuccessful in school work and was awaiting the day when he could leave school. He verbalized his concern for Johnny and his stutter; yet he dominated him as much as he could. In puppet play, Johnny had indicated a strong dislike for a brother several times and finally had told a former teacher of his antipathy toward his big brother. Because of this evident strong feeling, the school psychologist had been working with Johnny. The pyschologist and Mr. Howard favored sending Johnny to a summer camp, but the mother demurred, saying that while Johnny was young, she wanted him by her side. The psychologist hoped that this year Johnny's mother would send him to camp.

Miss Jones asked Mr. Howard what she could do to help Johnny, for he was the first stutterer she had had in class. Mr. Howard explained to her that she, the psychologist, and he must work together. He indicated that the previous year the school doctor had given Johnny a very careful physical checkup and that he would cooperate again this year. He explained that Miss Jones would play an important part in the therapy. She would get to know the family and the home and might well be the one who could reach Johnny's mother most successfully. She might be able to help her understand her child as a stutterer and help her in understanding herself and her relationship with the child. Johnny's mother might have more confidence in Miss Jones than in a specialist. He indicated to her ways of handling Johnny in the classroom. The correctionist, the doctor, the psychologist, and the teacher would work as a team to help Johnny.

The Stutterer in the Classroom. The psychologist, Miss Jones, and Mr. Howard discussed the kind of classroom atmosphere and activity that would help Johnny, with the following conclusions:

1. They hoped Johnny would feel that he was an integral, responsible part of the group, one who belonged with its members. They noted ways in which he could continue to be drawn into the activities of the group. They discussed how he could develop his sense of responsibility. He had already volunteered for, and carried through, certain tasks in the preparation for visits to a boat and a factory.

2. Miss Jones emphasized that she would set reasonable standards

that Johnny could reach, particularly since he tended to set too high standards for himself.

3. The psychologist stressed the point that the classroom must be a place where Johnny could find outlets. He had already found opportunity for expression through several media: he liked to be in plays; he enjoyed playing with puppets; he was interested in drawing. Miss Jones agreed to approve him for successful experiences. If, in his play, he expressed strong feelings, she was to view these as normal. She was not to frown on his reactions. While she would not try to "solve his problems," she would listen attentively to any recitation of his difficulties or to his narration of imaginary happenings involving personal or social troubles.

4. They agreed that Johnny was to be encouraged to develop along his own individual lines. He showed no aptitude for music. He gave evidence of little athletic ability. Miss Jones would capitalize on his interests and strengths in writing, drawing, and dramatics.

5. They discussed the necessity of maintaining and increasing the number of speech situations in which Johnny could find success. Miss Jones planned to continue choral speech with the group. Johnny was able to speak lines by himself without stuttering; therefore he was to participate on occasion as a soloist. In taking part in creative dramatics, his stuttering was less severe. The previous week, Johnny's group, inspired by the television show "I Remember Mama," had made up a story with the members of this family as characters. Johnny had taken on the Swedish dialect easily and had spoken as the Swedish papa without stuttering. He was, therefore, to be given opportunities to continue to engage in dramatic activity.

6. The correctionist stressed that Johnny and his classmates should accept his stuttering as his way of speaking. Fortunately, Johnny and Miss Jones were good friends. Because they were both interested in the learning taking place in the classroom, they enjoyed working together. Johnny had already spoken with Miss Jones about his problem of stuttering and some of his difficulties at home. Having established good rapport, she could help Johnny and his classmates accept his stutter. She would make him feel that she realized he was doing as well as he could. He and his classmates would recognize that many individuals have handicaps of one kind or another and that they can learn to live with them successfully. A second way Miss Jones could help Johnny accept his stutter was to be certain that both she and the children were

responsive listeners. When the work in the classroom is meaningful to the children, they are more likely to listen actively. A third way was to be sure that she did not hurry or interrupt Johnny in his speaking. Lastly, she could aid in keeping the environment as free as possible of distractions which might annoy Johnny when he was talking. She would attempt to make the classroom a place where the children speak purposefully and listen actively.

7. Miss Jones herself said that she thought it was important that she approve Johnny for tasks he does well and for his contributions to successful classroom living. She pointed out that she had already complimented him on his intelligent questioning of the captain of the boat, for his ability to portray "Papa," and for his creative writing. She also noted that when she had discovered that he liked to read, she had shown her delight in his interest in books. She had encouraged him to motivate other members of the class to read some of the books he had enjoyed. She indicated that she had shown her pride when Johnny had served as a very fair umpire in a basketball game and when he had given in gracefully to a group decision.

8. Lastly, the psychologist said that he noted that Miss Jones's classroom had a warm, friendly, calm atmosphere. He felt that this atmosphere was an important asset to Johnny's speech work. The correctionist pointed out that Miss Jones's voice was clear and pleasant and that she spoke slowly and rhythmically. Her manner of speaking would be a definite aid to Johnny.

The next question Miss Jones asked was "What are you going to do about Johnny's stutter?" The psychologist explained that he was trying to assist Johnny to live in his environment with less strain. The correctionist indicated that he was working with the psychologist in helping Johnny adjust to his environment. He noted that he was using a variety of approaches to help Johnny control his stuttering and described them to her.

Mr. Howard told her that various types of therapy are used with stutterers. He cited a study made by Loren Reid,[23] in which he analyzed the published material of a selected list of twenty authorities to show the extent to which they approve certain clinical procedures. Equal numbers work to modify the stutterer's environment so that he will feel secure and to modify the stutterer's attitude toward his speech. The next largest number use various rest and relaxation procedures. Others follow different therapies. Some clinicians encourage the stutterer to try

[23] Reid, *loc. cit.*

different patterns of speech in relation to pitch, loudness, duration, or quality. Others encourage social activity; still others set up simplified speech situations so that the student can participate successfully and gain confidence. There are those who still recommend strengthening the preferred hand. Psychoanalysis, rhythmical procedures, and moto-kinesthetic techniques are also utilized. Both the psychologist and the correctionist emphasized that clinical work with a stutterer must remain in the hands of a specialist.

The next comment of Miss Jones was that Johnny seemed to be a superior student. She asked whether stutterers were usually intellectually superior to other students. Mr. Howard answered that, in testing by language tests, there is no significant difference in intelligence between a group of stutterers and nonstutterers. When tested by non-language tests, the stuttering group is slightly higher in intelligence than a nonstuttering group.[24]

Johnny's ability and interest in reading also surprised Miss Jones. She wanted to know whether stutterers, as a rule, were superior readers. Mr. Howard pointed out that stutterers are in general less efficient silent readers than nonstutterers. Stutterers tend to be one grade below normal in comprehension of reading and two grades below in rate of silent reading.[25]

The correctionist helped Miss Jones understand Johnny as a stutterer. The psychologist aided both the correctionist and Miss Jones in understanding Johnny, his brother, and his mother as individuals. Miss Jones helped Mr. Howard know Johnny as a member of the group. All three worked as a team to help Johnny live happily and successfully in his environment with his stutter. They hoped he would learn to control his stuttering through their combined efforts.

HARD-OF-HEARING DIFFICULTY

Bobby was a third grader in whom Mr. Howard was interested. He had been a rather severe stutterer in kindergarten but, with help, had learned to control the difficulty unusually quickly. Each year, Mr. Howard asked about him to check his progress. This year, Miss King said that Bobby no longer stuttered but that he didn't seem a very alert

[24] E. D. McDowell, *Educational and Emotional Adjustments of Stuttering Children,* Teachers College Contribution to Education, No. 314, New York, Teachers College, Columbia University, 1928.

[25] E. Murray, "Disintegration of Breathing and Eye Movement in Stutterers during Silent Reading," *Psychological Monographs,* Vol. 43 (1932), pp. 218–275.

child. Mr. Howard was surprised, for Bobby had been a vivacious, energetic, imaginative five-year-old. Teachers in the first and second grades had reported that he was a bright, intelligent, well-adjusted youngster. Miss King said that Bobby didn't do well in school work, that he followed directions badly, and that he seemed to withdraw from the group. At times, she said, he seemed aggressive, for he spoke too loudly. After this report, Bobby came to see the correctionist, who, after a short conference, suspected that Bobby had become hard of hearing. He recalled that the mother had told him of hereditary deafness on the paternal side. Therefore, he checked the child's hearing with a pure-tone audiometer and found that he had a substantial hearing loss in both ears. When he called Bobby's mother, she said that she had just recently begun to suspect that Bobby did not hear well. An otologist to whom Bobby was referred diagnosed the condition as perception deafness due to damage to the nerve of hearing and made the prognosis that a further loss of hearing would occur. Since Bobby was destined to lose his hearing progressively, and since the otologist said a hearing aid would be of little value, Mr. Howard began to teach Bobby lip reading.

Miss King did much to help the child live with his handicap successfully. She helped him regain his feeling of social competence. He began to accept the fact that he could live normally in a normal environment. Because he had begun to withdraw and live within himself, the teacher encouraged him to become part of the group. She motivated him to take and carry responsibility. She influenced him to converse with others and to take part in discussion groups. She motivated him to participate in the activities of the playground and in creative dramatics. He had an interest in growing plants. Miss King furthered this interest and urged him to share it with his friends and family.

Mr. Howard and Miss King talked about how she could help Bobby understand what was going on in the classroom. She said that she was making sure that Bobby was seated where he could see her and where the light would shine on her face as she spoke. She said that Bobby had changed his seat to a table in the center of the room where he would be nearer to her and to his classmates whom he must hear. Mr. Howard suggested that she use gestures normally to help Bobby understand what she was saying. The correctionist was delighted when Bobby said, "Miss King is easy to understand. She talks with her face and her hands." He was allowed to move around the room so that he could hear what was going on more readily. Furthermore, Miss King watched Bobby for signs of lack of comprehension and, when she discovered he did not understand, she restated her directions and ideas in different words. Miss King emphasized that she did not repeat material but rather rephrased it. The adoption of these simple measures made hearing easier for Bobby.

VOICE PROBLEMS

Mr. Alexander, in charge of the seventh grade, referred two children with unpleasant voices to Mr. Howard. One was Alice, with a high-pitched, thin, light voice, and the other was Tony, with a denasal voice, one that sounded as if he had a bad cold.

Alice had recently moved into the school district. She came with no cumulative record but with a note from her former principal saying that her teachers had found her to be a delightful child, a good school citizen, and an excellent student, talented in art. She was a small, attractive twelve-year-old. She wore pretty clothes, inclined to frills and bows, and immaculately pressed.

When Alice first came to the seventh-grade classroom, she greeted Mr. Alexander pleasantly and was cordial to the students. Although her voice made her sound young, she appeared well poised and mature. Because no homework was assigned, she expressed concern, for she said that she was preparing for college. She volunteered for several tasks such as that of chairman of the bulletin-board committee. As she worked at it with her group, she made sure that the board contained what *she* felt important and looked the way *she* wanted it. When one of the boys on her committee remonstrated, saying that the board looked "sissy," she was hurt. As Mr. Alexander talked with her about accepting the ideas of committee members and resolving conflict within a group, she responded, "But those kids just aren't artistically inclined." But she did think the problem through with the teacher and probably did learn a little about accepting the ideas of the members of one's group.

Her achievement in school subjects was excellent. She read well and she wrote with a certain creative flair. Her papers were always very neat and carefully written. Although her writing was small, it was perfectly formed. Her main interest was in art. She drew and painted small representative pictures with many details. She did exquisite flowers in pastels. When the art instructor encouraged her to use large sheets of paper and to be bolder about her painting, she used the large sheet but painted small flowers in the middle of the paper.

Alice's voice was high-pitched, and she already sounded like a prissy old lady with every sound overly distinct. The correctionist agreed to see her and discovered that she was speaking one-fifth, or five tones, above her natural pitch. At first, Alice seemingly acquiesced but obviously was not really convinced that her voice was inadequate. Both adults and children feel this way; however, Alice was unusually adamant, although sweetly so, in her position of not hearing anything in her own voice different from other children. The correctionist recorded her voice. Her first reaction was that the recording did not sound like her; but when she discovered the machine was accurate, she said, "Well, I'll change that!" Within two months, she became accustomed to her new voice and almost never reverted to her old one. But her articulation remained too precise. She liked it, for she said after hearing the recording, "I do speak distinctly, don't I?"

Mr. Alexander not only praised Alice in her acquisition of her new voice but also assisted her to become a cooperative member of the group. Alice was chairman of the decorations committee for a class party. She planned the decorations minutely and carefully. Although she did not consult freely with members of her committee, they accepted her plan. When they did not execute it with care, however, she became angry and resigned from the chairmanship. Again the teacher talked with her to point out the similarities of this incident with the bulletin-board one. Shortly, one child suggested that Alice join the stage crew of the play. Alice was hesitant to accept the assignment of the group, but, as she saw that Mr. Alexander agreed, she acquiesced, for she was always anxious to achieve the teacher's approval. Strangely enough, she enjoyed pounding nails; and the crew members came to accept her as a working, cooperative member of the crew. One twelve-year-old said, "You're different when you got a hammer in your hand."

Alice became interested in science, a new field to her, and became an active and enthusiastic member of a group who were working on sound. She related the work to what she had done with the pitch of her voice. In this project, she was willing to accept directions from others, to offer her own suggestions cooperatively, and to work for the success of the project. Too frequently she tidied the worktable, but when another youngster said, "Mmmm, the tidy one at work," she laughed.

Alice's speech became less pedantic. Here the real therapist was the teacher. He had aided Alice in understanding herself. Further, he had helped her become a member of the group, accepting the other members as they were rather than trying to mold them to her pattern. Alice came to realize that she had a place in the group and that she should contribute to group living. She learned to enjoy her peers and they, her. She lived with herself and her classmates more easily.

Mr. Alexander helped Alice in several ways: by recognizing her voice difficulty, by referring her to the correctionist, and by helping her know herself and adjust to her group.

Difficulty in Voice Due to Physical Abnormality. The second child whom Mr. Alexander was concerned about was Tony. Tony was an eleven-year-old who sounded as if he had a bad cold. The sounds *m*, *n*, and *ng* were muffled, and they tended to sound like *b*, *d*, and *g*. He was a mouth breather. The previous summer, he had broken his nose playing football. The Doctor had set it, but Tony admitted that, when the "stick" had hurt, he had pulled it out. Tony was referred through school authorities to a nose specialist; upon examination, the specialist found that, because little air could pass through the nasal cavities, an operation was necessary. The school authorities helped to make the necessary arrangements.

SUMMARY

A child has a speech difficulty when his speech attracts attention to itself. In general, the teacher can try to understand the child as a whole, accept him as he is, create a classroom atmosphere that invites communication, build good human relationship with and among his students, and reinforce the teaching of the correctionist.

Articulatory defects include (1) substitution of one sound for another, (2) omission of sounds, and (3) distortion of sounds. The classroom teacher can assist by reporting speech which prevents adequate communication because of articulatory difficulties to the correctionist, by helping with articulatory and ear training under the direction of the correctionist, and by taking advantage of situations which promote successful communication and where the child can practice his new skills.

In impaired hearing, both voice and articulation may be affected. The hearing loss may be either conductive or perceptive. Conduction loss is the result of physical impairment of the ear; perception, of destruction or disease of the nerve of hearing. When a child speaks either too loudly or too softly, when he doesn't articulate clearly, when he responds to printed directions better than to oral ones, when he frequently turns his head, and when he complains of dizziness and earaches, the teacher should refer him to the speech correctionist and the school nurse. The correctionist will test his hearing. If the test shows a loss, he will be referred to an otologist. The correctionist will help the child with his voice and articulation and teach him lip reading when needed. The classroom teacher will help him gain a feeling of social competence in the group, develop his language abilities, and do what he can to assist him in hearing what goes on in the classroom.

Stuttering draws attention to itself and prevents the listener from receiving the ideas of the speaker. The symptoms vary from one individual to another. They include: repetition and prolongation of sounds, repetition of syllables and words, hesitations, blocking on some sounds, broken rhythm, use of a starter, excessive rapidity, excessive slowness, spasms of the articulatory and vocal mechanism, monotony, intermittence of the condition, and speaking on inhalation. Hesitations and repetitions, however, are normal in children's speech, and these characteristics alone should not be labeled "stuttering."

Three causes of stuttering are widely held: (1) A weakness of the neuromuscular system exists in the stuttering child which causes it to break down. (2) Adults and other children in the stutterer's environment have handled the child's normal hesitations and repetitions unwisely. (3) Emotional conflicts which show themselves in the symptoms of stuttering exist in the child.

Stuttering is complex and needs the understanding and help of a team composed of the parents of the stutterer, the doctor, the speech correctionist, the psychologist, the classroom teacher, and sometimes a psychiatrist. The therapy the stutterer receives from the correctionist varies according to the latter's beliefs concerning the cause of stuttering. Frequently, the correctionist will try several approaches.

The classroom teacher can aid the child in the classroom by (1) helping him to be an integral part of the group, (2) setting standards he can reach, (3) providing outlets for him, (4) encouraging him to develop along his own lines, (5) increasing the number of speech situations which he can meet successfully, (6) accepting his stuttering as his way of speaking, (7) approving him for tasks well done, and (8) keeping the classroom atmosphere calm, friendly, and easy.

Voice difficulties fall, in general, into three categories: (1) pitch, (2) volume, and (3) quality. Defects of pitch include the use of monotonous, too high, or too low pitch patterns. Each individual possesses a natural level of pitch where his voice is most efficient. Representative of defects of volume are too loud voices, too soft voices, and voices where the intensity remains the same. Defects of quality refer to characteristics of voices which are unpleasant and disagreeable, such as voices that are nasal, denasal, or hoarse. The causes of voice difficulties are (1) physical, (2) emotional, and (3) functional. The classroom teacher can assist by referring the child for correction, motivating the child to improve his voice and use his improved voice, and helping him adjust to his school environment and live successfully with his group.

Cleft palate is a fissure running through the lip, the teeth ridge, and the hard and/or soft palates. Any part of the palate may be cleft, or all of it may be. The cleft is normal at certain stages of fetal life, but the cause of the arrested development is not known. Cleft-palate speech has a high degree of nasality, since all sounds pass directly into the nose where normal modification is impossible. Many of the sounds are not articulated properly. Surgery or prosthetic appliances close the cleft. The speech training consists of directing the breath stream through the mouth and in training articulation.

One-half of the cerebral-palsied children born each year can be educated to be useful citizens. The cooperation of the physician, psychologist, speech therapist, physical therapist, and teacher is important in its treatment. Some do not require speech treatment; others do. The syndrome of speech symptoms cannot be accurately defined and classified; it usually includes hesitations, broken rhythm, abnormal voice quality, and articulatory errors. Inducing relaxation in the child is one of the tasks of the physical therapist and is a necessary adjunct to speech training.

The whole school personnel works to help a child with his speech difficulty. The classroom teacher, the school doctor, nurse, psychologist, and speech correctionist cooperate for the good of the child.

EXERCISES

1. Visit a school or clinic where you may observe a correctionist working with a child with a speech defect. Explain how you can reinforce in the classroom some of the learning you see taking place.

2. Visit a classroom. List the speech difficulties you hear.

3. Visit a kindergarten. Note the sound substitutions made by the children.

4. Explain how you can help children in the grade you plan to teach listen to sounds.

5. Indicate specifically how you can help a child who is hard of hearing understand directions for a specific activity.

6. Explain how you would use one of the drill books listed in the bibliography on articulatory defects to help a child with an articulatory defect.

7. Listen to voices you hear. Describe those you would consider seriously defective.

BIBLIOGRAPHY

GENERAL

Backus, O. L., *Speech in Education: A Guide for the Classroom Teacher*, New York, Longmans, 1943. Discusses speech rehabilitation from the viewpoint of the classroom teacher.

Bates, E. C., "Speech-centered School," *Education*, Vol. 62 (January, 1942), p. 309. Describes the work of a speech correctionist. Gives principles the speech correctionist follows in training children with speech difficulties.

Gray, L. G., "A Survey of Speech Defectives in the Indianapolis Primary Grades," *Journal of Speech Disorders*, Vol. 5 (September, 1940), pp. 247–258. Tells of a survey of 3,602 students, of whom 2.94 per cent were speech defectives.

Henry, L. D., "The Physician and the Speech Correctionist," *Journal of Speech Disorders*, Vol. 8 (March, 1943), pp. 9–26. Tells the part the physician plays in the speech correction program.

Hildreth, G., "Speech Defects and Reading Disability," *Elementary School Journal*, Vol. 46 (February, 1946), pp. 326–332. Analyzes the connection between defects of speech and ability in reading. Gives suggestions concerning preventive and remedial measures.

Johnson, W., "Ten Children You Should Know," *National Parent Teacher*, Vol. 38 (January, 1940), pp. 10–12. Defines types of speech defects and sets forth the influence of the classroom teacher on the child with a speech defect.

———, et al., *Speech Handicapped School Children*, New York, Harper, 1948. Tells how to supplement the work of the correctionist, if one is available, and contains suggestions for correction of speech difficulties if one is not available. Describes all the major speech difficulties and suggests what the teacher can do to help. Designed for the layman.

Mayfarth, F. (ed.), *Learning to Speak Effectively*, Washington, Association for Childhood Education, 1943. Translates speech problems into a language suitable to others than speech specialists.

Mills, A. W., and H. Streit, "Report of a Speech Survey, Holyoke, Massachusetts," *Journal of Speech Disorders*, Vol. 7 (June, 1942), pp. 161–168. Lists the number of speech defects of 4,685 children in the schools of Holyoke, Mass.

Routh, R. A., "Speech Adjustment Program," *Childhood Education*, Vol. 16 (March, 1940), pp. 304–306. Tells of the objectives of the program to adjust children to social living by speech work in social groups.

Schuell, H., "Working with Speech Defectives in Public Schools," *Journal of Speech Disorders*, Vol. 8 (December, 1943), pp. 355–362. Explains through the use of examples the cooperation among classroom teacher, nurse, speech correctionist, and other specialists.

Wood, K. S., "The Parent's Role in the Clinical Program," *Journal of Speech and Hearing Disorders*, Vol. 13 (September, 1948), pp. 209–210. Examines the environment of the child with a speech defect. Suggests training for the parents of speech-defective children in constructing a happier home as well as treatment in speech for the child.

ARTICULATORY DIFFICULTIES

Abney, L., and D. Miniace, *This Way to Better Speech*, Yonkers, N.Y., World, 1940. Includes a simple exposition of how sounds are made, followed by sentences and jingles. Usable for children in the second or third grade.

Baker, P., *A Primer of Sounds*, Boston, Expression Co., 1941. Gives exercises for relaxation and for drill on sounds.

Barrows, S., and K. Hall, *Games and Jingles for Speech Development*, Boston, Expression Co., 1936. Contains games and jingles for drill material for sounds.

Berry, M., and J. Eisenson, *The Defective in Speech*, New York, Crofts, 1942. Describes causes of articulatory defects and methods of treatment. Includes drill material.

Bryngelson, B., and E. Glaspey, *Speech Improvement Cards*, Chicago, Scott, Foresman, 1941. A set of cards with colored pictures. One group is for testing; the second group is for remedial work and includes sets of cards where names of objects in pictures contain specific sounds.

Case, I. M., and S. T. Barrows, *Speech Drills for Children in the Form of Play*, Boston, Expression Co., 1929. Describes games for speech drill that are fun for children in the primary grades.

Reid, G., "Functional Articulatory Defects," *Journal of Speech Disorders*, Vol. 12 (June, 1947), pp. 143–159. Analyzes the correlation between improvement in articulation and mental age, auditory memory span, ability to discriminate between speech sounds, kinesthetic sensitivity, personal and social adjustment.

Roe, V., and R. Milisen, "The Effect of Maturation upon Defective Articulation in the Elementary Grades," *Journal of Speech Disorders*, Vol. 7 (March, 1942), pp. 37–45. Reports the substitutions of children and their decrease with maturity.

Stoddard, C. B., *Sounds for Little Folks*, Boston, Expression Co., 1940. Contains drill for children who haven't learned to read.

Van Riper, C., *Speech Correction: Principles and Methods*, New York, Prentice-Hall, 1947, Chaps. 7, 8. Discusses causes and treatment of articulatory disorders.

Voegelin, C. F., and S. Adams, "A Phonetic Study of Young Children's Speech," *Journal of Experimental Education*, Vol. 3 (December, 1934), pp. 107–116. Shows inconsistency existing in children's articulatory errors. A study of the substitution of sounds made by children.

Wood, K. S., "Parental Maladjustment and Functional Articulatory Defects in Children," *Journal of Speech Disorders*, Vol. 11 (December, 1946), pp. 255–275. Examines the interrelationships between child and parents where the child has an articulatory defect.

Yedinack, J. G., "A Study of the Linguistic Functions of Children with Articulation and Reading Disabilities," *Journal of Genetic Psychology,* Vol. 74 (March, 1949), pp. 23–59. Describes a study of second-grade children with articulatory or reading problems which shows that articulation and reading difficulties are coexistent.

STUTTERING

Anonymous, "We Made Our Child Stutter," *Parents' Magazine,* Vol. 38 (April, 1949), pp. 131–132. Describes a home in which the pace is too great. Written by a mother who realizes she demanded too much of her child and who recognizes her responsibility in creating a favorable environment for her child.

Barber, V., "Studies in the Psychology of Stuttering," *Journal of Speech Disorders.* Vol. 4 (December, 1939), pp. 371–383. Shows that choral reading tends to be more effective in decreasing the frequency of stuttering when the stutterer receives more support, that is, when there are several persons reading along with the stutterer.

Barr, H., "A Quantitative Study of the Specific Phenomena Observed in Stuttering," *Journal of Speech Disorders,* Vol. 5 (September, 1940), pp. 277–280.

Glasner, P. J., "Personality Characteristics and Emotional Problems in Stutterers under the Age of Five," *Journal of Speech and Hearing Disorders,* Vol. 14 (June, 1949), pp. 135–138. Pictures stuttering children who frequently have a long background of overprotection, pampering, and overanxious, obsessively perfectionistic parents.

Hahn, E. F., *Stuttering: Significant Theories and Therapies,* Stanford, Calif., Stanford University Press, 1943.

Heltman, J. H., "Remedial Training for Speech Deviates in the Elementary School," *Elementary School Journal* Vol. 48 (January, 1946), pp. 283–287. Defines stuttering. Gives practical suggestions to the classroom teacher for handling the stutterer.

Johnson, W., "A Study of the Onset and Development of Stuttering," *Journal of Speech Disorders,* Vol. 7 (September, 1942), pp. 251–257. Deals with the onset and early development of stuttering. Propounds the theory that stuttering in its serious form develops after the diagnosis rather than before and is a consequence of the diagnosis.

Moncur, J. P., *Environmental Factors Differentiating Stuttering Children from Non-stuttering Children,* Ph.D. dissertation, Stanford University, August, 1950. States that, if there exists one causal factor which may account for the manifold differences between stuttering and nonstuttering groups with regard to adverse environmental influences and to which all other unfavorable factors are subordinate, it may be that the parents of the stuttering children are (as a group) dominating parents.

Van Riper, C., *Speech Correction: Principles and Methods*, New York, Prentice-Hall, pp. 265–367. A comprehensive, thorough treatment of stuttering.

VOICE DEFECTS

Anderson, V. A., *Training the Speaking Voice*, New York, Oxford, 1942, pp. 1–234. Gives practice program of voice development, including drills and exercises to perfect the functioning of the vocal mechanism. Contains background material dealing with the physical, physiological, and psychological bases underlying phonation.

Berry, M., and J. Eisenson, *The Defective in Speech*, New York, Crofts, 1942, pp. 148–176. Describes vocal difficulties and discusses their causes and treatment.

Fairbanks, G., *Voice and Articulation Drillbook*, New York, Harper, 1940, pp. 133–217. Discusses voice classified in terms of volume, time, pitch, and quality. Based on recent research.

Van Riper, C., *Speech Correction; Principles and Methods*, New York, Prentice-Hall, 1947, pp. 218–256. Discusses voice difficulties of pitch, quality, and volume. Extensive bibliography, carefully annotated.

CLEFT-PALATE SPEECH

Buck, M., and R. Harrington, "Organized Speech Therapy for Cleft Palate Rehabilitation," *Journal of Speech and Hearing Disorders*, Vol. 14 (March, 1949), pp. 43–52. Suggests relaxation and lip exercises, jingles, and games, for speech training for the cleft-palate patient.

Harkins, C. S., and H. Koepp-Baker, "Twenty-five Years of Cleft Palate Prosthesis," *Journal of Speech and Hearing Disorders*, vol. 13 (March, 1948), pp. 23–30. Discusses the major problems related to the application of the prosthetic methods for the complete restitution of the cleft-palate patient.

Phair, G. M., "Wisconsin Cleft Palate Program," *Journal of Speech Disorders*, Vol. 12 (December, 1947), pp. 410–414. Describes the program for cleft-palate patients in Wisconsin. Discusses the cooperation of surgeon, orthodontist, prosthodontist, and social-welfare worker.

Wells, C. G., "Practical Techniques in Speech Training for Cleft Palate Cases," *Journal of Speech and Hearing Disorders*, Vol. 13 (March, 1948), pp. 71–73. Shows the development of skill in control of movement and use of mechanism.

SPEECH OF THE CEREBRAL PALSIED

Carlson, E. R., *Born that Way*, New York, Doubleday, 1941. Autobiography of a spastic who became an authority on cerebral palsy. Tells of his own education and the meeting of his problems.

Crosland, J., "Some Wider Aspects of Cerebral Palsy," *Occupational Therapy and Rehabilitation*, Vol. 27 (June, 1949), pp. 227–230. Tells of the rehabilitation of children who have had cerebral palsy and their problems of adjustment. The role of the parent in helping the child with cerebral palsy.

Huber, M., "Letter to the Parents of the Cerebral Palsied Child," *Journal of Speech and Hearing Disorders*, Vol. 15 (June, 1950), pp. 154–158. Gives good, simple suggestions to parents. Shows how to make language attractive and meaningful to children. Might well be read by teachers.

Snidecor, J. D., "The Speech Correctionist on the Cerebral Palsy Team," *Journal of Speech and Hearing Disorders*, Vol. 13 (March, 1948), pp. 67–70. Represents the cooperation of the physician, psychologist, physical therapist, teacher, and speech correctionist in the treatment of cerebral palsy.

HEARING PROBLEMS

Berry, M. F., and J. Eisenson, *The Defective in Speech*, New York, Crofts, 1942, pp. 321–339. Depicts types of hearing losses, speech symptoms, and treatment.

Gardner, W. H., "History and Present Status of the Education of the Hard-of-hearing," *Journal of Speech Disorders*, Vol. 8 (September, 1943), pp. 227–236. Gives history of treatment in schools. Discusses use of lip reading, special seating arrangements, effort of teacher to help the children understand her, tutoring, vocational guidance, individual and group hearing aids, and lip reading. Correlation with class subjects when groups are small.

Huber, M., "A Child's First Books," *The Crippled Child*, Vol. 28 (August, 1950), pp. 23–29. A bibliography with annotations of materials for reading aloud to the speech-handicapped child.

Keller, L. K., "Hearing Survey in Detroit Schools," *Journal of Exceptional Children*, Vol. 11 (March, 1945), pp. 168–183. Describes a survey of 23,347 children in Detroit schools and indicates the number and age of those with impaired hearing.

Miller, E., "A Public School Program for Hard-of-hearing Children," *Journal of Speech and Hearing Disorders*, Vol. 13 (September, 1948), pp. 256–259. Discusses use of audiometer, segregation of hard-of-hearing and deaf children, adjustment of the deaf child, responsibilities of the classroom teacher, speech-conservation program, and vocational and educational placement.

Pintner, R., J. Eisenson, and M. Stanton, *The Psychology of the Physically Handicapped*, New York, Crofts, 1941. Contains a chapter on the deaf which follows this plan: intelligence, educational achievement, personality, and special abilities. A clear summary of the essential differences between the psychological profile of the normal child and that of the handicapped one.

Sprunt, J. S., and F. W. Finger, "Auditory Deficiency and Academic Achievement," *Journal of Speech and Hearing Disorders*, Vol. 14 (March, 1949), pp. 25–32. A study which shows that, when hearing loss and academic achievement are measured objectively and when intelligence is considered in terms of a nonverbal test, the hard-of-hearing child will progress more slowly in the typical school situation than will the normal-hearing child.

12 Improving the Child's Voice and Diction

By example, the teacher establishes acceptable patterns of voice and diction for the child. Teachers influence the voice quality of their students. A college student had a very pleasant, well-modulated voice. During a discussion of experiences that had influenced her speech, she recalled the effect of a junior high school teacher. She said that at that time she herself had tended to shout and to speak in strident tones, while her teacher, who had a particularly pleasing personality, spoke in a clear, resonant, well-pitched voice. The teacher had suggested that she tone down her shouting. She believed that she now had her pleasant voice partly because she had wanted the approbation of this teacher and partly because she had imitated her. How a teacher says a word also affects children. A college sophomore always used the *ah* sound in *orange*, although she had lived all her life in a community whose members used the *aw* sound. When talking about pronunciation, she volunteered the information that her second-grade teacher had always used the *ah* sound and that from then on she had used it. She remembered clearly changing her way of saying *orange*. Teachers subtly influence children's voice and diction through their own usage. For this reason, the teacher's speech should be that of a cultivated, educated person regardless of the region he comes from.

REGIONAL DIFFERENCES IN PRONUNCIATION

Differences in speech among educated persons are not so wide as those among persons with less education. No educated person from one area has difficulty understanding an educated person from a different area, although pronunciations in the three main regional divisions of American pronunciation (Southern, Eastern, and General American) are somewhat varied. Geographically, the East includes New York City and its immediate vicinity and New England east of the Connecticut River. The South includes Virginia, North Carolina, South Carolina, Tennessee, Florida, Georgia, Alabama, Mississippi, Arkansas, Louisiana, Texas, and parts of Maryland, West Virginia, Kentucky, and Oklahoma. General American includes the rest. The vast majority of Americans speak General American. More accurately, seven major areas exist, which C. K. Thomas[1] lists as eastern New England, New York City, the Middle Atlantic area, the Lowland South, the Southern Mountain area, the Western Pennsylvania area, and the General American area. He notes the geographic distribution of the seven areas on a map.

A New Englander and a Southerner may say *bahn;* an Ohioan, *barn.* A New Englander approaches *pahth* for *path;* the Ohioan uses the same vowel in *path* as he does in *cat.* In the South, the *o* in *glory* is the same *o* as in *tote;* whereas, in other regions, it may be the *aw* sound as in *law.* The vowel in the word *scarce* in the General American and Eastern areas may be either the vowel found in *hat* or the one in *let;* in the South, in the word *scarce,* the vowel in *hat* is heard most frequently. The teacher and the child use the cultivated pronunciations of their particular area.

Teaching children to accept the speech of a child from a different area. The teacher helps the child accept the pronunciations of the child from a different region. Katy, a six-year-old New Englander, had recently moved to New York State. When, early in the year, the children teased her about her "accent," the teacher helped the children see that they need not all speak alike. After explaining how New Englanders talk, he played a record to show that Katy's speech was typical of the region where she had lived. He also invited to the classroom a music teacher who had originally come from New England and who still used a broad *a* and the intrusive *r* in *idear.* The children quickly discerned ways in which Katy spoke like the music teacher. Since Katy was interested in trucks, the group enjoyed seeing her collection and hearing what each kind was used for. The children became interested in what Katy had to say rather than in her New England speech. By the end of the year her pattern of speaking had changed and she sounded much like the rest of the children in her room.

[1] C. K. Thomas, *An Introduction to the Pronunciation of American English*, New York, Ronald, 1947, Chap. 21.

PRONUNCIATION

SOUND REPRESENTATION

Spelling today is not highly phonetic. *Ei* in *weigh, a* in *late, ea* in *bear, ay* in *tray, ai* in *chair* all represent the same sound. The sound usually spelled *c* in *cat* has spellings as different as *x* in *tax, ch* in *chorus,* and *k* in *cake.* During the last few centuries, the sounds of speech have changed considerably, but the spelling has changed only slightly. Many letters are silent in such words as *write, right, knight, calm,* and *island.* Spelling, therefore, is of some but no great value as an aid to pronunciation.

DICTIONARIES

Dictionaries assist students in pronouncing unfamiliar words, for their editors have recorded the current pronunciations. A pronunciation given in the dictionary is a generalization of the manner in which many people say a word. Obviously then, a dictionary with an old date does not accurately guide the child's pronunciation, because the pronunciation of words changes. Dictionaries frequently record more than one pronunciation. In some dictionaries, the first pronunciation is the one held to be more widely used; in others, the editor makes no attempt to show which pronunciation is more prevalent. Some dictionaries indicate pronunciations current in regional areas. The teacher may well read the introduction to a dictionary to learn what its procedures are.

Some dictionaries adopt for representation the style of formal platform speech. For example, Webster's *New International Dictionary,* second edition, is a dictionary which exemplifies this representation. Other dictionaries include less precise pronunciations. Kenyon and Knott's *A Pronouncing Dictionary of American English* is "a dictionary of colloquial English, of the everyday unconscious speech of cultivated people—of those in every community who carry on the affairs and set the social and educational standards of those communities."[2] The differences in recording between the two dictionaries, however, are not too great, because the majority of English words are pronounced alike in colloquial and in formal speech. Pronunciations, however, are somewhat different at different levels of speech and in connected speech, for the pronunciation of words is influenced by the phonetic effect of one

[2] J. S. Kenyon and T. A. Knott, *A Pronouncing Dictionary of American English,* Springfield, Mass., 1944, p. vii.

word on another and by the rhythm, tempo, intonation, and meaning intended by the speaker.

LEVELS OF PRONUNCIATION

A child learns pronunciation, to a large degree, by imitating other children. Pronunciation varies according to the occupations and social standing of the people using it. If a child lives in a neighborhood with a low socioeconomic level, he will probably hear vulgate pronunciations. Vulgate pronunciations, typical of the speech of people with little education, are appropriate in the daily lives of those using this level but are not appropriate in groups using other levels. Education influences people to drop vulgate pronunciations, for they are social hindrances.

At the other extreme is formal pronunciation, used mainly in lectures and addresses by ministers, teachers, and governmental officials. Those using it tend to speak more slowly, to utter vowel sounds more distinctly, and to stress more heavily.

Informal pronunciation lies between the two extremes. It is the conversational speech of educated, cultivated people. It shows more regional flavor; its stresses are lighter; its vowels are less distinct; it is faster than formal speech. Many of the consonants that are hard to say in their position are dropped or assimilated with other sounds. For example, *Mary and John* is often *Mary 'n John*. Informal pronunciation is sometimes called colloquial speech. The child's pronunciation should be appropriate for his audience. Too conscious attention to pronunciation or the use of too many vulgate pronunciations handicaps the speaker's relationship with his listeners.

One teacher compares the wearing of different kinds of clothes for different occasions to the levels of pronunciation. He says that the use of vulgate pronunciation is like wearing overalls and is perfectly appropriate in many situations. He then relates that men also wear tuxedos and full dress suits on certain state and rare occasions. The wearing of dress suits he compares with formal usage. Finally, he explains that most of the time people wear comfortable, everyday clothes and that, also most of the time, people use the informal level of language. He draws the analogy further in that in both informal dress and speech the important characteristics are that they are comfortable and practical. He further points out that within informal dress and speech wide variations exist.

SOUNDS IN CONVERSATION

STRONG AND WEAK FORMS

Sounds in words change as they appear in conversation. For example when a child reads *to* in a list of words, he pronounces it as he does *two*. But if he reads the sentence "I went to the bank," the vowel in *to* is no longer a long *u* but a short one or even the schwa, the sound in the first syllable of *about*. When a child says the alphabet, he pronounces *a* to rhyme with *play*. But when he reads "I saw a tree," he reads the *a* as the schwa, the first sound in *about*. The vowel in *the* in "The doll is beautiful" is usually the schwa. But if the *the* refers to a particular doll to distinguish it from other dolls, the speaker pronounces the *the* as *thee*. The *the* with the schwa is the weak form; the *the* pronounced as *thee* is the strong form. Ordinarily, the speaker or reader uses the weak forms of pronouns, prepositions, articles, auxiliaries, and conjunctions. In strong forms, the vowel is stressed; in weak forms, it is not.

ASSIMILATION

One sound is changed because of the sound next to it. For example, the past tense of *joke* is spelled *joked*. The final sound, however, is not a *d* but a *t*. Sounds such as *b*, *d*, *z*, and *g* are made with voice; others, such as *p*, *t*, *s*, and *k*, are made without voice. In *joked*, the *k* is made without voice and influences the *d* to become a *t*, a change that exemplifies the change from a voiced to an unvoiced sound. The same type of assimilation happens to plurals of nouns. For example, the word *pads* is spelled *pads* but is pronounced *padz*. The voiced *d* influences the voiceless *s* to become the voiced *z*. *Handkerchief* frequently becomes *hangkerchief*. The *k* influences the *n* to become *ng*, which is made in the same place as *k*; the back of the tongue touches the soft palate in both sounds. On the other hand, sometimes the word is pronounced *hankerchief*. In this case the *n* assimilates the *d*; both sounds are made in the same place; the tip of the tongue is on the ridge behind the upper teeth. The longer sound, *n*, takes over the *d*, a short, plosive sound.

Assimilation also takes place in phrases like *woncha go* for *won't you go*. Some persons accept this assimilation, while others reject it. The use of *pungkin* for *pumpkin* and *lemme* for *let me* are examples of assimilations generally considered unacceptable. Speech with too many unacceptable assimilations draws attention to itself.

ARTICULATORY ERRORS

Articulatory errors usually fall into six classes: (1) substitution of sounds, (2) voicing and unvoicing errors, (3) omission of sounds, (4) addition of sounds, (5) transposition of sounds, and (6) distortion of sounds.

SUBSTITUTION OF SOUNDS

The correctionist works with those substitutions of sounds which are definitely speech difficulties. For example, a ten-year-old boy may use a *w* for *l* and *r*. In this instance, the correctionist teaches the boy to say *l* and *r* correctly, and the classroom teacher reinforces the teaching. But the classroom teacher handles those substitutions which are more easily corrected. These substitutions are often those identified with vulgate speech and are frequently the results of environmental influences.

The following are typical of the type of substitution errors the teacher corrects:

Consonants: *n* for *ng*, as *comin* for *coming*
 t and *d* for the two *th*'s, as *tank* for *thank* and *dem* for *them*
 w for *wh*, as *wen* for *when*
Vowels: short *i* for short *e*, as *git* for *get* and *min* for *men*
 long *o* for short *o*, as *ohcassion* for *occasion* or *ohfense* for *offense*
 short *i* for short *a*, as *kin* for *can*
 short *i* or *e* for short *u*, as *sich* or *sech* for *such*, *jist* or *jest* for *just*
 short *e* for short *i*, as *ben* for *been*
 long *o* for long *a*, as *dork* for *dark*
 short *oo* for short *i*, as *mulkman* for *milkman*
 er for *oy*, as *berl* for *boil*
 oy for *er*, as *oil* for *earl*

Correcting the Substitution of One Sound for Another. The first step is to help the child recognize his own substitution. He must hear what is wrong. David, a nine-year-old, said *dis*, *dese*, and *trow* for *throw*. When, one day, David corrected another child who said *ayg* for *egg*, the teacher complimented him on hearing sounds well. She then told him about his saying *dis* for *this*. By saying *dis* and *this*, she pointed out to him the difference in his pronunciation from that of other people. She also recorded his speech so that he could hear the errors in his own speech.

Next, she showed him how to make the two *th* sounds. She demonstrated the *th* in *these* and told him she made the sound by putting the tip of her tongue against the cutting edge of her upper teeth. She explained the difference between the voiceless *th* in *thin* and the voiced *th* in *then*. David repeated the sounds after her.

David and she decided that he would make a list of words with the two *th* sounds in them and practice saying them. Shortly, he began to work hard at incorporating the newly acquired sounds into conversation. Admittedly, when he became excited, he forgot and slipped back into his old habits. By the end of the year, however, the occasions when he slipped were rare. The teacher was happy when on the baseball diamond he yelled not "Trow it" but "Throw it."

VOICING AND UNVOICING ERRORS

Voicing and unvoicing errors are errors of substitution, for they are the substitution of a voiced sound for an unvoiced sound or of an unvoiced sound for a voiced sound. *T* and *d* are made in the same place (tip of tongue on ridge behind upper teeth), but *t* has no voice, whereas *d* does. *Z* is the voiced counterpart of *s*. *J*, as in *judge*, is voiced; *ch*, as in *chair*, is unvoiced; otherwise, the two sounds are the same.

The following are errors in which a voiced sound has replaced the unvoiced sound: *d* for *t*, as *cidy* for *city*, *lader* for *later*, *liddle* for *little*, *moundain* for *mountain*; *z* for *s*, as in the words *decrease*, *lease*, where the final sound should be *s* not, as some speakers make it, *z*.

The following are errors in which an unvoiced sound has replaced a voiced sound: *s* for *z*, as in the words *lose*, *rose*, *raise*, *hers*, *ease*, where the final sound should be *z*, not, as some speakers make it, *s*; *ch*, as in *charge*, for *j*, as in *judge*, as in *langwitch* for *language* and *collitch* for *college*; *sh* for *zh*, as *pleashure* for *pleazhure* (plĕsh′ẽr for plĕzh′ẽr); voiced *th* for the voiceless *th*, as troo̅th for troo̅th or lăth for lăth.

Correcting Voicing and Unvoicing Errors. The first step in correcting voicing and unvoicing errors is to help the child hear the difference between the voiced and unvoiced sound. Sylvia always said *cidy* for *city*, and *moundain* for *mountain*. The teacher had listed the words in which Sylvia made the error: *little*, *better*, *latter*, *later*, *fatter*, *fainting*, *better*, *heating*, *written*, *tenting*, *plenty*, *fifty*, *question*, and *faulty*. The teacher first explained the difference between *t* and *d*; he told her that both sounds are made in the same place but that *t* has no voice, whereas *d* does. When he said *tin* and *den*, Sylvia recognized the difference between the two words. After he had said *city* and *cidy*, he asked her to tell him how his two pronunciations differed and which one was correct. Sylvia recognized the difference and the correct *city*.

The second step included Sylvia's saying first *cidy* and then *city*. She then went down the list of words and said each one incorrectly and then correctly. She was able to hear her own inaccuracy and was able to say the words properly. After she had obtained from the teacher the list of words on which she had made errors, she practiced saying them correctly.

The last step was incorporating the correction in her speech. Sylvia did well on this step, for she was the kind of girl who is anxious to speak well. The teacher commended her when she said the words correctly and called her attention to her inaccuracies. He did not correct her when she was speaking but after she was through.

OMISSION OF SOUNDS

Children frequently omit necessary sounds. Admittedly, children and adults do not pronounce every sound in a word. Many are obviously silent as the *k* in *knife* and the *b* in *lamb*. In other words, certain omissions are acceptable; for example, Kenyon and Knott note that the first *n* in government is omitted by leading statesmen in both America and England even in formal address.[3] Dictionaries do not all agree on whether or not sounds are acceptably omitted in some words. For example, the *American College Dictionary* (1947), Funk and Wagnalls' *New College Dictionary of the English Language* (1947), and *Webster's New Collegiate Dictionary* (1949) all agree that the first *r* in *February* is pronounced. But Kenyon and Knott indicate that the pronunciation with the *r* and the one without are both frequently used; they note that the loss of *r* is due to dissimilation and the influence of *January*.[4]

Before a teacher insists on the inclusion of a sound, he may well check his own pronunciation. For example, some adults insist on the *y* sound, as in *you*, before $\overline{oo}$ in *duty*, *news*, and *student*. The pronunciations, without the *y* sound, are, however, listed in both the *American College Dictionary* and the Kenyon and Knott dictionary. *Webster's* points out in the introduction: "After d(duty), t(tune), n(new)— tongue point stops and nasals—the u sounds are also accepted generally

---

[3] *Ibid.*, p. 188.
[4] *Ibid.*, p. 163.

but here too in America, at least, the $\overline{oo}$ sound is widely used by the educated."[5]

The following are examples of unacceptable omissions of sounds:

artic for *arctic*
libarian for *librarian*
lemme for *let me*
genlemen for *gentlemen*
member for *remember*
longer without the *g* sound after the *ng* sound
probly for *probably*
generly for *generally*

Teaching the Child to Include the Necessary Sounds. Again, the first step is to aid the child in hearing what he says unacceptably. The teacher may repeat what the child has said, or he may point out the errors in a recording of the child's speech. Next, he teaches him to say the word accurately, and, lastly, he encourages him to incorporate the correct pronunciation in his speech.

ADDITION OF SOUNDS

A child may add sounds which do not belong in a word. Again, the teacher should make sure that he is not being too demanding. Some dictionaries now recognize such pronunciations as *almond* with an *l*, *often* with the *t*, and *forehead* with the *h*. Many additions, however, exist which are not acceptable. They include such additions as:

wisht for *wish*
acrosst for *across*
efen for *if*
elum for *elm*
singging for *singing*
plumber (with the *b*) for *plumber*
egshibit (with the *h*) for *exhibit*
umberrella for *umbrella*
athalete for *athlete*

Teaching the Child to Omit the Added Sound. The steps are identical to those in teaching him to add the necessary sounds. The teacher (1) helps the child to hear the sound or syllable that he is adding, (2) shows him how to omit it, and (3) encourages him to carry over the correct pronunciation into his speech.

[5] J. P. Bethel (ed.), *Webster's New Collegiate Dictionary*, Springfield, Mass., Merriam, 1949, p. xvi.

TRANSPOSING SOUNDS

Children sometimes transpose sounds. Some teachers object when children say *childern* for *children* and *hunderd* for *hundred;* other teachers accept these transpositions, since both are listed as variant pronunciations in Kenyon and Knott.[6] Other transpositions are clearly unacceptable: *prespire* for *perspire* and *plubicity* for *publicity*. The teacher follows the same steps in helping the child correct the transposition as he does in teaching the child to omit or add sounds.

DISTORTION OF SOUNDS

Sometimes the child is approximating the sound but distorts or changes it slightly. For example, he may make his *t*'s and *d*'s with the tip of his tongue on his teeth rather than on his teeth ridge, so that the *t*'s and *d*'s sound heavy and are more noticeable. He may raise his tongue on a sound. For instance, sometimes *cat* tends to sound somewhat like *cet*. Or the first part of the diphthong of *cow* is the same vowel sound as in *hat*, so that the *ow* sound becomes somewhat distorted. Once again the teacher follows the same three steps: (1) helping the child to recognize his error, (2) teaching him to make the sound correctly, and (3) motivating him to incorporate it in his speech.

IMPROVING VOICE

The teacher is concerned with four aspects of voice: (1) volume—is the volume adequate for communication and is it controlled?—(2) pitch—is it appropriate and does the child use a variety of pitches?—(3) tone—is it clear?—and (4) rate of speaking—does the child's tempo interfere with the reception of ideas by his listeners?

VOLUME

Some children always speak too loudly; others speak too softly. Still others do not adjust their voices to the size of the room. When the problem is a serious one, the teacher needs the help of other specialists.

Jerry was a child who always spoke too loudly. All of Jerry was noisy. His books landed on the table with a bang. He moved his easel for painting with energy and consequently with much scraping and pulling. The teacher helped Jerry realize that, if he were to live with

[6] Kenyon and Knott, *op. cit.*, pp. 80, 210.

others easily, he must do it with less noise. When he was about to read aloud, the teacher said, "Now let's take it easy this time." When, in conversation, his volume would mount, he would say, "Let's keep the voice down." By the end of the year, Jerry was a quieter Jerry and his voice was not so loud. Sheila, on the other hand, spoke very softly. She moved quietly and gently, often even timidly. The teacher helped her to have confidence in herself and in her abilities. Frequently he reminded her, "Sheila, we all want to hear."

When children speak in small auditoriums or large rooms, the teacher helps them to adjust the volume of their voices so that they are heard. Often the teacher asks a child to sit in the rear of the auditorium and to indicate to the speakers in the group the need for more or less voice.

PITCH

The classroom teacher does not ask a child to lower or to raise his habitual pitch without advice from a correctionist. Because physical factors fix the pitch of the child's voice, some children normally speak at pitches higher or lower than others. Each child has an approximate pitch at which he uses his voice most effectively.

The teacher helps the child realize the capacities of his own voice for expressing meaning and emotion. He encourages the student whose voice is monotonous to express himself with friendliness and warmth. Sometimes the teacher uses the simple phrase "Good morning." Children talk about making their good mornings mean "I'm glad to see you." The teacher may ask one child to play Grumpy and to grunt "Good morning," and another to play Happy, who gaily says, "Good morning." Other phrases serve the same purpose. "You're a clever fellow" may communicate sarcasm, surprise, pleasant agreement, admiration, annoyance, or dislike. Children say the phrase in different ways to indicate different meanings. The meaning is partly communicated through the use of a variation in pitch. An effective speaker controls the pitch of his voice; his control helps him to express both his meaning and feeling.

QUALITY

Quality is the tone that distinguishes one voice from another. Some voices are resonant, clear, pleasant; others are nasal, metallic, breathy, hoarse, or thin. The quality of voice depends on the size, shape, condition, and manipulation of the resonating cavities, that is, the throat, mouth, and nose. Where the voice attracts attention to itself, the teacher asks the correctionist for help.

Relaxation often furthers good voice quality. In the lower grades, the teacher attacks the problem through play. The children are rag dolls which flop. After the teacher has lifted a hand, he lets it fall limp. Or the children are leaves being blown about by the wind. In the later grades, the teacher can approach the problem directly by encouraging the children to relax the muscles of the throat and neck.

RATE OF SPEAKING

The child may speak too fast, too slowly, or too monotonously. He must control his rate of speaking to meet the needs of his listeners rather than his own inclination. Alex was a boy who never walked when he could run, who usually finished his paintings first, and who completed the construction of his birdhouse before anyone else. He always worked and played at high speed, and he talked the same way. The

FIG. 22. The child hears himself. (*University State Teachers College, Geneseo, N.Y.*)

teacher made him see that his listeners could not always understand him and frequently could not follow him because of his rate of speaking. He worked hard at making sure that his classmates both understood and followed him; finally, he succeeded in speaking and reading more slowly.

The child must be trained to hear his own voice and to listen to it discriminatingly. A good recording machine is an asset; as the teacher works with the child, the latter can hear his own vocal improvement.

SUMMARY

The teacher's speech serves as a pattern for children's speech. Regional differences, levels of pronunciation, and the degree of assimilation affect the way the teacher and the children speak.

Dictionaries record the current pronunciations and word usages.

Articulatory errors fall into six classes: (1) substitution of sounds, (2) voicing and unvoicing errors, (3) omission of sounds, (4) addition of sounds, (5) transposition of sounds, and (6) distortion of sounds. The teacher helps the child recognize his error and say the sound or word correctly, and he encourages him to incorporate the correction in his speech.

The teacher is concerned with four aspects of voice: (1) volume, (2) pitch, (3) quality, and (4) rate of speaking. He helps the child hear his own voice and improve it so that his listeners will more readily understand and appreciate what he is talking about.

EXERCISES

1. Visit a classroom. List the articulatory errors that you hear.

2. Visit a classroom of children. Note the voices that need improving. Indicate the ways, if any, in which the classroom teacher helps the children speak more pleasantly.

3. Indicate specifically how you can improve the articulation of a particular child.

4. Find a list of frequently mispronounced words. Look up ten of them in three different recent dictionaires. Show the agreement or disagreement on how to pronounce the words that exists in the three dictionaries.

5. Read the introduction to *Funk and Wagnalls, American Collegiate Dictionary*, or *Webster's*. Note the information that is helpful to you in your use of the dictionary.

6. Read briefly in a book on the history of the language. Show how the pronunciation of a particular word has changed over the centuries.

BIBLIOGRAPHY

SOURCES OF FURTHER READING

Baldridge, M., "Three Decades of Language Study," *Childhood Education*, Vol. 26 (November, 1949), pp. 117–121. Discusses the studies of language that are significant in teaching children.

Eisenson, J., *Basic Speech*, New York, Macmillan, 1950, Chaps. 2, 5, 6, 7. Contains a description of the speech mechanism and how it works. Includes suggestions for improving the speech sounds and voice and an introduction to phonetics.

Fairbanks, G., *Voice and Articulation Drillbook*, New York, Harper, 1940. Includes material on improving voice and diction.

Kenyon, J. S., "Levels of Speech and Colloquial English," *The English Journal*, Vol. 37 (January, 1948), pp. 25–31. Distinguishes between "cultural level of English" and "functional varieties of standard English." Points out that it is impossible to draw a strict dividing line between the colloquial and the literary or formal diction.

———, *American Pronunciation*, 9th ed., Ann Arbor, Mich., Wahr, 1944.

Kenyon, J. S., and T. A. Knott, *A Pronouncing Dictionary of American English*, Springfield, Mass., Merriam, 1944. Provides the best source for the pronunciation of American English words. Based on the pronunciations of cultivated, educated speakers of America.

Pooley, R., "Contributions of Research to the Teaching of English," *English Journal*, Vol. 27 (April, 1948), pp. 170–175. Indicates the influence of research on teaching of usage.

Thomas, C. K., *An Introduction to the Phonetics of American English*, New York, Ronald, 1947. Treats individual sounds and pronunciation in various areas.

Appendix

THE GRADE PLACEMENT OF SPEECH ACTIVITIES

To guide the young teacher, a list of speaking activities, of aims of speech education in terms of the child, and of items about the growth of children in language are included. They have been listed for four levels: the kindergarten, the primary grades, the middle grades, and the upper grades.

The speaking activities contained in this list are not exhaustive; they are suggestive. In some instances children, because of their level of maturity, will reject them. In other instances, the teacher will find they do not fit into the program which he and the children have planned. The major role of the teacher in promoting oral communication is to supply nurture for the development of children's ability to communicate. He stresses the ability of all his children to speak and listen better; but he recognizes that all will not attain the same level. He makes use of those speaking activities which help each child to speak alone and with others according to his level of language development. He provides for a wide range in kind and difficulty of speaking experiences, so that each child finds success in speaking. While playing house helps one kindergartner grow in language, talking to the policeman who helps the children cross the street helps another.

Children grow differently; they react to environment differently. But growth does not occur in a vacuum. The teacher must supply the child with a variety of experiences from which to choose. W. C. Olson and B. L. Hughes say, "The child is not a passive stimulant. He reaches out for it according to the maturity of his total and partial growth and the energy at his disposal. He reacts selectively to the surroundings that are supplied and creates his own world of experience within them. He tends to reject the experience for which he is not ready."[1] The teacher insures an environment that is adequate to the speaking needs of all the members of the class and adjusts how much he expects from each child according to the child's level of development.

The same philosophy applies to the aims. These expressed are ideals to represent the kinds of things a teacher would like to see children able to do. How soon the learning is brought about differs with individuals and with groups. For some groups, some of the aims are impractical. As children mature, they investigate, share ideas, and think cooperatively. Inherent in this statement are aims of speech education. But how far children go in achieving these aims is dependent on many factors, such as their rate of growth, their previous school environment, their home environment, and their group characteristics and interactions. The teacher in setting up the aims, however, recognizes that he must insure an environment wherein the aims can be reached and wherein the needs of all the children can be met.

[1] W. C. Olson and B. L. Hughes, "Concepts of Growth: Their Significance to Teachers," *Childhood Education*, Vol. 21 (October, 1944), p. 10.

Lastly, pertinent items about growth in language collected from various authoritative sources are listed. They are listed to give the teacher a feeling of trends of growth and of what to expect in children at the various age levels. It is important to remember that these facts are approximate averages of many children. Because each child is an individual, he develops in his own way. The individual may not fit the norm. Some age groups will not fit the pattern, for the groups are made of widely varying individuals. The purpose of listing the facts is to acquaint the teacher better with what the average child does with language. He must not expect all his children to fit the pattern.

In considering the chart, one other fact is important: ability to speak is but one facet of the child's development. The teacher does not separate this ability from the other abilities of the child. He capitalizes on all the child's strengths, whether they be to throw a ball, paint a picture, or act a part. In many instances, ability to speak goes along with another ability. Tommy, a nine-year-old, could not read well, did not excel at spelling or arithmetic. Yet, when the fourth grade gave a party, he was its best host. He was considerate of his guests, was able to make them comfortable, and was completely charming. Part of this charm was a knack for saying the right thing to the right person. Furthermore, he was somewhat bigger than the other third graders. He was one of the few who frequently shot a ball into the basket. When he sat on the sidelines, he cheered well and enthusiastically. Tom's strengths and weaknesses in language were part and parcel of his whole make-up. The teacher's job is to build on all his strengths, including those in language.

BIBLIOGRAPHY

1. Gesell, A. H., and F. L. Ilg, *The Child from Five to Ten*, New York, Harper, 1946.
2. Jenkins, G. G., "Six Year Olds: Their Characteristics and Needs," *The Supervisor's Notebook*, Vol. 12 (Spring, 1948), pp. 1–4.
3. Jenkins, G. G., H. Shacter, and W. Bauer, *These Are Your Children*, Chicago, Scott, Foresman, 1949.
4. Ohio State University Faculty, *How Children Develop* (a revision of *Child Development Study*), Columbus, Ohio, The Ohio State University Press, 1946.
5. Watts, A. F., *The Language and Mental Development of Children*, London, George G. Barrap, 1944.

Aims in teaching oral communication in the kindergarten	Language growth of five-year-olds based on norms found in literature	Speaking activities
	ITEMS APPLICABLE TO CONVERSATION	CONVERSATION
To speak freely and listen to others.	The five-year-old exchanges ideas with others (4, p. 13).*† The conversation of the five-year-old centers around disputes (5, p. 69). The five-year-old likes to talk and will talk to anyone (1, p. 445).‡ He loves to tell about what happened at home (3, p. 24).	Participation in conversation about such topics as pets, weather, birthdays, holidays, and home activities.
	ITEMS APPLICABLE TO SPEAKING IN SOCIAL SITUATIONS	SPEAKING IN SOCIAL SITUATIONS
To use speech to adjust to the social situations of the kindergarten. To take advantage of rich opportunities for developing language through a variety of experiences.	Some children of five years of age are able to greet friends. They verbalize about "please" and "thank you" (1, p. 350).	Serving as hosts and hostesses to children from other grades. Greeting each other and strangers. Saying "thank you" and "please" upon occasion. Dictating to the teacher a letter to be sent to an absent member who is ill, to the manager of a factory expressing gratitude for his making a visit to his factory pleasant, or to a parent for helping with the transportation of children.

284

To listen to stories appreciatively. To tell a short, simple story.	ITEMS APPLICABLE TO STORYTELLING	STORYTELLING
	The five-year-old likes to be read to. He likes stories of animals who behave like human beings (1, p. 371). Children of five can narrate a complete occurrence and repeat a familiar story (4, p. 13). The child of five enjoys stories about the things he sees around him—steam shovels and engines, grocery stores and boats (3, p. 22.)	Listening to the teacher tell stories. Listening to the teacher read stories. Listening to the teacher read stories and watching the illustrations which help tell the stories. Making up stories and dictating them to the teacher. Repeating with the teacher refrains of nursery rhymes or parts of stories. Retelling a short, simple story.
To begin to take part in group planning of activities.	ITEMS APPLICABLE TO DISCUSSION	DISCUSSION
	Environmental influences play an important part in the speech development of the five-year-old (4, p. 13.) The five-year-old makes up his mind. He decides quickly what he wants (1, p. 415). The five-year-old exhibits an increasing willingness to share (4, p. 11).	Planning to go on trips to such places as the firehouse, the toy store, the seashore, or the lumber yard. Discussing what the children have seen and done on the trip. Planning the work of the class together, such as the building of a farm and stocking it with animals. Planning the work of small groups of children. Discussing the work small groups have done.

* Numbers at the ends of items in this column refer to books listed in the bibliography preceding this section.

† Ohio State University Faculty, *How Children Develop*, Columbus, Ohio, The Ohio State University Press, 1946. Used by permission.

‡ A. H. Gesell and F. L. Ilg, *The Child from Five to Ten*, New York, Harper & Brothers, 1946. Used by permission.

SPEECH IN THE KINDERGARTEN—(Continued)

Aims in teaching oral communication in the kindergarten	Language growth of five-year-olds based on norms found in literature	Speaking activities
To contribute information to the class.	ITEMS APPLICABLE TO GIVING TALKS The five-year-old asks innumerable questions; he really seeks information (1, p. 445). The five-year-old is interested in using new and large words (1, p. 445).	GIVING TALKS Explaining the work of small groups; for example, the group who stocked the farm explains what it has done. Explaining how to get to certain places or how to do a certain task. Telling why they painted pictures the way they did.
To express oneself in dramatic play.	ITEMS APPLICABLE TO DRAMATIZATION Children of five years of age are highly dramatic (4, p. 7). Five-year-olds like rhythmic play (4, p. 7). The play of five-year-olds centers around the house and imitates adult activities. Girls play with dolls, play house, store, and hospital. Boys play war games (1, p. 367). Both boys and girls like home-centered dramatic play (3, p. 23). Children of five have difficulty in distinguishing between fact and fancy (1, p. 445). The five-year-old loves dramatic play. He is ready to act out the story that he has heard (3, p. 23).	DRAMATIZATION Dramatization of everyday experiences like getting supper, or washing dishes. Dramatization of stories such as *The Three Little Pigs* and of nursery rhymes like "Little Jack Horner." Using stick puppets to tell nursery rhymes like "Old King Cole" and stories, such as *Three Billy Goats Gruff*.

SPEECH IN THE PRIMARY GRADES (GRADES 1 TO 3)

Aims in teaching oral communication in the primary grades	*Language growth of six-, seven-, and eight-year-olds based on norms found in literature*	*Speaking activities*
		CONVERSATION
	ITEMS APPLICABLE TO CONVERSATION	Participation in conversation concerning class activity or topics of mutual interest.
To talk freely and easily about experiences.	Children of six and seven are interested in almost everything of the present time and of the immediate environment (4, p. 26).*†	Relating personal experiences.
To listen with increasing ability to get the other person's point of view.	The six-year-old uses language aggressively (1, p. 446).‡	
	The six-year-old is very talkative (1, p. 446).	
To increase the fund of ideas through trips, listening to music, looking at pictures, reading, and listening to children's literature.	The seven-year-old likes to talk, although his conversation centers about himself (3, p. 65).	
	The seven-year-old uses language complainingly (1, p. 446).	
To use clear, intelligible language.	The eight-year-old talks a great deal.	
	He boasts, exaggerates, tells tall tales (1, p. 446).	
	Some eight-year-olds carry on real social conversations with adults (1, p. 351).	
		TELEPHONING
	ITEMS APPLICABLE TO TELEPHONING	Using the telephone to give and receive invitations.
To use the telephone with consideration for others.	The six-year-old uses the telephone. Some can dial (1, p. 446).	

* Numbers at the ends of items in this column refer to books listed in the bibliography preceding this section.
† Ohio State University Faculty, *How Children Develop*, Columbus, Ohio, The Ohio State University Press. Used by permission.
‡ A. H. Gesell and F. L. Ilg, *The Child from Five to Ten*, New York, Harper & Brothers, 1946. Used by permission.

SPEECH IN THE PRIMARY GRADES (GRADES 1 TO 3)—(Continued)

Aims in teaching oral communication in the primary grades	Language growth of six-, seven-, and eight-year-olds based on norms found in literature	Speaking activities
	The seven-year-old does considerable social telephoning (1, p. 446). The eight-year-old makes much social use of the telephone (1, p. 446).	Taking of simple messages over the telephone. Ordering materials over the telephone.
	ITEMS APPLICABLE TO SPEAKING IN SOCIAL SITUATIONS	SPEAKING IN SOCIAL SITUATIONS
To respond easily to simple social situations.	The six-year-old has difficulty in formal social situations. But he can offer and receive hospitality from contemporaries (1, p. 350). The seven-year-old can listen for twenty minutes courteously and pleasantly (1, p. 351). The eight-year-old uses language fluently (1, p. 446).	Giving and receiving invitations. Making introductions. Serving as hosts and hostesses to outsiders. Greeting guests.
	ITEMS APPLICABLE TO STORYTELLING	STORYTELLING
To listen appreciatively to stories.	Children in the primary grades begin to appreciate various types of humor (4, p. 27).	Listening to stories read or told by the teacher. Telling stories the children have read.
To re-create stories for others.	A six-year-old tells a story moving his whole body (2, p. 3). First grades like to be read to (1, p. 380). Six-year-olds like to hear stories about themselves and the activities of children (1, p. 371). The seven-year-old is interested in books about chil-	Telling stories the children have created.

dren, animals, and nature. Boys like books about the army and the navy. Seven-year-olds like fairy tales, myths, and legends (1, p. 371).

The eight-year-old is beginning to be interested in people who lived long ago (4, p. 28).

The eight-year-old still enjoys books about children, animals, and fairies. He is becoming interested in faraway places (1, p. 371).

The eight-year-old favors exciting and humorous stories (1, p. 183).

ITEMS APPLICABLE TO GIVING TALKS

Six-year-olds show a marked interest in transportation and construction (1, p. 121).

The second grader acquires knowledge of natural and social science through projects, excursions, and the celebration of holidays. "Centers of interest" organize knowledge concerning nutrition, biology, and geography (1, p. 383).

The third grader makes a more rational approach to nature, to foreign peoples and strange lands (1, p. 385).

ITEMS APPLICABLE TO READING ALOUD

The eight-year-old likes to read aloud (1, p. 382).

GIVING TALKS

Participation in "show and tell" period.

Explaining pictures the children have painted.

Explaining a game or process.

Reporting on material read.

Reporting on events seen or heard.

Reporting on group activities.

READING ALOUD

Reading aloud a story or a poem.

Reading aloud material necessary for classroom activities.

Participation in choral speaking, with the children selecting the poem and deciding on the interpretation.

To tell an experience or to report an event or activity in an orderly fashion.

To stick to a point in talking and to develop the point by means of a simple sequence of ideas.

To read aloud a simple poem or story so as to share it with the group.

Aims in teaching oral communication in the primary grades	Language growth of six-, seven-, and eight-year-olds based on norms found in literature	Speaking activities
	ITEMS APPLICABLE TO GROUP DISCUSSION	DISCUSSION
To select a topic for discussion and stick to it. To share information by means of group discussion. To settle issues through group discussion.	While there is a growing realization of time, children of this age cannot plan far in advance (4, p. 26). The six-year-old finds decisions and choices hard. It is wise not to expect too many decisions (2, p. 3). The six-year-old has difficulty making up his mind. He will not change it when it is made up (1, p. 415). The seven-year-old finds it easier to make up his mind but hard to change it (1, p. 415). Children do not collaborate in thought before the age of seven. At seven, they engage in genuine argument in which reasons are advanced in support of assertions (5, p. 69). The seven-year-old likes to plan his day. Many enjoy using a chart (1, p. 151). The eight-year-old makes up his mind easily. He can listen to reason and then change his mind (1, p. 415). The eight-year-old verbalizes ideas and problems. He begins to understand cause-and-effect relationships (1, p. 446). Children in this age group take sincere criticism with grace. They are not blocked in artistic efforts by it (4, p. 24). The seven-year-old criticizes his own performance (1, p. 446).	Participation in planning the activities of the class (includes work of the entire group and of smaller groups). Participation in planning and preparation for trips and excursions. Talking about the trips. Talking about the benefits derived from the trips. Discussing the work of the members of the class. Settling an issue of the group through participation in group discussion.

	ITEMS APPLICABLE TO DRAMATIZATION	DRAMATICS
To engage in dramatic play. To dramatize a story so that the listeners can follow it readily.	Children of six to nine years of age enjoy dressing up and playing appropriate parts, which they not only play but live (4, p. 20). Dramatic presentation of stories is an activity that several children work together on over a considerable period of time (4, p. 27). The six-year-old increases in ability to distinguish between fact and fantasy (1, p. 446). The child of six becomes self-conscious in overly directed dramatic play (2, p. 3). Six-year-olds engage in imaginary play. They pretend to be a horse or that a piece of furniture is a boat (1, p. 368). Six-year-old girls play school, house, and library. The boys play war games, cowboys, and cops and robbers (1, p. 368). The seven-year-old demands more realism in play (1, p. 151). The seven-year-old plays library, train, and post office. The girls play house and school; the boys, cops and robbers and gunplay (1, p. 369). The eight-year-old arranges and produces shows (1, p. 369). The eight-year-old likes to dramatize. He dramatizes air raids, accidents, fighting, and bombing. He impersonates characters in movies which he has seen or books that he has read (1, p. 180).	Dramatic play of everyday occurrences. Pantomiming. Playing a story or a poem. Playing a story or poem with stick or hand puppets.

Aims in teaching oral communication in the middle grades	Language growth of nine-, ten-, and eleven-year-olds based on norms found in literature	Speaking activities
	ITEM APPLICABLE TO ALL SPEECH SITUATIONS	CONVERSATION
To converse intelligently, to know what to talk about and how and when to talk.	At nine, language is used as a tool and not for its own sake (I, p. 447).*†	Participation in conversation. Knowing what to talk about, how to talk about a topic, how to change the subject, and how to interest listeners.
To respond wholeheartedly to the other person's conversation.		Demonstrating this knowledge.
To listen carefully and critically.		
		TELEPHONING
To speak on the telephone courteously and effectively.		Taking messages accurately. Asking for information over the telephone.
To know the forms of opening and closing a conversation.		Conducting business over the telephone.
		Asking permission to visit a plant or institution over the telephone.
		INTERVIEWING
To interview to gain the desired information graciously.		Participation in interviews.

292

	ITEMS APPLICABLE TO SPEAKING IN SOCIAL SITUATIONS	SPEAKING IN SOCIAL SITUATIONS
To participate in social situations with consideration of guests.	There are marked individual differences in social activities. Some children of this age are ready to shake hands (1, p. 351). At this age, classmates supply standards of manners (4, p. 32).‡ Children from nine to eleven are ready for a widening of social contacts (4, p. 33).	Serving as quite mature hosts and hostesses to schoolmates and to strangers. Keeping the guests comfortable and happy. Expressing sympathy and congratulations.
	ITEMS APPLICABLE TO STORYTELLING	STORYTELLING
To tell a story effectively. To listen to stories appreciatively.	Nine-year-olds tell long, detailed, strung-out stories about radio programs or movies (1, p. 207). For children of nine to eleven story and drama begin to help the child understand relationships between factors such as time, place, ideas, and happenings (4, p. 37).	Telling personal experiences, myths, biographies, folk, and fairy tales. Listening appreciatively to stories read and told by others.
	ITEM APPLICABLE TO ORAL READING	ORAL READING
To read from the printed page so as to interpret the meaning and feeling intended by the author.	The nine-year-old likes mysteries and biographies (1, p. 371).	Reading directions for others to follow. Reading to impart information to others. Reading a quotation to support a statement.

* Numbers at the ends of items in this column refer to books listed in the bibliography preceding this section.

† A. H. Gesell and F. L. Ilg, *The Child from Five to Ten*, New York, Harper & Brothers, 1946. Used by permission.

‡ Ohio State University Faculty, *How Children Develop*, Columbus, Ohio, The Ohio State University Press. Used by permission.

SPEECH IN THE MIDDLE GRADES (GRADES 4 TO 6)—(Continued)

Aims in teaching oral communication in the middle grades	Language growth of nine-, ten-, and eleven-year-olds based on norms found in literature	Speaking activities
		Reading children's stories and poetry for the enjoyment of the listener. Participation in choral speaking.
	ITEMS APPLICABLE TO GIVING TALKS	GIVING TALKS
To be able to instruct, impress, entertain, or inform one's classmates.	At nine, the child's reasoning is based on direct observation (4, p. 37).	Giving oral reports.
To collect and arrange material for a talk.	Between eleven and twelve, children make assumptions, generalize, make deductions (4, p. 37).	Construction of simple outlines. Finding facts for talks from magazines or books.
To support adequately what is said.	Children between nine and eleven begin to see the importance of clarity in expressing their ideas (4, p. 35).	Giving short talks to inform, persuade, impress, or entertain, as the occasion demands.
To learn to outline ideas.	Children of this age use reference books (4, p. 36).	
To know where to look to find information in a reference book.	Children of this age are interested in factual information about the building of culture (4, p. 38).	
	ITEMS APPLICABLE TO DISCUSSION	DISCUSSION
To cooperate in group planning.	Children of nine to eleven are ready for a program which gives them opportunities to make decisions and face the consequences of their mistakes (4, p. 35).	Planning activities of the class. Pooling information.
To think critically of what others are saying.	At nine, there is an emergence of independent, critical thinking (1, p. 447).	Participating in various forms of discussion.
To be willing to change one's mind.		Leading discussions of small groups.

To stick to a point.

To participate in group discussion constructively.

To follow the five steps in group discussion in solving a problem.

To be beginning to serve as an effective discussion leader.

To conduct a meeting by means of simple parliamentary procedure.

The nine-year-old makes up his mind easily. Some nine-year-olds change their minds in response to reason (1, p. 415).

In planning, nine- to eleven-year-old children set up "blueprints" before they act. The eleven-year-old can make tentative plans for several weeks and keep them (4, p. 35).

The nine-year-old relates himself to his immediate environment, to his community, his country, and even other countries (3, p. 99).

The nine-to eleven-year-old recognizes the value of pooled thinking (4, p. 35).

Nine- to eleven-year-old children form clubs like those of adults as far as children are familiar with, and understand, their organization (4, p. 33).

Following the five steps of discussion.

Organizing into a club.

Conducting meetings following the right order of business and using the form of making a main motion.

ITEMS APPLICABLE TO DRAMATICS

Nine-year-olds build elaborate drama. They may enact an entire day's routine (1, p. 369).

Children at the ages of nine to eleven are less interested in imaginative play. They are interested in facts, and their interest in realism increases (4, p. 36).

DRAMATICS

Playing a story or an original story.

Participating in pantomime.

Participating in the production of a play.

Writing a script for a play and playing it.

Putting on a puppet, marionette, or shadow show.

To act in plays.

To write and act in plays.

To make a story into a play.

To adapt an experience for a play.

To make hand puppets and marionettes and put on a show.

SPEECH IN THE UPPER GRADES (GRADES 7 TO 8)

Aims in teaching oral communication in the upper grades	Language development of eleven-, twelve-, and thirteen-year-olds based on norms found in literature	Speaking activities
To be able to participate in conversation with peers and adults about ideas with an interplay of minds.		CONVERSATION Conversing with strangers. Direct study of what makes conversation successful.
To use the telephone in a mature manner.		TELEPHONING Arranging interviews by telephone. Expressing sympathy over the telephone. Asking a favor. Planning an activity. Making a business complaint.
To ascertain the purpose of an interview, to plan it, and to carry it through graciously and effectively.		INTERVIEWING Direct study of interview techniques.
To be an effective social member of a group, considerate of other persons' feelings.	ITEM APPLICABLE TO SOCIAL SITUATIONS Children from eleven to thirteen years of age learn the niceties of social relations quickly (4, p. 44).*†	SPEAKING IN SOCIAL SITUATIONS Direct study of the speech required in different social situations.

	ITEMS APPLICABLE TO GIVING TALKS	STORYTELLING
To tell a story creatively.		Participation in storytelling to entertain. Telling stories to younger children.
		GIVING TALKS
To inform, persuade, impress, and entertain listeners.	Children of eleven to thirteen years of age are increasingly better able to use book lists, books on how to do and make things, etc. (4, p. 46).	Giving talks to persuade, impress, inform, and entertain as the occasion demands.
To find, select, and organize material for talks.	Children of this age have a continued interest in factual information concerning the building of the culture (4, p. 48).	Collecting material for talks. Using the library resources.
To support one's ideas effectively.	Children of this age have an intense interest in scientific aspects of the culture (4, p. 48).	Evaluating the material collected. Organizing the material for a talk. Making an outline. Supporting the main idea.
To analyze one's audience.		Analyzing the listeners to whom the talk is to be given.
To adapt the content of the talk to the audience.		Adapting the talk to the listeners.
To listen critically to the talks of other children.		Listening to the speaker and analyzing what he is saying.
		ORAL READING
To listen critically to the reading of others.	The preadolescents like nature stories and books on science, travel, and mechanics (5, p. 118).	Getting at the meaning intended by the author. Studying his purpose and his background.

---

* Numbers at the ends of items in this column refer to books listed in the bibliography preceding this section.

† Ohio State University Faculty, *How Children Develop*, Columbus, Ohio, The Ohio State University Press. Used by permission.

Aims in teaching oral communication in the upper grades	Language development of eleven-, twelve-, and thirteen-year-olds based on norms found in literature	Speaking activities
To interpret the thought and meaning of the author to the listeners. To be able to talk about a piece of prose or poetry in terms of its meaning and mood.		Using the techniques of oral reading, such as pausing and phrasing, to establish meaning for the audience. Establishing the mood for the audience. Reading to own group. On occasion, the talented members will read to other groups. Choral speaking. Working out the interpretation of the poem and selecting the material to be read.
ITEMS APPLICABLE TO DISCUSSION	ITEMS APPLICABLE TO DISCUSSION	DISCUSSION
To participate in discussion in a mature manner. To listen critically. To participate in group reflective thinking. To lead a discussion.	Children this age like to feel that their ideas are important in group planning (4, p. 45). An increasing understanding of cause and effect helps these children to predict and plan with greater effectiveness (4, p. 46). Children of these ages are best able to solve problems involving concrete situations within their own experiences (4, p. 46).	Planning work of the group in units. Planning activities of the group. Discussing topics such as the causes of the American Revolution, recent courses of action taken by the common council, causes of juvenile delinquency.

To conduct a meeting.
To participate in parliamentary procedure.

To interpret a role in a play creatively.
To study the characterizations and the interplay of characters.
To analyze the motives of the characters.
To accept responsibility for various phases of play lighting, costuming, make-up, scenery, and management.

Children of this age are now able to analyze situations verbally. They show increasing ability to "talk out" problems and clarify group thinking (3, p. 46).
The attention span of children this age is short in group discussion (4, p. 46).
These children tend to draw conclusions from scanty and improperly observed data (4, p. 47).

ITEMS APPLICABLE TO DRAMATICS

Imaginative play has virtually disappeared in this group (4, p. 47).
Imagination of eleven- to thirteen-year-olds is active, but the scenes must be relatively true to life (4, p. 47).

Following the five steps of discussion.
Participating in group reflective thinking.
Talking about the use of reasoning by students.
Serving as a discussion leader.
Conducting a meeting, sometimes using the different types of motions.

DRAMATICS

Development of individual talent and abilities through planning and participation in plays written by children.
Participation in play production.
Study of consumption of radio and television programs and of moving pictures.
Production of a puppet or marionette show, depending on the interests of the group.

Visual Aids

The motion pictures listed below and on the following pages can be used to supplement the material in this book. For the convenience of users the films have been grouped under two headings—those primarily for teachers and those for students—but since some films can be used in the study of two or more chapters, it is recommended that each one be reviewed, before use, in order to determine its suitability for a particular group.

Immediately following the film title is the name of the producer; and if different from the producer, the name of the distributor. Abbreviations are used for names of producers and distributors, and these abbreviations are identified in the list of sources at the end of the bibliography. In many instances, the films can be borrowed or rented from local or state 16-mm film libraries. (A nation-wide list of these local sources is given in *A Directory of 2,660 16mm Film Libraries*, available for 50 cents from the Superintendent of Documents, Washington 25, D.C.) Unless otherwise indicated, the motion pictures are sound and black-and-white films. All are 16mm.

This bibliography is a selective one, and film users should examine the latest annual edition and quarterly supplements of *Educational Film Guide*, a catalog of 11,000 films published by the H. W. Wilson Co., New York. The *Guide*, a standard reference book, is available in most college and public libraries.

FILMS PRIMARILY FOR TEACHERS

Child Development (EBF) Eleven films produced at Yale, under the direction of Gesell, showing stages in the development of children. Individual titles, 10–11 minutes each, are:

Baby's Day at 48 Weeks
Baby's Day at 12 Weeks
Behavior Patterns at One Year
Early Social Behavior
From Creeping to Walking
Growth of Infant Behavior: Early Stages
Growth of Infant Behavior: Later Stages
Learning and Growth
Life Begins
Posture and Locomotion
Thirty-six Weeks Behavior Day

Child Development (McGraw) Five films, correlated with Hurlock's text "Child Development," portraying characteristic interests, attitudes, and behavior patterns of children. Titles and running times of the individual films are:

> *Child Care and Development* (17 min)
> *Children's Emotions* (22 min)
> *Heredity and Pre-natal Development* (21 min)
> *Principles of Development* (17 min)
> *Social Development* (16 min)

Children Growing Up with Other People (BIS/UWF, 30 min) Illustrates stages in the growth of children and in the transition from self-centered individuality to recognizing the responsibilities of social behavior.

Children Learning by Experience (BIS/UWF, 40 min) Illustrates how children learn through many and various experiences.

Four Ways to Drama (Calif, 33 min) A short dramatic episode is presented in four different versions—for stage, radio, television, and motion pictures. Compares and contrasts the requirements of the four methods.

Good Speech for Gary (USC/McGraw, 22 min color or b&w) Features of a well organized speech program with emphasis upon the need for understanding children's speech difficulties and the contribution of the school to helping children speak clearly and understandably.

It's a Small World (BIS/Columbia, 38 min) By means of hidden cameras, the film shows spontaneous actions and reactions of children during a full day of nursery school life.

Marionettes—Construction and Manipulation (Brandon, 10 min) Demonstrates the construction of Bobo, a clown marionette, and then the manipulation of the strings.

New Voices (Cleveland, 20 min) Training film in the development of esophageal speech, portraying the chance discovery of cancer of the larynx, confirmation by diagnosis, pre-operative training, and post-operative care and re-training.

Report on Donald (Minn U, 20 min) Story of Donald Carter, his bad speech block, and his going to the speech clinic for help; history and the causes of his difficulty; and work at the clinic to overcome his difficulty.

Shadowland (Brandon, 12 min color or b&w) Step-by-step demonstration of the creation of transparent shadow figures by Jero Magum, artist-puppeteer.

FILMS PRIMARILY FOR PUPILS

Background for Reading and Expression (Coronet) Stories and poems to create background for reading, discussion, and singing activities in the primary grades. Titles and running times are:

> *Mary Had a Little Lamb* (11 min)
> *The Toy Telephone Truck* (10 min)
> *What the Frost Does* (10 min)

Fundamentals of Public Speaking (Coronet, 10 min color or b&w) Explains the importance of public speaking in school situations, and the steps to planning and delivering a successful speech.

How Not To Conduct a Meeting (GM, 10 min) Colonel Stoopnagel burlesques common errors made in holding luncheon meetings. Primarily for adults.

Learn to Argue Effectively (Coronet, 10 min color or b&w) Explains when arguments are purposeful, what subjects are good and bad, and what is a basis for a profitable argument.

Learning from Class Discussion (Coronet, 10 min color or b&w) Explains the ingredients of a good class discussion and emphasizes the values of such a discussion.

Let's Make Puppets (Library, 10 min) How to make puppets out of newspapers, flour paste, crayons, and ingenuity.

Literature Appreciation: How To Read Plays (Coronet, 14 min) Suggestions on how to read a play in order to communicate its visual, aural, and dramatic content.

Speech: Conducting a Meeting (YAF, 11 min) Demonstrates and explains the basic parliamentary procedures which contribute to a successful meeting.

Speech: Function of Gestures (YAF, 11 min) Explains the value of gestures and gives examples of commonly used gestures.

Speech: Planning Your Talk (YAF, 11 min) Emphasizes the importance of planning and organizing a talk, and demonstrates the basic steps in such preparation.

Speech: Platform Posture and Appearance (YAF, 11 min) Emphasizes the importance of the speaker's appearance and demonstrates good platform posture and movement.

Speech: Stage Fright and What To Do About It (YAF, 11 min) Explains the causes of stage fright, gives typical examples, and shows what can be done to conquer it.

Speech: Using Your Voice (YAF, 11 min) Points out common speech and voice faults in formal and informal speaking, and explains how to correct such faults.

Ways to Better Conversation (Coronet, 10 min color or b&w) Illustrates the characteristics of a good conversation and explains how skill in conversation can be improved.

LIST OF FILM SOURCES

BIS—British Information Services, 30 Rockefeller Plaza, New York 20.

Brandon—Brandon Films, Inc., 200 W. 57th St., New York 19.

Calif U—University of California, Berkeley.

Cleveland—Cleveland Hearing and Speech Center, 11206 Euclid Ave., Cleveland 6.

Columbia—Columbia University Press, 1115 Amsterdam Ave., New York 27.

Coronet—Coronet Films, Inc., Coronet Bldg., Chicago 1.

EBF—Encyclopaedia Britannica Films, Inc., Wilmette, Ill.

GM—General Motors Corp., Film Section, 3044 W. Grand Blvd., Detroit 2
and 405 Montgomery St., San Francisco 4.

Library—Library Films, Inc., 25 W. 45th St., New York 19.

McGraw—McGraw-Hill Book Co., Text-Film Dept., 330 W. 42nd St.
New York 36.

Minn U—University of Minnesota, Audio-Visual Education Service, Minneapolis 14.

UWF—United World Films, Inc., 1445 Park Ave., New York 29.

YAF—Young America Films, Inc., 18 E. 41st St., New York 17.

Index